A HANDBOOK ON THE PAPACY

A
HANDBOOK
ON THE
PAPACY

The Rt. Rev.
WILLIAM SHAW KERR
Bishop of Down and Dromore

London
MARSHALL MORGAN & SCOTT
Edinburgh

LONDON
MARSHALL, MORGAN AND SCOTT LTD.
1-5 PORTPOOL LANE
HOLBORN, E.C.1

AUSTRALIA AND NEW ZEALAND
117-119 BURWOOD ROAD
MELBOURNE, E.13

SOUTH AFRICA
P.O. BOX 1720, STURK'S BUILDINGS
CAPE TOWN

CANADA
EVANGELICAL PUBLISHERS
241 YOUNGE STREET
TORONTO

PRINTED IN GREAT BRITAIN BY
LOWE AND BRYDONE (PRINTERS) LTD., LONDON

FOREWORD

To all Christian people the divisions of the Church are a distressing scandal. The separation between the Roman and non-Roman communions is one of the most momentous and far-reaching. We who remain outside the Roman unity are bound to ponder the causes that explain our position. Only reasons of a compelling nature—obligations of loyalty to the truth as we know it—can justify us.

Controversy is often foolishly decried. A contentious spirit is to be condemned. But the defence of the truth against hurtful error is a manifest duty. Much of St. Paul's writings and those of the early Fathers—Irenaeus, Hippolytus, Athanasius, Hilary, Basil, Augustine, etc.—were devoted to combating false doctrines. In the Anglican Church many of its most illustrious and learned sons in every age have found it necessary to defend the faith against Romanist errors —Jewel, Cosin, Overall, Laud, Andrewes, Usher, Jeremy Taylor, Bramhall, Barrow, Pusey, Palmer, Whately, Littledale, Salmon, Gore, Bright, Puller, Denny, etc.

Romanist writers are continually challenging what they call our schism. Their aggressiveness is natural and, from their point of view, meritorious. We do not resent their trying to show us that we are mistaken, so long as their arguments are fair. The venerable heads of the Church of Rome have again and again appealed to us to return to their communion. Pope Leo XIII in his letter to the English people (*Ad Anglos*) besought us to join with him in furthering the reunion of Christendom. He implored us as we value our eternal salvation to offer prayers to God that we may be given "light to know the truth in all its fullness".

Pope Pius XI, in his encyclical *Lux Veritatis*, hoped for those outside his Church that, "moved thereby by the desire of truth, it may well be that, taught by history, the guide of life, they will at least be affected by a longing for the one fold and the one Shepherd, and for embracing that genuine faith which is ever preserved safe and whole in the Roman Church". In a previous encyclical on *Fostering True Religious Union* the same Pope besought the children of the

5

Reformation to "return to their common Father, who, forgetting the insults previously heaped on the Apostolic See, will receive them in the most loving fashion".

It would be unseemly not to respond to such imposing appeals. It would be wrong for us stubbornly to adhere to our inherited theological tenets without patiently studying the grounds for our beliefs. We should indeed discover what light "history, the guide of life" has to throw on the grave issues in dispute. The appeal is to the words of Christ, the teaching of His apostles, the beliefs of the early Church, the lessons of history and the behests of conscience and intellect.

In the following pages an attempt is made to investigate the validity of one crucial doctrine of Romanism—the claims of the Roman Pontiff to supremacy and infallibility. The result of the study is to demonstrate that such claims are inconsistent with the teaching of the New Testament, are a contradiction of history and a monstrous distortion of the Christian Faith. These are hard words, not lightly used. The evidence will decide whether they are justified. Much as we value unity, we cannot subscribe to doctrines that we honestly feel outrage our conscience and intellect. We cannot accept as truth what we believe false. One of our devout and competent scholars, Dr. Neville Figgis, described ultramontanism as "destructive, as I believe it ultimately to be, of the true social and organic conception of the Church, dangerous to the individual conscience which it supersedes, ultimately productive of widespread infidelity, and opposed alike to the teaching of experience and the whole method and Spirit of our Lord Jesus Christ".[1] It was not a Protestant who wrote, "Sooner or later the historical lie of the Papacy must be realised by every educated Romanist." [2]

In dealing with one dogma of Romanism it is not to be supposed that the objections to other parts of that system are overlooked— such as, for instance, worship of the Virgin Mary, Transubstantiation, Purgatory, Indulgences, the traffic in Masses. But the claim for the absolute authority of the Papacy is crucial. Let that claim be granted and then we have no remedy but to accept every doctrine the Pope cares to promulgate and to submit unreservedly to his complete autocracy.

No appeal to the clearest words of Christ has validity in

---

[1] *Hopes for English Religion*, p. 81.
[2] George Tyrrell, *Life*, vol. ii, p. 383.

determining belief or prescribing conduct unless they are interpreted according to the sense approved of by the infallible Teacher. "For a Catholic the Papacy is the key to the whole religious question. For—to put it concisely—we believe the doctrines of our faith not because we fancy we discover them set forth in the New Testament, nor because a vague entity called 'the Church' has held them, but because the visible teaching Church—the *Corpus Christi* or Body of Christ—has taught them and continues to teach them through its Head on earth, the Pope, the successor of St. Peter, the Vicar of Christ."[1]

Papal utterances, meant to be conciliatory, leave us in no uncertainty as to the necessity of unquestioning obedience to their dictatorship. Pope Pius XI, in an encyclical referred to, discredits the attempt to know the truth apart from the unerring teacher. "All who are truly Christ's believe, for example, the Conception of the Mother of God without stain of original sin with the same faith as they believe the mystery of the August Trinity and the Incarnation of our Lord, just as they do the infallible teaching authority of the Roman Pontiff, according to the sense in which it was defined by the Oecumenical Council of the Vatican." "In this one Church of Christ no man can be or remain who does not accept, recognise and obey the authority and supremacy of Peter and his legitimate successors."[2]

It is difficult to understand how the Pope's claim to be God's vicegerent can be soberly advocated after the papal record in the last war. Then, if ever, positive outspoken guidance should have been given. We may take Cardinal Hinsley's exposition of the issues at stake. He broadcast that "we are pitted against the powers of darkness which have unleashed a satanic campaign against God". "For or against God . . . that is now the supreme issue of this conflict." "Christian civilisation was menaced by the fiercest anti-Christian violence that mankind has ever endured."[3]

What part did the "Vicar of Christ" take? He constantly proclaimed his neutrality. He announced his "full consciousness of our absolute impartiality towards the belligerents" (14th May 1942). "The impartiality we have assumed towards everyone without distinction of nationality or religion" (12th November 1943). He

[1] Rev. Hugh Pope, O.P., S.T.M., Doct. S. Script., *The Papacy* (edited by Rev. C. Lattey, S.J.), p. 5.
[2] *Fostering True Religious Union*, pp. 12, 13.
[3] 23rd March 1941.

enunciated copious pious generalities, but was careful to specify it was always "without taking sides" (24th December 1942). The papal claim to be God's vicegerent might be credited if the Deity was indifferent to moral standards. Vatican policy in 1939–45 does not invalidate Bishop Hensley Henson's verdict: "Not the moral courage of Peter standing before the Sanhedrim, but the cynical expediency of Caiaphas as he counselled the condemnation of Jesus has commonly marked the procedure of the Vatican. . . . It is the continuing deadness to moral obligation which shocks the student of papal history."[1]

When the conscience of mankind was shocked by Mussolini's barbarous attack on Abyssinia Cardinal Hinsley tried to excuse the Pope's silence by pleading, "He is a helpless old man with a small police force to guard himself and the priceless treasures of the Vatican"; that to employ spiritual sanctions against Mussolini would involve "upsetting the peace and the conscience of the great mass of Italians" and would risk "active reprisals".[2]

How can that be reconciled with the Pope's claims as set forth in the *Pastor Aeternus*? Is the Papacy neutral where Italy is concerned? Mr. William Teeling, M.P., a member of a family highly honoured by the Papacy, wrote in 1937 that Pius XI "has thrown his weight on the side of the totalitarian leaders and he has felt that the imperial policy of Italy must mean an advance for his own Church in the conquered countries. . . . He raised no finger to stop Italian bishops up and down the country from going on Fascist platforms and doing everything possible to support Italian armies. . . . The Vatican has thrown in its lot to a very considerable extent with Mussolini, as every well-informed person in Europe knows". "The Pope on numerous occasions specifically referred to his great loyalty to Italy as an Italian."[3]

That he who, *jure divino*, rules on earth in Christ's stead must be always Bishop of Rome remains destitute of proof. Still more perplexing is it that he must generally be an Italian. Since the fifteenth century with one exception no one but an Italian has been made Pope. The cardinals and the great Congregations have been predominantly Italian. Members of the Roman Catholic Church are becoming increasingly unhappy about this Italianisation of the Papacy. "The fact, however, must be faced, that the Catholic Church

[1] *Retrospect of an Unimportant Life*, vol. ii, pp. 131, 132.
[2] *The Universe*, 18th October 1935.
[3] *The Pope in Politics*, p. 129.

cannot go on indefinitely having an Italian Pope and a majority of Italian cardinals."[1] "Those in important positions in the College (of Cardinals) are almost entirely Italian."[2]

Regretfully I have to refer to another subject—the common and unscrupulous misrepresentation of history and falsification of documents by Roman Catholic writers. No one who has not experience of the methods of Roman Catholic controversialists can understand how general is this want of candour and honesty. Bishop Gore's protests against this have abundant justification. "Perhaps there is nothing which gives to the mind of intelligent and truth-loving men so invincible a prejudice against the ultramontane system and temper—nothing which so radically convinces him it is not divine —as the certainty that ultramontane writers will always be found manipulating facts and making out a case, will never behave as men who are loyally endeavouring to seek the light and present facts as they are."[3] Newman's cry is referred to *infra*: "Nothing would be better than an historical Review for Roman Catholics—but who would bear it? Unless one doctored all one's facts one should be thought a bad Catholic." Coulton quotes the Liberal Catholic Fogazzaro's words: "The spirit of lying is one of the worst enemies of the Roman Church."[4] Lord Acton, the most learned Roman Catholic of his generation (Professor F. W. Maitland believed Acton could himself have written all the twelve volumes of the *Cambridge History*), declared that the ultramontane claims are founded "on unremitting dishonesty in the use of texts".[5] It is impressive to find a man of his rare erudition and conspicuous fairness of judgment writing that ultramontism "not only promotes, it inculcates distinct mendacity and deceitfulness. In certain cases it is made a duty to lie. But those who teach this doctrine do not become habitual liars in other things".[6]

The late Dr. G. G. Coulton was distinguished for his immense learning and scrupulous accuracy. He devoted much time to challenging errors in Roman Catholic writers. The most famous of his exposures was that of the mis-statements in the works of Cardinal Gasquet. Gasquet's book on the English monasteries won him considerable reputation. It was placed on the Ecclesiastical History

[1] *The Pope in Politics*, p. 3.
[2] Ibid., p. 89.
[3] *Roman Catholic Claims*, p. 112.
[4] *Romanism and Truth*, vol. ii, p. 237.
[5] *History of Freedom*, p. 512.
[6] *Correspondence of the First Lord Acton*, vol. i, p. 43.

Prize list which I read in Dublin University. Coulton, after futile private correspondence with him, repeatedly called public attention to his grave departures from the truth, and challenged him to correct or justify them.[1] Coulton, with irrefutable evidence, charged Dr. Gasquet with publishing numerous errors and republishing them after responsible journals like the *Times Literary Supplement*, the *Church Times* and the *Church Quarterly Review* had called attention to them. Of one astounding, obvious untruth Coulton wrote: "Yet not only did he offer no apology but five years later when a new edition was called for he allowed his printers to set up afresh in cold blood, word for word, this utterly indefensible falsehood. . . . Moreover, other mis-statements almost as gross, which had been similarly exposed, were reprinted again without alteration."[2] Yet Dr. Gasquet, Abbot-General of the English Benedictines, was promoted to be cardinal.

Dr. Coulton, from his long experience of Romanist controversial methods, wrote: "After a good deal of reading I have no hesitation in saying that it is impossible to trust a Romanist book as one naturally trusts other books by educated men. I do not of course mean for one moment that there are not trustworthy Romanist writers; but experience convinces me that such accuracy and impartiality as is normal in modern literature of the first class is rather exceptional in Romanism." If this be thought excessively severe let the reader study the evidence adduced in chapter xvii and the following pages in *Romanism and Truth*, vol. ii.

Dr. J. V. Simcox was until 1944 Professor of Canon Law at St. Edmund's College, Ware, the R.C. ecclesiastical seminary for the Archdiocese of Westminster. He had held that post for twenty-three years. The penalties he suffered after his protests against intellectual dishonesty in his Church impel him to declare: "God does not need our lies; and Catholics who fear truth in matters of religion confess that they do not really believe Catholicism to be from God."[3]

---

[1] *The Roman Catholic Church and the Bible* (1921); *Romanism and Truth*, vol. ii, chap. xviii (1931); *The Scandal of Cardinal Gasquet* (1937); *Sectarian History* (1937); *A Premium upon Falsehood* (1939), etc.

[2] *Sectarian History*, p. 6.

[3] *Is the Roman Catholic Church a Secret Society?*, p. 30.

CONTENTS

CHAPTER I

PAPAL CLAIMS TO SUPREMACY

In the third chapter of the Vatican Decrees the absolute sovereignty of the Pope over the Church is enunciated. It is declared that he is Vicar of Christ with divinely given power to rule, feed and govern the universal Church; that he has immediate jurisdiction over all the Church; that all are bound to submit to and obey him not only in matters of faith and morals but in matters of discipline and Church government. "This is the teaching of Catholic truth from which no one can deviate without loss of faith and salvation." The Roman Pontiff is the supreme judge of the faithful. Recourse may be had to his tribunal in all Church causes, and from it there is no appeal even to an Oecumenical Council. Anathema is pronounced on all who deny these tremendous claims.

The succeeding Pope, Leo XIII, in his encyclical *Satis Cognitum*, enforced this claim. The Roman Pontiffs have, he states, supreme power in the Church, *jure divino*. Christ "assigned to Peter and his successors that they would be His Vicars and would for ever exercise the same power in the Church that He Himself exercised in His mortal life". In a compendium, *The Catholic Faith*, authorised by the next Pope, Pius X, we are told that "the Roman Pontiff is the Vicar of Jesus Christ because he represents Him upon earth and takes His place in the government of the Church".[1]

These claims may be compared with the self-assertions of medieval Popes. Innocent III taught that the Lord committed to Peter not only the government of the universal Church but also of the whole world.[2] "As God, the Creator of the Universe, placed two great lights in the firmament of heaven, the greater light to rule the day and the lesser light to rule the night, so for the firmament of the universal Church which is called by the name of heaven he had appointed two great dignitaries, the greater to rule souls, as it were days, and the lesser to rule bodies, as it were nights. These are the pontifical authority and the royal power. Further, as the moon

---

[1] p. 24.   [2] *Ad Patr. Const.* P. L. 214: 759.

obtains its light from the sun and is indeed less than it both in size and quality, though alike in place and effect, so the royal power obtains the splendour of its dignity from the pontifical authority."[1]

Boniface VIII, in his bull *Unam Sanctam*, gave other specimens of Scriptural interpretation. We learn from the Gospels that there are two swords in the power of the Church, the spiritual and the temporal. When the apostle said, "Behold here are two swords", the Lord answered, "It is enough". He who denies that the temporal sword is in the power of Peter misunderstands the words of the Lord, "Put up thy sword into the sheath". The material sword is to be used for the Church, the spiritual by the Church—the spiritual by the priest, the material by kings and knights, but at the bidding and permission of the priest. The temporal authority is to be subject to the spiritual. "Furthermore we declare, state, define and pronounce that it is altogether necessary to salvation for every human creature to be subject to the Roman Pontiff."

The papal prerogatives as set out in the Vatican Decrees show some significant variations from those proclaimed in the thirteenth and fourteenth centuries. They do not venture to renew the claims of superiority in temporal affairs over secular monarchies. They are silent about the power—so frequently resorted to—of deposing kings. Boniface VIII boasted that his predecessors had deposed three kings of France and that he would if need be depose King Philip as though he were a groom[2] (*sicut unum garcionem*).

The medieval and present-day claims coincide in positing an absolute sovereignty of the Pope over the Church. Here is a doctrine that contradicts Scripture and history. It is in flat opposition to all we learn of the nature of the Church from the words of Christ and the teaching and practice of His apostles. It is simply the arrogant intrusion of a dictatorship over the rights of Christian people. It substitutes an arbitrary despotism for the original freedom of the members of the Church. It is the introduction of a Caesarism that is alien to the whole true spirit of Christianity—the changing the brotherhood into a vast imperialistic system. Professor N. P. Williams scarcely exaggerates when he writes that the official theory of the position of the Pope asserts him to be "the one and only sovereign and autocratic ruler, teacher, owner and proprietor of the

---

[1] *Ad Acerbum* P. L. 214: 377.
[2] Gieseler, *Ecclesiastical History*, vol. iii, p. 146.

whole Church militant here on earth".[1] Our sense of Christian citizenship revolts against such a tyranny. Bunyan's simile of Giant Pope is not out of date.

The mystical body of Christ, indwelt by His Spirit, cannot be coerced into a subservient state dominated by an earthly ruler. Membership in it is determined by allegiance to Christ, not by obedience to an Italian prelate. Our Lord repudiated such thraldom when He said: "The kings of the Gentiles have lordship over them and they that have authority over them are called Benefactors. But ye shall not be so" (Luke xxii. 25).

It is easy to follow the steps by which the constitution of the Church was changed from its original freedom and association of equal leaders to become a servile state with one bishop usurping supreme jurisdiction over the rest. History shows the deplorable divisions and weakness of the Eastern Churches—the destruction of the great African Church, and the overwhelming of Eastern Church by Mohammedanism. The position of the Bishop of Rome—the metropolis of the world and sole Apostolic See of the West—was always one of immense influence. The fall of the Western Roman Empire and the absence of the emperors from the imperial city gave the Bishops of Rome a sort of succession to the prestige of the Caesars. These bishops, ambitious and able men, were eager to seize their advantageous position. Hobbes was justified when he wrote that the Papacy is only the ghost of the deceased Roman Empire sitting crowned upon the grave thereof. Civil power was brought in through imperial rescripts at the instigation of ambitious overbearing prelates, like Leo the Great, to crush down opposition of bishops to the rapidly advancing aggressiveness of Rome. In the dark ages there was scope for unfounded claims to gain credence. Ignorance provided a fruitful field for such impositions. Crude forgeries could not be detected as spurious until the revival of learning. The acceptance of the forged decretals and the stress laid by Thomas Aquinas on patristic forgeries are typical instances of this. The historic sense was lost through centuries of superstition and turmoil. The ascendancy of Rome came to its highest point in these ages when the consciousness of the Christian revelation was at its lowest. Ruthless persecution obliterated those who raised their voices against papal domination.

There has always been one great witness against the usurpation of

[1] *Our Case as Against Rome*, p. 13.

Roman autocracy—the protest of the Eastern Church. In the East Christianity began. There all the Oecumenical Councils were held. There were situated four of the five patriarchates—Constantinople, Alexandria, Antioch, Jerusalem. The claim of Rome to ecclesiastical sovereignty was the real reason of the division between the Eastern and Western Churches in 1054. The Eastern Church continues to this day unmoved in its rejection of the supremacy of the Bishop of Rome. Chrysostom, Archbishop of Athens, wrote in his reply to the *Lux Veritatis* encyclical: "The Fathers of the Eastern Church acknowledged the Bishop of Rome as the first in rank and bishop of the first see, as being the bishop of 'Great Rome', the old capital of the state and as such possessing great prestige"; but his position was that of "hierarch of the first see, not that of an absolute monarch and sovereign of the Church, ruling it by divine right and infallibly deciding the dogmatic and universal questions of the Church".[1]

The attitude of the Anglican Church is in full harmony with the Oriental Church regarding papal claims. We recognise the great position of the Bishop of Rome as prelate of the first see in Christendom. We acknowledge he is entitled to a primacy of honour among other bishops. We also deplore "all that has crept in to the Roman Church contrary and alien to the teaching and practice of the primitive Church."[2]

[1] *The Third Oecumenical Council and the Primacy of the Bishop of Rome*, p. 50.
[2] Ibid., p. 53.

CHAPTER II

PAPAL CLAIMS TO INFALLIBILITY

1

I n the fourth chapter of the Vatican Decrees the startling novel claim of the Pope to infallibility is defined. It is declared to be "a dogma divinely revealed that the Roman Pontiff when he speaks *ex cathedra*, that is when in discharge of the office of Pastor and Doctor of all Christians, by virtue of his supreme apostolic authority he defines a doctrine regarding faith or morals to be held by the universal Church, by the divine assistance promised him in blessed Peter, is possessed of that infallibility with which the divine Redeemer willed that His Church should be endowed for defining doctrine, and that such definitions of the Roman Pontiff are irreformable of themselves and not from the consent of the Church".

Thus in 1870 the whole basis of knowledge of Christian doctrine was radically altered. The former methods of ascertaining the true belief were rendered obsolete. All that now is required is acquiescence with what the infallible Teacher propounds. The evidence of Scripture and history is irrelevant. Such tests as that of St. Vincent in the fifth century, for the securing of a right faith, "first by the authority of the Divine Law, secondly by the tradition of the Catholic Church"—that which has been believed "everywhere, always, by all"; or the appeal of Bishop Jewel to the Holy Scriptures; the example of the primitive Church, the teaching of the Fathers, the decisions of General Councils, no longer are allowed as valid. All Christian doctrine depends on the utterance of the one divinely authorised and miraculously safeguarded spokesman—he who has "the supreme power of teaching". The Pope alone is the final authority—the medium for making known the truth of God, the never-erring oracle. Pius IX naturally, therefore, taught in a letter to the Archbishop of Munich that this dogma is "the fundamental principle of Catholic faith and doctrine".[1] Cardinal Bourne similarly

---

[1] Döllinger, *Declarations and Letters*, p. 101.

described it as "the fundamental doctrine of the Catholic Church".[1]
The revolutionary and anarchical effect of all this is obvious.
Döllinger was justified in declaring that "In future every Catholic
Christian when asked why he believes this or that can and may give
but the one answer: I believe or reject it because the infallible Pope
has bidden it to be believed or rejected".[2]

On the papal theory Cardinal Manning was entirely logical when
he asserted that "all appeals to Scripture alone, or to Scripture and
antiquity, whether by individuals or by local Churches, are no more
than appeals from the divine voice of the living Church and therefore essentially rationalistic".[3] "The appeal to antiquity is both a
treason and a heresy. It is a treason because it rejects the divine
voice of the Church at this hour, and a heresy because it denies that
voice to be divine."[4] He subsequently enforced this by asserting:
"The appeal from the living voice of the Church to any tribunal
whatsoever, human history included, is an act of private judgment
and a treason because that living voice is supreme; and to appeal
from that supreme voice is also a heresy because that voice by divine
assistance is infallible."[5]

Mr. Adrian Fortescue, in articles originally published in the
Tablet, denounces the appeal to Scripture and the Fathers. "We
cannot admit that it is necessary for a Catholic in 1920 to examine
the documents of the year 1 to 451 in order to know what is the
nature of the primacy Christ gave to His Church. . . . To be obliged
to hark back some fifteen hundred years to judge for yourself,
according to the measure of your scholarship, what the documents
of that period imply would be the end of all confidence in a living
authority. It is a far worse criterion for religion than the old Protestant idea of the Bible only." Dealing with ecclesiastical disputes,
he points out that an appeal to Rome "costs twopence halfpenny".[6]

A Catholic Truth Society pamphlet teaches similarly: "The
Catholic Church is essentially, and by divine institution, papal in
its nature; that it is a body which is visibly one, under one visible
head, who is the infallible spokesman of God in his official pronouncements to the Church on matters of faith and morals; that to

---

[1] *Lenten Pastoral*, 1924.
[2] *Declarations and Letters*, pp. 100, 101.
[3] *Temporal Mission of the Holy Ghost* (4th edition), p. 29.
[4] Ibid., p. 238.
[5] *Daily Telegraph*, 8th October 1875, p. 5.
[6] *The Early Papacy*, pp. 3, 4, 14.

be a Catholic means precisely to be in communion with the Pope and nothing else."[1]

The official teaching of the Popes fully corroborates this attitude to the standards of belief. The statement of Pius XI,[2] already referred to, that all Christians must believe the Immaculate Conception of the Virgin Mary and the infallible teaching authority of the Roman Pontiff with the same faith as they believe the Trinity and the Incarnation, is a disturbing example. The Immaculate Conception and the Infallibility were decreed by the Pope in the nineteenth century (a Council approving of the latter). To hold that they are as vital to the faith as belief in the Trinity and the Incarnation inevitably tends to making the doctrines of the Trinity and the Incarnation to be no more authentic than they. The tendency of predominantly Roman Catholic countries to be overrun with infidelity is not hard to account for.

2

The attempt of modern Romanists to discredit the appeal to the Bible and history is clearly an evidence that they cannot find support for their dogmas there. It is a significant admission of defeat. We often read how a general whose defences have been stormed has taken up a new, shorter line in the rear. The present policy of Roman defenders to fall back for a guarantee of their teaching to the mere *ipse dixit* of their Oracle in Rome is a desperate one that will not avail them.

They do not themselves really trust in it. In practice they are still continually endeavouring to demonstrate that Scripture and tradition can be made to support their theories. Pius IX in the *Pastor Aeternus* was careful to maintain that the Vatican dogmas are in accordance with the ancient and constant faith of all ages, according to the testimony of the Gospel: resting on the plain testimonies of the Sacred Writings, adhering to the tradition received from the beginning of the Christian faith, and so on. Similarly the *Satis Cognitum* of Leo XIII is an elaborate effort, with many citations from Scripture and the Fathers to prove that Papalism is the venerable and constant belief of every age—what not one race or age but all ages, East and West, acknowledged—what has the *consensus antiquitatis*.

[1] Rev. P. H. Malden, *Anglo-Catholics, Have They Grasped the Point?*, p. 12.
[2] Encyclical on *Fostering True Religious Union*, p. 12.

The most confident proclaimers of the all-sufficiency of the Living Voice to establish their tenets find it necessary to resòrt to the authority of Scripture and tradition. Mr. Adrian Fortescue, for example, gives much labour to the testimony of the Fathers. The Rev. Hugh Pope at Cambridge, after his high-flying words about the Pope, proceeds to discuss at length "the Papacy in the New Testament". We have seen how in *Lux Veritatis* we are exhorted to attend to "history, the guide of life". The attempt to make papal pronouncements the sole authoritative criterion of doctrine is a convenient one for hard-pressed apologists but one that is a complete begging of the question and one that they themselves in practice do not venture to depend on.

3

There is another logical development of the acceptance of such claims. Since the Pope possesses such a unique relation to God, he is lifted above normal human categories. Hence it is natural to address him in terms of extreme devotion or even adoration.

La Croix of 22nd November 1912 published what it called not a literal but a sufficiently complete and faithful reproduction of a discourse of Pius X: "The love of the Pope is effectively a necessary means of sanctification. . . . He is the chief under whom no one feels himself tyrannised over because that he represents God Himself."[1] Pope Pius XI informed a number of Maltese pilgrims that the Pope was the rope that Jesus Christ threw to the world in order that every one might stay with Him.[2]

The volume of addresses given at the Cambridge School of Catholic Studies has a preface by the editor, Rev. C. Lattey, S.J., entitled, "The Light of the World". He teaches: "If Christ be the Light of the world, the Vicar of Christ also sheds that same divine light upon the world."[3]

It is only a step from this to the pamphlet *De la Devotion au Pape*, published in 1904 with the imprimatur of the Archbishop of Tours. The Pope honoured it with a letter sent through Cardinal Merry del Val, in which the pamphlet is praised for its "very intelligent filial piety" of a "true Catholic and exemplary priest". It is taught in this that the Pope is "the Father of all humanity"; that though

---

[1] *Spectator*, 4th January 1913.
[2] *Irish Catholic*, 30th August 1930.
[3] *The Papacy*, p. 2.

there is not an absolute parity, yet in a sense one may say, as the tabernacle is the home of Jesus the Victim, so the Vatican is the home of Jesus the Teacher; that from this Sanctuary the Lord Jesus now speaks to the world by the mouth of His Vicar, whether he be Peter or Pius IX or Pius X. "When we fall at the Pope's feet to offer him the homage of our mind, and to accept his teaching, it is again, in a certain way, Jesus Christ whom we adore in his Doctrinal Presence." Obedience is necessary, for "every objection will be silenced, every reasoning will go for nothing, every hesitation will yield before this unanswerable argument: 'God wills and commands it because the Pope wills and commands it.' Let us enter into the joys of the Pope. . . ." By the fact "that he is the Vicar of Christ and His principal co-operant he is an elect victim and he is ex-officio nailed to the cross".

In a book by Mgr. Gay we read: "All the devotion to Jesus as Priest, Shepherd and Father that enlightened faith can inspire is summed up practically and effectively in devotion to the Pope. . . . If one would have a devotion to the sacred Scriptures, the Pope is the living and speaking Bible. If it is a duty to be devout to the Sacraments, is not the Pope the Sacrament of Jesus by the mere fact that he is His Vicar?"[1]

In 1931 Dom Lucien Chambat published a book, *La Royauté du Christ*. The Bishop of Autun wrote a preface felicitating the author on having faithfully set forth the doctrine of the Church. The book is written to advocate the *Ligue Universelle du Christ Roy*. One of the rules for the members is "a spirit of total submission to the directions of the Sovereign Pontiff, submission born from the conviction that every word of the Pope is a word of God".

Abbé Houtin in his *Une Vie de Prêtre* quotes from a pastoral letter of his bishop (Bishop of Angers, 30th June 1900). The Pope "has received from Jesus Christ the investiture as Pastor of Pastors; he possesses the plenitude of priesthood, he is the Sovereign-Priest. His ministry is so indispensable that without him there would be neither episcopate nor priesthood, nor power to ordain nor power to adjudicate. At the same time his power as Pontiff is so universal that it embraces the future as well as the present life. The Church of this world exists only through him. Suppress the Pope and you destroy the unity of the Church of which he is the centre, the holiness of the Church of which he is the source".[2]

---

[1] M. D. Petre, *Modernism*, pp. 189, 190.   [2] E. T., p. 126.

B

George Tyrrell wrote to Cardinal Mercier in 1908: "Your Eminence, on the communion-tessera of this year, approved by the Archbishop of Milan, I find Mary and the Pope twice put side by side: *Gloria alla madre Immaccolata: Gloria al santo Padre!* I have seen one of the crosses sold to the faithful of Rome on which the figure of Christ is replaced by that of the Pope. I admit the logic of it all, but I ask myself: where is it to end?"[1]

A few years ago Rev. Albert Gillo, S.J. ("Father Jerome"), protested against the "childish endeavour to raise the Pope to the level of a demigod. . . . This campaign of fulsome flattery. . . . Our hero worship is growing into a disease. . . . If it is not stopped the Popes in a hundred years will be as sacred as the Lamas of Tibet".[2]

[1] *Medievalism*, p. 71.   [2] *A Catholic Plea for Reunion*, pp. 46, 47.

CHAPTER III

PRIVATE JUDGMENT

1

Romanists are accustomed to contrast the security enjoyed by their members, protected against false doctrine by an inerrant authority, with the hazardous uncertainty of others who have to depend on their own reasoning faculties. The wrongfulness of such dependence on private judgment is constantly warned against.

But the attempt to disallow private judgment is foredoomed to failure. "We can never attain to any higher certainty than whatever that may be able to give us. We may talk about the right of private judgment, or the duty of private judgment, but a more important thing to insist on is the *necessity* of private judgment. We have the choice whether we will exercise our private judgment in one act or in a great many; but exercise it one way or another we must." "Absolute certainty can only be had on the terms of being infallible one's self. A man may say, 'I am absolutely certain that I am right in my religious opinions, because I believe what the Pope believes, and he is absolutely certain not to believe wrong.' But then comes the question, 'How come you to be absolutely certain that the Pope is absolutely certain not to be wrong?'"[1]

Roman Catholics adopt the extraordinary position that private judgment is to be depended on when it leads one to accept Romanist theology but is never again to be listened to. The Rev. Vernon Johnson's arguments about this are peculiar. He has come to the discovery that "it is the function of reason to guide us to where the divine authority rests, and that the authority itself must be able to meet the challenge of reason, one of God's greatest gifts to man, or else cease to exist, for only truth can prevail".[2] Yet he condemns the Anglo-Catholic view of authority inasmuch as it "leaves room for independence and private judgment". The Catholic "view of

---

[1] Salmon, *Infallibility of the Church* (3rd edition), pp. 48, 53.
[2] *One Lord—One Faith*, p. 42.

authority leaves no room for private judgment".[1] What then has been done with "one of God's greatest gifts to man"?

The Rev. F. Woodlock, S.J., puts forward the same view: "The Catholic theory of the use of reason in religion is this. A man uses his reason, his private judgment to reach the Church as the mouth-piece of God's message. Once that is found he uses his reason, not to criticise and reject, but to understand and assimilate what doctrinal authority proposes to him as God's truth."[2]

This dependence on private judgment in a supremely grave issue, and scrapping it for the rest of one's life is as illogical as anything can be. "You can trust your private judgment up to the point of making this tremendous surrender to the claims of Rome. In making this particular act of private judgment you can be certain that it is a perfectly true and reliable guide. But if you do not make this particular act of your own private judgment, you have nothing left to rely on but—your own private judgment! It is really a little ridiculous. Can we seriously believe that a power which will enable us to decide aright on an issue of such tremendous importance will fail to guide us aright on issues of lesser importance? A faculty given for the purpose of performing one single act of submission and never to be used again seems a little improbable."[3]

Archbishop Whately well showed the momentous task laid on private judgment before a man submits to Rome. "He must first have judged: (1) that there is a God; (2) that Christianity comes from God; (3) that Christ has promised to give an infallible authority in the Church; (4) that such authority resides in the Church of Rome. Now to say that men who are competent to form sound judgments upon these points are quite incompetent to form sound judgments about any other matters of religion is very like saying that men may have sound judgments of their own before they enter the Church of Rome, but that they lose all sound judgment entirely from the moment they enter it."[4] Nowadays a man has to judge another question of great difficulty—that the infallible authority of the Church is vested in the Bishop of Rome.

It amounts to this. A man can never have any more valid basis of surety that the Pope will infallibly guide him right than he has in concluding that the Pope is infallible. Everything rests on private

[1] *One Lord—One Faith*, pp. 51, 52.
[2] *Constantinople, Canterbury and Rome*, pp. 3, 4.
[3] Milner-White and Knox, *One God and Father of All*, p. 87.
[4] *Cautions for the Times*, p. 21.

judgment. However a convert may decide to jettison his reason at a certain stage of his life and so commit a sort of intellectual suicide, he is actually always dependent on that particular exercise of his judgment.

Not a few of those who make the sacrifice find out the requirements are more than they can endure. Some years ago Mr. Alfred Noyes was enjoined to withdraw all copies of his book on Voltaire and write something equivalent to a reparation. He complained in a manner nearer to Protestant self-assertion than Romanist submissiveness that "no submission can have any value when the free will of the author was completely eliminated by the procedure which had already been taken". He was determined to "answer with my own conscience to any requirements that are made of me. . . . I I would feel myself traitor to one of the greatest English traditions if I were to shrink from saying it honestly and clearly". He declared he reverenced his "conscience as his king". Here was a convert of eleven years' standing who had not realised that his submission to Rome meant substituting an infallible authority for his own private judgment.

George Tyrrell was driven to the position in which he announced: "I must go by my own moral certainties."[1] Unqualified obedience, he came to see, was "the profoundest idolatry and immorality".[2]

2

It is maintained that the absolute authority of the Church demands "in the name of our Lord a complete submission of the individual".[3]

This is a statement to be denied with indignation. Our Lord made no such demand on the individual intellect in His own name. He called for the exercise of men's judgment. The appeal of St. Paul is to men's individual judgment. "Prove all things: hold fast that which is good" (1 Thess. v. 21). "Let each man be fully assured in his own mind" (Rom. xiv. 5). His method of teaching was "by the manifestation of the truth commending ourselves to every man's conscience in the sight of God" (2 Cor. iv. 2). "I speak as to wise men; judge ye what I say" (1 Cor. x. 15). It is St. Peter who exhorts the church officers how they are to tend the flock of God, "neither

[1] *Life*, vol. ii., p. 405.
[2] Ibid., vol. ii, p. 293.
[3] Rev. Vernon Johnson, *One Lord—One Faith*, p. 52.

as lording it over the charge allotted to you, but making yourselves ensamples to the flock" (1 Pet. v. 3). We dare not surrender
the use of our own reason. We are dishonouring our noblest
faculties if we transfer our consciences to any external authority.
Such spiritual self-mutilation is abhorrent. Loyalty to God and
ourselves forbids abandoning what makes us responsible rational
beings. "The spirit of man is the candle of the Lord" (Prov.
xx. 27).

Absolute despotism in the state, obliging unconditional obedience,
is rightly abhorred as outraging the inherent rights of the individual
personality. Is not ecclesiastical despotism a more crushing and
enslaving bondage? The imprisonment of the soul is a deadlier
affliction than of the body. The status of the members of Christ's
Society is that of sons, not of slaves. The obedience due from responsible beings must be voluntary and rational, not blind and passive.
"I have ever," wrote Bishop Gore, "since I was an undergraduate
been certain that I must in the true sense be a free-thinker, and that
either not to think freely about a disturbing subject or to accept
ecclesiastical authority in the face of the best judgment of my own
reason would be an impossible treason against light. I must go
remorselessly where the argument leads me."[1]

It is easy to set forth the mistakes arising from the misuse of
private judgment. These mistakes no more justify its suppression
than do the evils arising from the misuse of freedom justify keeping
people perpetually under restraint. Because some men think wrongly
is not sufficient excuse for forbidding others to think at all. Charles
Leslie's words deserve remembrance. The not allowing the free use
of reason to a man he compares to persuading him to prefer to be
led blindfold by others, since "there is less danger of stumbling than
if his eyes were open, because every man's sight is not good, and has
deceived many. Have I not taken a horse for a man at a distance?
And does not a stick look crooked in the water? Why then should
I trust my eyes any more? This is all the reason ever I could hear
for not trusting to our reason. And what is the remedy proposed?
If it were to give us rules whereby to judge of true reason, to help
it, and to trim this lamp which God has lighted for us, this would
be rational like clearing our eyes if they were dim. But the remedy
you propose is to shut reason quite out, to make no more use of it,
to silence, to extinguish it, and take implicit faith in its room; like

[1] *Belief in God*, preface.

pulling out one's eyes because they are not good, and choosing to be led by the hand and never examine our way any more".[1]

3

It is not difficult to see how even within the Roman fold the exercise of private judgment cannot in practice be dispensed with. Leo XIII, in his encyclical *Immortale Dei* (1885), copiously denounced private judgment and its consequence, freedom of conscience. He cites with approval the encyclical *Mirari Vos* of his predecessor, Gregory XVI (1832). This is the encyclical that described the claim that the freedom of conscience of each individual ought to be asserted and vindicated as madness (*deliramentum*). Leo XIII also appealed to Pius IX's condemnation of false theories in the Syllabus, "in order that in this sea of error Catholics might have a light which they might safely follow".

Are the *Mirari Vos* and the Syllabus infallible utterances? The hesitations and contradictions of Romanists on this illustrate how hollow are the protestations about the necessity for infallible guidance and also how orthodox Romanists cannot eliminate their private judgments even in determining their attitude to solemn papal pronouncements. W. G. Ward, editor of the *Dublin Review*, wrote: "If Gregory XVI denounced as an 'insanity' the tenet that 'liberty of conscience is to be vindicated for each man,' Pius IX no less emphatically declares (prop. lxxix) that the liberty of worship and of the Press conduces to the corruption of morals and the propagation of a pestilential indifferentism. . . . We have no hesitation in maintaining . . . that its doctrinal deductions possess absolute infallibility in virtue of the promise made by Christ to St. Peter's chair."[2] Ward presses his dissentient co-religionists with unsparing logic. The *Mirari Vos* was in response to an appeal from the episcopate for "a solemn decision from the infallible mouth of St. Peter's successor". The encyclical claimed "universal submission to the Vicar of Jesus Christ". Gregory, in an encyclical of 10th July 1834, used the critical word "definimus", in speaking of "that Catholic doctrine which he had delivered in the *Mirari Vos*".[3] The cardinal who sent the encyclical to the bishops announced that the Pope

---

[1] *The Case Stated* (1840 edition), pp. 128, 129.
[2] *Dublin Review*, April 1865, p. 443.
[3] *Dublin Review*, January 1865, p. 58.

required obedience to the utterances of "Peter's infallible mouth". Those Romanists who refuse to admit its infallibility show a daring exercise of private judgment.

The Syllabus of 1864 is a collection of errors condemned in allocutions and encyclicals by Pope Pius IX. Later in the year he issued an encyclical, *Quanta Cura*, condemning other errors. In the presence of the bishops assembled from all parts of the world in Rome for the eighteenth centenary of St. Peter the Pope confirmed solemnly the Syllabus and the encyclical as the rule of their teaching. The bishops later declared that unanimous concurrence with what the Pope "judged fit to reprove and reject".

Dr. Ward wonders how anyone can doubt the *ex cathedra* character of the Syllabus. Cardinal Manning declared the bishops "recognised the voice of Peter in the voice of Pius and the infallible certainty of all his declarations and condemnations in virtue of the supreme and singular prerogative of Doctor of the universal Church given by our Lord Jesus Christ to Peter and through Peter to his successors". The bishops renewed their adhesion to the encyclical *Quanta Cura* and the eighty condemnations in the Syllabus as "part of the supreme teaching of the Church through the person of its head which by the special assistance of the Holy Ghost is preserved from all error. They did not add certainty to that which was already infallible".[1]

This seems entirely clear and emphatic. The flock of the Roman Catholic Church has been given guidance by the Living Voice. The members are bound by its infallible authority to reprobate such opinions as that "the Church has not the power of availing herself of force or of any direct or indirect temporal power"; or that "in the present day it is no longer necessary that the Catholic religion should be held as the only religion of the state to the exclusion of all others".

Do present-day Roman Catholics use their private judgment in declining to be bound by these authoritative and—according to Cardinal Manning—infallible declarations? Cardinal Newman, in his letter to the Duke of Norfolk (1875), shows how deftly he can eliminate formulas of their natural meaning. Thirty years in the Roman Church had not caused the hand of the writer of *Tract Ninety* to lose its cunning. He proves to his own satisfaction that the Syllabus need be no more accepted "as *de fide*, as a dogmatic docu-

[1] *Petri Privilegium*, pp. 33, 34 (centenary of St. Peter).

ment, than any other index or table of contents".[1] He goes on to argue that propositions that are correct have been condemned because they are false as the offending author used them.[2] The cardinal falls back on the reprobated principle: "In discussions such as these there is a real exercise of private judgment and an allowable one."[3] He even admits that there are extreme cases in which conscience may come into collision with the word of a Pope and is to be followed in spite of that word.[4]

The *Catholic Encyclopaedia* leaves the infallibility of the Syllabus in doubt. Many theologians, we are told, ascribe to it an infallible authority, others do not. "So long as Rome has not decided the question every one is free to follow the opinion he chooses"[5]—in other words, decide the grave issues involved by his own judgment. It would seem that, after all, Romanists cannot entirely dispense with private judgment.

[1] p. 83.   [2] p. 92.   [3] p. 121.
[4] p. 55.   [5] vol. xiv, p. 368.

CHAPTER IV

AUTHORITY

The question of the rights of private judgment is inseparable from that of the place of authority in religious matters. A man is, of course, not justified in depending altogether on his own uninformed judgment. It is senseless arrogance to ignore the respect due to the corporate belief of the Church, the decisions of the assembled Church leaders of former days, that have stood the test of time and come to us ratified by the experience of the Christians of all ages. The collective Church is the pillar and ground of the truth. We are bound to listen in a deferential and teachable spirit to those who are wiser and more learned than we.

From our infancy we are instructed by the knowledge and experience of others. Our attainments in any study are founded on the discoveries of those before us and on the erudition of teachers and experts. We are the heirs of the accumulated knowledge of the ages. It would be as foolish for a person to attempt to make a system of theology by his own unaided interpretations of the Bible as it would be to make a system of astronomy by his own unaided observation of the stars. But always the authority of a teacher over his students or of physicians, lawyers, financiers over those who consult them, is based on the assumed possession of superior knowledge. Such authority is not merely official. It cannot subsist if it is not justified by greater erudition or wisdom. There is no such conception in any branch of science as infallibility in an expert, much less in the holder of an official position such as the presidency of the Royal Society or of the College of Physicians.

As in all secular subjects, we accept the precepts of teachers because we believe these precepts are capable of being proved, so in religious matters we accept the conclusions of our teachers because we believe they also can justify themselves before the enlightened understanding. The ultimate authority in the Christian religion is the Personality of Christ. We believe in Him as one entitled to be given our full obedience and devotion. The ordinances of His Church have no final, arbitrary authority apart from it being known they can be proved to be truly representative of His teaching. The great Christian doctrines were arrived at by the exercise of men's judgment, under the influence of the Holy Spirit, after careful examination of the teaching of our Lord and His apostles and the beliefs of the primitive Church.

The true function of the teacher is to lead the enquirer to be able to understand the reasons for the instruction imparted. Church authority is very different from the absolutism that announces but will not demonstrate. As Bishop Gore has written: "True authority does not issue edicts to suppress men's personal judgments or render its action unnecessary, but is like the authority of a parent, which invigorates and encourages, even while it restrains and guides the growth of our own individuality."[1] With this view of authority Salmon is in agreement: "I maintain that it is the office of the Church to teach; but that it is her duty to do so, not by making assertions merely, but by offering proofs; and again, that while it is the duty of the individual Christian to receive with deference the teaching of the Church, it is his duty also not listlessly to acquiesce in her statements but to satisfy himself of the validity of her proofs."[2] Religion that cannot approve itself to the intellect will not survive.

The principle of authority in the Church, far from being opposed to private judgment, derives its valid sanction from the free consent of thoughtful men. The authority that requires the sacrifice of intellect, the suppression of conscience, is only a fantastic spiritual despotism. Not so did Christ our Lord impose a body of dogmas on His followers. He allowed and trained their minds to respond to His appeal. He waited for their unenforced decision. When they had sufficient grounds for knowledge He asked them: "Who say ye that I am?" He trusted in the spiritual discernment of men. "My sheep hear My voice"; "He that is of God heareth God's word"; "If a man love Me he will keep My word". The unity He prayed for was first of all a spiritual unity resulting in a visible unity. "That they may all be one; even as Thou, Father, art in Me and I in Thee, that they also may be in Us" (John xvii. 21).

The demand of the Roman Church for absolute obedience to its authority is constantly founded on such words of our Lord: "He that heareth you heareth Me" (Luke x. 16); "I am with you alway,

---

[1] *Roman Catholic Claims* (5th edition), p. 54.
[2] *Infallibility of the Church*, p. 116.

even unto the end of the world" (Matt. xxviii. 20). The former of these sayings was spoken to the seventy; the latter to the eleven disciples. Our Lord's words must be either taken as applicable to all faithful followers of His or only as applicable to the specific groups who heard them. It will not be argued that their purport is confined to their first hearers. Therefore they are meant for His Church as a whole. On what right, then, does the Roman Church limit them to its own communion exclusively? Why are they not true of all those who faithfully love and follow Him in the Oriental, Anglican and other Churches? Such an interpretation as the Roman is childish. The Roman Church really interprets them not as spoken to the disciples as a group but to one of them. The Pope has usurped to himself the teaching authority belonging to the episcopate and to the whole Church. The episcopate has lost its function in the Roman Church of being part of the *Ecclesia docens*.

The Anglican Church does not, as often represented, ignore the rightful authority of the Church. Our Twentieth Article of Religion states: "The Church hath power to decree rites or ceremonies and authority in controversies of faith."

Finally, we reject the authority claimed by the Church of Rome because of its practical working out in history. We reject it not only because it is based on impossible assumptions but also because of the many and terrible blunders and abominations it has committed.

"The Papacy," writes Bishop Headlam, "as authority is inconsistent with the very essence of Christianity." After referring to its interference with the rights of conscience, its opposing Christian principles by force, etc., he writes: "Again and again in its history the Papacy has adopted such methods and violated the rules which should guide Christian action."[1] "We may find in this imperialistic ambition the worst perversion that Christianity has ever undergone."[2]

[1] *The Doctrine of the Church*, p. 194.
[2] Inge, *Christian Ethics and Modern Problems*, p. 189.

CHAPTER V

CERTITUDE

1

One of the most common arguments for papal claims is the *a priori* one: that it is reasonable and necessary to conclude God would not have left the Church without a supreme Ruler and Teacher. This argument in various forms is continually advanced by Romanist advocates. "There must therefore be some living authority on earth, commissioned by God, to decide the meaning of the revelation which God has given us. Such an authority must be infallible . . . without such infallibility there would be no certainty of faith."[1] "The question resolves itself into these two: does the world need a trustworthy teacher? and does the doctrine of papal infallibility supply it with one in a suitable manner?"[2] There is higher sanction for this *a priori* plea. Leo XIII taught: "Since He willed [His kingdom] to be visible He was obliged [*debuit*] to designate who would be His vicegerent after that He Himself had ascended to heaven"; and quoted St. Thomas Aquinas' words: "For the same reason, therefore, when He was about to withdraw His visible presence from the Church it was needful [*oportuit*] for Him that He should commission some one who in His stead would have charge of the universal Church."[3]

It is futile to argue that because it seems fitting to us that God should govern the world in a certain way therefore that must be the course He has willed. *Decuit ergo fecit.* Bishop Butler sufficiently dealt with that sort of wishful thinking. He showed the errors of forming "notions of God's government upon hypothesis"; of indulging in "vain and idle speculations how the world might possibly have been framed otherwise than it is". By such a process of thinking we would be led to some such conclusions as, "that all creatures should at first be made as perfect and happy as they were capable of ever being; that nothing to be sure of hazard or danger should

---

[1] Di Bruno, *Catholic Belief* (24th edition), p. 36.
[2] Rev. Sydney F. Smith, S.J., *Papal Supremacy and Infallibility*, p. 20.
[3] *Satis Cognitum.*

be put upon them to do"; that effectual care should be taken that they always do what was right and most conducive to happiness. We should see "that we have not faculties for this kind of speculation . . . we are far from being able to judge what particular disposition of things would be most friendly and assistant to virtue". While we know that regularity, order and right must prevail finally in God's universe, "we are in no sort judges what are the necessary means of accomplishing this end".[1]

The world as it is, with all its evil and pain, all its injustice and tragedies, defeated hopes and blighted lives, ravages of war and physical catastrophes, is not the ideal world we might expect under the providence of the almighty and all-loving God. Butler has reminded us of the sagacious saying of Origen, that "he who believes the Scripture to have proceeded from Him who is the Author of nature may well expect to find the same sort of difficulties in it as are found in the constitution of nature".[2] From the facts of experience we have no grounds for imagining that God would make miraculous provision to safeguard us from theological mistakes.

Experience shows that the way to knowledge is by the honest exercise of our faculties. There is no infallible authority anywhere in life whereby we can be divinely safeguarded from sin or suffering, intellectual or moral error. Man has to search, to adventure, to discover. By that struggle his personality is developed. Risk is involved, but the risk is part of his training. Improvement in character is the supreme end. A sheltered, protected existence where is no necessity to think for oneself, to choose according to conscience, to hold convictions because we personally believe them true, is not worthy of the dignity of man. Whether we like it or not we have to examine and decide.

"Live thou! and of the grain and husk, the grape and ivy berry
        choose.
        . . . . Thou art thou,
    With power on thine own act and on the world."[3]

The conception of life as a perpetual tutelage so far as the knowledge of the highest truths is concerned, where painful stumbling, endeavour towards the light, is superfluous because of inerrant official announcements is not one to be desired. The promise of

---

[1] *Analogy of Religion*, introduction.   [2] Ibid.
[3] Tennyson, " De Profundis ".

the Master is that His Spirit will guide us to the truth. There is point in the story of the Roman Catholic who said of an Anglican: "He believes the same things that we believe, but he believes them for the wholly irrelevant reason that he thinks them true." The beliefs that we value are those which our mind and conscience attain to, not those handed out to us from some final external bureau of information.

The method of Rome can produce—for a time—uniformity, but it is a cast-iron uniformity purchased at too high a cost. It is the stepping in line at the behest of the drill sergeant. The different points of view among Protestants are at all events signs of vitality, of spiritual life. If we are not to use our intellects in religious questions we are not likely to go astray. "Agreement in a body which allows no difference with itself is no proof of divine authority; it is proof of skilful policing. The Church in the apostles' days, in the early undivided days, in medieval days, did not take refuge from the questions of its time in oracular infallibility. It tackled the questions."[1] The machinery for the regulating of doctrinal beliefs in the Roman Church produces acquiescence rather than certainty. Conviction that is of value does not evolve through such regimentation of thought.

Milton's message should not be forgotten: "Truth and understanding are not such wares as to be monopolised and traded in by tickets and statutes and standards. We must not think to make a staple community of all knowledge in the land, to mark and licence it like our broad cloth and our wool pecks. What is that but a servitude like that imposed by the Philistines, not to be allowed the sharpening of our own axes and coulters."[2]

2

The New Testament has nothing to say about any authoritative human source of truth. Such a conception is alien to its whole outlook. Our Lord called on His followers to use their minds (Luke xii. 57). When the question was asked Him, "Art Thou He that should come?" instead of making a positive declaration He referred His questioners to the conclusion to be drawn from the works He did (Luke vii. 22). He did not authoritatively secure His followers from falling into errors, as about His second coming. His disciples

[1] Milner-White and Knox, *One God and Father of All*, p. 24.
[2] *Areopagitica*.

often misunderstood Him. He taught not so much by laying down formulated doctrines as by the revealing of Himself. He gave them no access to truth other than the leading of His Spirit. "He shall guide you into all the truth. . . . He shall glorify Me: for He shall take of Mine, and shall declare it unto you" (John xvi. 13, 14). "As a matter of fact there is not a word in the New Testament to suggest that our Lord ever promised His Church an oracular infallibility. . . . The whole conception of a Church which has been entrusted with a fixed set of doctrines and an oracular authority to interpret them is utterly without support in the New Testament. The authority of the New Testament is the Person of our Lord and the guidance of the Holy Spirit, working through His followers, leading them to the truth in so far as they seek it sincerely, and giving them power to convince the world that God is with them. But this guidance depends not on their acceptance of the authority of the Church but on their loyalty to the example and Spirit of the Lord Himself."[1]

The one-sided Roman concentration on ecclesiastical security against wrong doctrines is a strange perversion of the Christian religion. The teaching of Christ was almost entirely on a good life, on overcoming sin. "He shall save His people from their sins." His call was: "Follow Me." His main commandment was love. It is by love that discipleship is proved. It is not underrating the importance of right belief to point out how the chief insistence of our Lord was on a right life. The regarding it as necessary that He should provide a series of Vicars with "plenitude of power" "to defend the truth of faith" is utterly out of keeping with His life. It is due to this fundamental misconception that the promise that the gates of hell shall not prevail against His Church is deflected to the excluding of heresy. "The question is whether God hates error so very much more than He hates sin, that He has taken precautions against the entrance of the one which He has not seen fit to use in order to guard against the other. . . . His great gift to His people, that of the Holy Spirit, is equally their safeguard against sin and against error. He is equally the spirit of Truth and the Spirit of Holiness."[2]

It is taught that the Pope cannot fall into heresy. But why should he not also be protected by "divine assistance" from falling into

---

[1] Milner-White and Knox, *One God and Father of All*, pp. 44, 45, 46.
[2] Salmon, *Infallibility of the Church*, p. 103.

sin? Why should the Vicar of Christ who rules in His stead be fortified by divine intervention doctrinally but nor morally? Is it in
accordance with the mind of Christ that His representative on earth
may be a vicious scoundrel but must be always doctrinally orthodox?
If infallible in theology, why not impeccable in character?

3

The theory of the all-importance of certitude of belief being provided through an infallible Teacher is sufficiently confuted by the
fact that it was not adopted by the Church for nearly one thousand
nine hundred years. This will be referred to again. It will be seen
how history presents abundance of positive disproofs. The evidence
destructive of the theory meets one in many forms. The great disputes about the basal truths of Christianity were not settled by pronouncements from the official spokesman of God. Not one of the
great heresies was put down in this way, but always by a Council or
by some private theologian. Sometimes the Popes were on the wrong
side. Sometimes the Popes are careful not to give a definite decision
while the need for it is greatest but to wait until the question settles
itself. The theory of the Immaculate Conception of the Blessed
Virgin Mother aroused fierce controversy for hundreds of years. St.
Bernard, St. Bonaventura, St. Thomas Aquinas opposed it. The
Franciscan and Dominican orders were in bitter opposition about it.
Universities were convulsed with the hostile parties. So the centuries
passed, and the question, like many others once eagerly debated,
ceased to rouse animosity. Then in 1854 the Pope made it a dogma
of faith. He declared, pronounced and defined in the bull *Ineffabilis
Deus* that the doctrine "is revealed by God". "Why should men
of today be forced to believe 'under pain of eternal damnation'
what St. Thomas and St. Bernard denied with impunity?"[1]

In the thirteenth century the Franciscan order was convulsed by a
controversy about holding to the principles of their founder. Gregory
IX in 1231 issued a bull that it was not lawful for them to have
property. In 1279 the bull of Nicholas III, *Exiit*, endorsed this and
stated that Christ taught it by word and example. Pope John XXII,
however, in his bull *Cum inter nonnullos*, 1332, denounced the tenet
of the absolute poverty of Christ as contrary to Scripture and
heretical. Where is certitude to be found?

[1] Tyrrell, *Medievalism*, p. 49.

C

CHAPTER VI

PAPAL CLAIMS AND THE SCRIPTURES

The dogma of the universal supremacy of the Pope as Vicar of Christ is asserted in the Vatican Decrees to rest "on plain testimonies of the Sacred Writings".[1] This doctrine of the supremacy was declared by Bellarmine to be "the principal matter of Christianity" (*de summa rei Christianae*).[2] A law so tremendous for the Christian Church must have been revealed in the clearest way by our Lord Himself. "This highest principle of faith must never have been obscured in the Church, as it must of necessity have been stated as clear as daylight in the Scriptures; it must have ruled the whole Church like a brightly shining star and that at all times and for all nations; it must have been put at the head of all instruction."[3]

Romanists, of course, profess to find the dogma in Holy Scripture. "If the Catholic doctrine of the Papacy is true it must find solid justification in the New Testament—the charter of Christianity."[4]

Now if this doctrine be plainly taught in Scripture how strange is the fact that the greater part of the Christian Church has been not only unable to find it but is firmly convinced that it is not there. Protestants are the most diligent students of the Bible. Their scholarship has been pre-eminent in defending and elucidating it. Yet they resolutely deny the papal dogma to be in accordance with Scriptural teaching.

Rome pronounces anathema on any who do not admit that the Bishop of Rome has full and supreme jurisdiction over the universal Church. Our first difficulty is that there is no authority whatever ascribed in the Bible to the Church of Rome. Rome is only referred to incidentally as other cities and places are. It is true in one book of the New Testament she is symbolically singled out but it is for the fiercest denunciation (Rev. xvii, xviii).

[1] chap. iii.
[2] *De Potestate Summi Pontificis* (1628 edition), praefatio, p. 128.
[3] Döllinger, Letter to Archbishop of Munich, *Declarations and Letters*, p. 101.
[4] Rev. Dr. Pope, O.P., *The Papacy*, p. 6.

On what Scriptural evidence, then, is the Bishop of Rome asserted to be the sovereign of the Church? The texts that are brought forward are amazingly insufficient and irrelevant. It is an involved line of proof. We are told, in the first place, that our Lord appointed St. Peter to be the prince of all the apostles with true and proper jurisdiction, the visible Head of the whole Church militant. Secondly, it is assumed that in this headship St. Peter was to have a perpetual series of successors. Thirdly, it is assumed that St. Peter was Bishop of Rome; and, fourthly, that Roman bishops are such successors.

Just as no mention of the Roman bishop is to be found in the Bible, so neither is there any mention of St. Peter ever being Bishop of Rome. Neither is there any mention in Scripture of his ever having been at Rome. Neither is there any mention of his having successors in his alleged primacy of jurisdiction. The Vatican Decrees do not even attempt to cite any scriptural proof for three of these four essential links. They have to fall back on pure assumptions and argumentation. What St. Peter was, it is urged, must remain united with the Church (*jugiter durare necesse est*).[1] "No one indeed can doubt, yea, it is known to all ages", that Peter lives, presides and judges in his successors, the Bishops of Rome. On these grotesquely inadequate grounds the conclusion is promulgated, "whence whosoever succeeds to Peter in this See does by the institution of Christ Himself obtain the primacy of Peter over the whole Church".[2] The breakdown of vital steps in the papal claim is obvious. It is not on such imaginary bases that the fundamental constitution of the Church can be erected.

Pope Leo XIII issued his *Satis Cognitum* twenty-six years later than the Vatican Council. It is a lengthy and comprehensive document, but he utterly fails to find any better Scriptural authority than Piux IX did for there being successors to St. Peter. He is reduced to pleading that since Christ "willed that His kingdom should be visible He was obliged to designate [*designare debuit*] who would be his vicegerent on earth after that He had returned to heaven". Then Leo XIII announces the totally unproven conclusion that our Lord transferred Peter's rulership to successors by inheritance (*hereditate*). For the further doctrine that the Roman bishops are Peter's successors by divine right it is claimed that "the consent of antiquity without any doubt" so acknowledged them.

It is thus apparent that whatever were St. Peter's prerogatives

---

[1] chap. ii. [2] Ibid.

there is not a vestige of legitimate proof that there were successors to them or that the Bishops of Rome are those successors.

It has often been pointed out how the Romanist theory, that God would not have left His Church without a supreme ruler and guide, is rebutted by the fact that diligent seekers cannot discover any such authorised guide. "A guide is useless if those who want his services cannot make him out." "To guard Christians against error He (God) works a perpetual miracle in order to provide them with an infallible guide to truth and yet He neglects to furnish that guide with sufficient proof of his infallibility."[1]

Isaac Barrow repeatedly enforced the same argument. "If this point be of so great consequence as they make it; if, as they would persuade us, the substance, order, unity, and peace of the Church, together with the salvation of Christians, do depend on it; if, as they suppose, many great points of truth do hang on this pin; if it be, as they declare, a main article of faith, and not only a simple error but a pernicious heresy, to deny this primacy; then it is requisite that a clear revelation from God should be producible in favour of it, for upon that ground only such points can firmly stand."[2]

[1] Salmon, *Infallibility of the Church* (3rd edition), pp. 85, 100.
[2] *Treatise on the Pope's Supremacy,* p. 85.

CHAPTER VII

THE FOUR GOSPELS

If St. Peter was appointed by our Lord to have "full and supreme power of jurisdiction" over the other apostles, then that rulership must be seen operative in the New Testament. There is no recognition of the divinely constituted sovereignty of Peter. No disputed question is settled by any appeal to his infallible authority. On the contrary, there is much recorded that conclusively proves the other apostles were far from recognising such a system in the Church.

St. Matthew (xviii. 1), St. Mark (ix. 33), and St. Luke (xxii. 24) all record a dispute among the disciples as to which of them would have the chief place. St. Luke's account is: "There arose also a contention among them which of them is accounted to be greatest. And He said unto them, The Kings of the Gentiles have lordship over them: and they that have authority over them are called Benefactors. But ye shall not be so; but he that is the greater among you let him become as the younger; and he that is chief as he that doth serve." Our Lord went on to speak about their place in His kingdom and their thrones, making no distinction between them.

It is apparent that if our Lord had already endowed one of them with kingly authority He could not have thus condemned the very idea of lordship or relative superiority among them. It is apparent if one of them had been given such authority there could have been no dispute about who would have the chief place. The Roman hypothesis is shown to be unfounded both by the words of our Lord and by the contentions of His disciples.

This is evidenced again by the request of James and John and their mother that these two disciples would have the two highest positions in His kingdom (Matt. xx. 20; Mark x. 35). They were unaware that Peter had been appointed to the supreme place. Our Lord did not inform them of Peter having jurisdiction over them. It is told that the other ten disciples were indignant with them, but

41

no reference is made to any special prerogative of Peter being invaded. Isaac Barrow's comment is apposite: "Would St. Peter among the rest have fretted at that idle overture whereas he knew the place of our Lord's immutable purpose and infallible declaration assured him? And if none of the apostles did understand the words to imply this Roman sense, who can be obliged so to understand them? yea, who can wisely, who can safely so understand them? For surely they had common sense, as well as any man living now; they had as much advantage as we can have to know our Lord's meaning; their ignorance therefore of this sense being so apparent is not only a just excuse for not admitting this interpretation, but a strong bar against it."[1]

After His resurrection our Lord gave a solemn commission to His disciples to carry on His work. All were treated as on an equality. "As the Father hath sent Me, even so send I you. And when He had said this He breathed on them and saith unto them, Receive ye the Holy Ghost; whose soever sins ye forgive, they are forgiven unto them; whose soever sins ye retain, they are retained" (John xx. 21–3). These words exclude any dependence on Peter, or any special powers that the others did not receive as fully as he. "To all the apostles after His resurrection He gives equal power (*parem potestatem*) and says, 'As the Father sent Me so I send you.' "[2]

Again, the final commission of our Lord makes the apostles as a whole His representatives on earth. The charge admits no sovereignty of one of them over the others. "All authority hath been given unto Me in heaven and on earth. Go ye therefore and make disciples of all the nations . . . and lo, I am with you alway, even unto the end of the world" (Matt. xxviii. 18–20).

In the discourse in the upper room our Lord gave His apostles His parting counsels. If He had appointed a viceroy in obedience to whom they were to act, in conforming to whose infallible directions they were to teach, in cleaving to whom they were to secure unity, how is it that He remained silent about such a vital matter? He spoke of the all-importance of unity, of how they would have to act when He went away from them, of the difficulties they would have to face, but He did not designate any one of them to be their teacher and head. Every word spoken then implies the equality of His disciples. On every occasion when we should expect our Lord

---

[1] *Treatise on the Pope's Supremacy* (1852 edition), p. 88.
[2] Cyprian, *De Unitate*, 4.

to enforce "the fundamental principle of Catholic faith and doctrine" He gives no indication of it.

One of St. Peter's unwise utterances was the query to our Lord: "Lo, we have left all and followed Thee, what then shall we have?" (Matt. xix. 27). The answer gave no hint of any unique place for Peter—nothing beyond what all the disciples were to be given— "you [*plural*] who have followed Me".

The Gospel of St. John is believed to have been written after the death of St. Peter. If Peter was the "Prince of the Apostles, true Vicar of Christ, Head of the whole Church, Father and Teacher of all Christians", then surely some mention of the event of his death should have been made and of the appointment of his successor, the new Vicar of Christ, and of the duty of submission to him. The mere suggestion of such formal sovereignty brings the sense of how foreign it would be to the whole tenor of the New Testament.

The Rev. Hugh Pope tells us that St. John at the time he wrote his Gospel was inferior "to Peter's successors".[1] The same authority on Scripture in the Roman Church states of the unity Christ prayed for: "Without the Petrine promises Christ's creative prayer for the unity of His Church would seem little more than an ideal suspended in the air, as it were, since incapable of realisation, owing to the absence of the organisation necessary for securing it."[2] Dr. Pope does not explain why our Lord omitted to mention the one factor that, *ex hypothesi*, could make the prayer effectual.

[1] *The Papacy*, p. 17.   [2] Ibid., p. 18.

CHAPTER VIII

ST. MATTHEW XVI. 18

1

There are three sayings of our Lord put forward as justifying the theory that Peter was appointed prince of the apostles with true and proper jurisdiction, Vicar of Christ and infallible Teacher. These are the three cited in the Vatican Decrees. (No words of our Lord are even appealed to in proof that the Bishops of Rome succeed to Peter's prerogatives.)

The first passage is the all-important one—Matthew xvi. 17–19. St. Peter had declared, on behalf of the apostles, his belief that Christ was the Son of God. This utterance marked a crucial development in the minds of the apostles. Our Lord signalised its importance by saying: "Blessed art thou, Simon Bar-Jonah, for flesh and blood hath not revealed it unto thee, but My Father which is in heaven. And I also say unto thee, that thou art Peter [*Petros*] and and upon this rock [*petra*] I will build My Church; and the gates of Hades shall not prevail against it. I will give unto thee the keys of the kingdom of heaven: and whatsoever thou shalt bind on earth shall be bound in heaven: and whatsoever thou shalt loose on earth shall be loosed in heaven."

No special authority can be made to depend on the last verse, for our Lord gave similar powers to all the apostles later on: "What things soever ye shall bind on earth shall be bound in heaven: and what things soever ye shall loose on earth shall be loosed in heaven" (Matt. xviii. 18); and again similarly after His resurrection (John xx. 23). The promise of the keys was fulfilled when St. Peter opened the Church to the multitude at Pentecost and when he admitted the Roman centurion, Cornelius.

When we consider the "rock" text we may well be astounded at what the Roman Church reads into it. It is to be remembered these words are relied on as legislating for the allegiance of all believers to the vicegerent of God and for their submission to the infallible Pastor of the flock.

(i) The most likely meaning of this figurative expression is that the Church was to be built on the truth Peter had expressed. In actuality the Church is founded on the belief in the deity of Christ. This is the rock-base without which it would crumble away. The *petra* in that which is the object of the verb "revealed" in the preceding verse. "Flesh and blood did not reveal *it*, i.e. the Messiahship and divine sonship of Christ. Upon this rock of revealed truth I will build my Church."[1]

(ii) Some understand Peter himself to be the "rock". It is a possible meaning and has had many adherents. It is the meaning the whole superstructure of the Roman Church depends on. So interpreted, it is their charter text. Without this particular and doubtful interpretation of this one saying of our Lord the vast fabric of Papalism would never have been constructed. Romanism is like one of those eccentric sects that owe their origin to a single text.

(iii) Some ancient writers, notably St. Augustine, understand the "rock" to be Christ Himself. They have scriptural parallels as "Jesus Christ Himself being the chief corner stone" (Eph. ii. 20); "That rock was Christ" (1 Cor. x. 4); "Other foundation can no man lay than that is laid, which is Jesus Christ" (1 Cor. iii. 11). This interpretation is sanctioned by St. Peter (1 Pet. ii. 4–8).

(iv) Another interpretation is that the Church is built upon all the apostles whom St. Peter represented.

Even if we accept the second sense as the right one, the papalist requirements from it are entirely unmet. For as has been pointed out, a foundation stone cannot have successors. One can speak of an institution as being founded by or on the men who were its first members and who first proclaimed its tenets. They were the first stones on which the rest were built. It is in this sense we read of "being built upon the foundation of the apostles and prophets" (Eph. ii. 20). Peter was not only the first to profess faith in Christ as God, but he was the first to enlarge the Church on the day of Pentecost and to open it to the Gentiles. In all this he could not have a successor, any more than Adam could have a successor as the first man, or Columbus as the first to discover America.

When the Romanists go beyond this permissible way of understanding Peter to be personally the foundation, the "rock", and assert that he thereby became the infallible Ruler of his brethren,

[1] Ven. W. C. Allen, "St. Matthew", *International Critical Commentary*, p. 176.

the Vicar of Christ, Head of the whole Church and Father and Teacher of all Christians, and that in such offices he was to have successors to the end of time, they are departing wildly from what is written. Immediately after our Lord had spoken the words in question He went on to tell of His death at Jerusalem. Peter immediately rejected the doctrine of the cross, and received from our Lord the terrible rebuke: "Get thee behind Me, Satan; thou art a stumbling block unto Me: for thou mindest not the things of God but the things of men." Could there be a more startling refutal of the papalist interpretation? Where was the infallible leadership when Peter denied his Lord?

This passage is on the Romanist hypothesis one of transcendent significance deciding what all Christians must conform to if they are to be saved eternally. Why, then, is it only to be found in this one place in Holy Writ? If it was of the vital importance alleged surely some of the other evangelists would have recorded it. The silence of the others is the more remarkable since St. Mark and St. Luke both record the conversation and give Peter's answer to our Lord's question. The fact they do not mention the "rock" promise shows that they did not regard it as of great importance or did not know of it. St. Mark, it is supposed, wrote his Gospel under the direction of St. Peter, so his omission gives grounds for believing St. Peter did not attach to the words the meaning that Romanists read into them.

To be certain that the Church was built on Peter there is necessary a plain direct statement of our Lord such as "On thee, Peter, I will build My Church". Then there would not be the necessity for all this precarious deduction from a metaphor. But even if such a statement existed we would be no nearer to the further totally unsupported deduction that Peter was to have successors.

2

In the creed of Pope Pius IV, which is obligatory on all ecclesiastics and on all "who promise and swear that they will continue in obedience to the Church of Rome", it is professed, concerning Holy Scripture, "nor will I ever understand or interpret it, except according to the unanimous consent of the holy Fathers". The "rock" text, on the Romanist theory, is one that the Fathers are bound to be in agreement on. The doctrine of the appointing of a vicegerent of God is so fundamental that it is inconceivable the Fathers did not perceive this. Again, in practice the Church must have respected this vicegerent, and so from the beginning have recognised the meaning of the text that was his divine authorisation.

But the fact is that there are extraordinary differences of inter-pretation among the Fathers about it. The majority do not even believe the "rock" to be Peter. This is in itself at once destructive of papal claims. Even of those who do there is no recognition in the early centuries that this made him the indefectible ruler of his brethren—much less that it gave the Roman bishop lordship over the Church.

Their freedom and variations in explaining the text show beyond doubt that they were entirely unaware of its supreme importance. Some of them interpret it one way at one time; in another way at another time. Their comments "will convince any candid reader of what is certainly significant, namely, that they did not think the interpretation of this word a matter which at all affected the basis of Church authority, or indeed a very important question at all".[1]

Maldonatus, the eminent Jesuit scholar of the sixteenth century (whose commentaries have been described as "the best ever pub-lished"),[2] writes: "There are among ancient authors some who interpret 'on this rock', that is 'on this faith' or 'on this confession of faith in which thou hast called Me the Son of the living God', as Hilary and Gregory Nyssen, and Chrysostom, and Cyril of Alexandria. St. Augustine, going still further away from the true sense, interprets 'on this rock' that is, 'on myself Christ, because Christ was the Rock'. But Origen, 'on this rock, that is to say, on all men who have the same faith'."[3]

The lists compiled by the Roman Catholic scholar Launoy have often been quoted. He found that there are seventeen Fathers in favour of the rock meaning Peter; forty-four for it meaning the faith Peter confessed; sixteen for it being Christ Himself, and eight for it all the apostles. Archbishop Kenrick, in the speech prepared for the Vatican Council, adopted this summary. He wrote: "From this it follows either that no argument at all, or a very feeble one, can be drawn in proof of the primacy of Peter from the words 'on this rock I will build My Church'. . . . If we ought to follow the greater

---

[1] Gore, *Roman Catholic Claims*, p. 85.
[2] See *Catholic Encyclopaedia*, vol. ix, p. 567.
[3] Quoted by Salmon, *Infallibility of the Church*, p. 335.

number of the Fathers on this question then certainly it is to be held that we should understand by the rock the faith professed by Peter and not Peter professing the faith."[1]

Space allows only a few of the comments of the Fathers to be quoted.

(1) Origen[2] held that the rock is every faithful disciple of Christ. "But if you think that the whole Church was built by God upon Peter alone, what would you say about John, the son of thunder, or each of the apostles? Or shall we venture to say that the gates of hell shall not prevail against Peter but shall prevail against the other apostles and those that are perfect? Are not the words in question 'the gates of hell shall not prevail against it' and 'upon this rock I will build My Church' said in the case of all and each of them?"

(2) Cyprian: "Certainly the rest of the apostles were what Peter was, endued with an equal fellowship of dignity and power."[3]

(3) Jerome: "But you say that the Church is founded upon Peter although the same thing is done in another place upon all the apostles, and all receive the kingdom of heaven, and the solidity of the Church is established equally upon all, nevertheless among the twelve one is therefore chosen that by the appointment of a head an occasion of dissension may be taken away."[4]

(4) Chrysostom explains the words thus, "that is, upon the rock of the confession".[5] He describes Paul visiting Peter "not as needing anything of him nor of his voice but as being his equal in honour".[6]

(5) Cyril of Alexandria: "Calling, I suppose, nothing else the rock, in allusion to his name, but the immovable and firm faith of the disciple on which the Church of Christ is founded and established."[7]

(6) St. Hilary: "Upon this rock of the confession is the building up of the Church. . . . This faith is the foundation of the Church."[8] (*Haec fides Ecclesiae fundamentum est.*)

(7) St. Ambrose: "Faith is then the foundation of the Church,

[1] Friedrich, *Documenta*, vol. i, pp. 195 f.
[2] *Com. in Matt.*, xvi, 18 (Migne). P. G. 13: 1000.
[3] *De Unitate*, 4.
[4] *Adv. Jovianum*, 1: 26 (Migne). P. L. 23: 258.
[5] Hom. liv. *in Matt.* xvi. 2.
[6] *In Gal.* i. 18. P. G. 61: 631.
[7] *De SS. Trinitate*, dial. iv. P. G. 75: 865.
[8] *De Trinitate* vi, 36, 37. P. L. 10: 186–7.

for not of the human person of St. Peter but of faith is it said that the gates of hell shall not prevail against it."[1]

(8) Pope Gregory I: "Establish your faith on the rock of the Church, that is on the confession of the blessed Peter, prince of the apostles."[2]

The testimony of St. Augustine, luminously exposing the untenableness of the papalist interpretation, is referred to elsewhere.[3] The belief of the early Church can also be seen in its liturgical formulas. The Eastern Liturgy of St. James in the solemn *Anaphora* has the words: "Thy holy Church which Thou hast founded upon the rock of faith that the gates of hell may not prevail against it."

The ancient liturgical witness of the Western Church is still preserved in the Roman Missal in the Collect for the Vigil of SS. Peter and Paul: "Grant, we beseech Thee, Almighty God, that Thou wouldst not suffer us whom Thou hast established on the rock of the Apostle's Confession to be shaken by any disturbance."

Bishop Gore (admitting that a universal statement is hazardous) expressed his belief that none of the Greek Fathers of the first six centuries connects the position of the Bishop of Rome with the promise to St. Peter.[4] Dom Chapman's unconvincing attempt to answer this only strengthens the bishop's contention. The Roman apologist has to fall back on such irrelevancies as that in the East Rome was spoken of as "the Apostolic See" and the reception alleged for the ambitious claims of the papal legates at the Councils of Ephesus and Chalcedon.

[1] *De Incarn.*, v. 34. P. L. 16: 827.
[2] Ep. 4: 38, ad Theodelind. P. L. 77: 713.
[3] See p. 139 f.
[4] *Roman Catholic Claims*, p. 91.

CHAPTER IX

ST. LUKE XXII. 32

The words of our Lord in Matthew xvi. 18, even if they meant Peter was the foundation of the Church, by no means constituted him its supreme ruler, or its infallible teacher. The Vatican Decrees appeal to another text when claiming infallibility for him and for the Popes. All the venerable Fathers and holy orthodox Doctors, it is said, "knowing most fully that the See of Holy Peter remains ever free from all blemish of error according to the divine promise of the Lord our Saviour made to the prince of His disciples. I have prayed for thee that thy faith fail not, and when thou art converted confirm thy brethren"[1] (St. Luke xxii. 32).

To see in these words of our Lord a guarantee that Peter was to be divinely protected from error is nearly as preposterous as to see in them a similar guarantee for the prelates of the Roman See. In the first place the word "faith" here used does not refer to the orthodoxy of Peter's doctrine but to his trust in our Lord. In the second place, Peter was not preserved from the most grievous apostasy. We know that he subsequently denied his Lord in a shocking manner. If the prayer did not secure Peter's faith from failure how can it be imagined it secures his alleged successors for whom it was not offered? Again, why use some words from our Lord's utterance, as applying to the supposed successors of Peter, and omit the remaining ones? Archbishop Kenrick in his famous Vatican Council speech put this concisely: "If the former words 'I have prayed for thee' and the latter words 'confirm thy brethren' prove that the heavenly power and office passed to the successors of Peter, it is not evident why the intermediate words 'when thou art converted' ought not also to belong to them."[2]

The injunction to "confirm" or "strengthen" his brethren conferred no peculiar prerogative on Peter. The word is often used in the New Testament. St. Paul sent Timothy to the Thessalonians

---

[1] chap. 4.   [2] Friedrich, *Documenta*, vol. i, p. 200.

to "strengthen" their faith. St. Paul himself longed to go to Rome for the "strengthening" of the Christians there (Rom. i. 11).

St. Peter denounced those who "wrest" or "twist" the Scriptures to their own destruction (2 Pet. iii. 16). The Romanist interpretation of Luke xxii. 32 is a most astounding instance of such perverting the Scriptures. The words of our Lord to His unstable and over-confident disciple are quite clear. They lay the future duty on Peter as one who had fallen and been restored to be active in comforting and establishing others who might be wavering or who had gone astray like himself. It is fantastic to find in them a transcendent dogma conferring doctrinal infallibility, not only on him but also on a perpetual series of "legitimate successors". The attempt to deduce such a dogma from this text is an outrage on reason.

As was to be expected, none of the ancient Fathers of the Church perceived in these words the infallibility of Peter or of the Bishops of Rome. The exposition of Chrysostom may be cited as representative. "For this He said sharply reproving him and showing that his fall was more grievous than that of the rest and needed more help. . . . Is it not plain that it is for the reason I have mentioned before, that is, as reproving him and showing that his fall was more grievous than that of the rest, that He directs His words to him? . . . He said not that thou mayest not deny but that thy faith fail not, that thou perish not utterly."[1]

The impossibility of finding patristic authority for the Romanist interpretation is demonstrated by the fact that, as Denny points out,[2] of twenty citations which Melchior Cano gives, eighteen are from the False Decretals. The other two from St. Athanasius are equally bogus. It is significant that the first clear claim based on Luke xxii. 32 for the inerrancy of the Roman See is from a bishop of that See, Pope Agatho, A.D. 680. He makes it in a letter sent to the emperor at the sixth General Council. But this was the Council that condemned and anathematised his predecessor, Pope Honorius, for having ratified heresy, and which ordered his "soul-destroying" writings to be burned.

---

[1] Hom. lxxxii, *in Matt.* xxvi (Migne). P. G. 58: 746.
[2] *Papalism*, p. 78.

CHAPTER X

ST. JOHN XXI. 15–17

The third text relied on to prove the Petrine supremacy is that from John xxi. The Vatican Decrees assert: "It was upon Simon alone that Jesus after His resurrection bestowed the jurisdiction of chief Pastor and Ruler over all His fold in the words: Feed My lambs: feed My sheep."[1]

Again, it is to be said that the words of our Lord on this occasion to St. Peter cannot, in their plain and natural sense, be made to imply the meaning thus ascribed to them. St. Peter had boasted: "If all shall be offended in Thee, I will never be offended" (Matt. xxvi. 33). In a little while he three times made his denial of his Master. The boast was made publicly: so was the denial. Now after Peter's repentance our Lord publicly restored him to his office as an apostle. The question: "Simon, son of Jonas, lovest thou Me more than these?" alludes to the boast in the upper room. The threefold query and the threefold charge "Feed My lambs"; "Tend My sheep"; "Feed My sheep" correspond to Peter's threefold denial. It is the definite assurance that Peter had not finally forfeited his pastoral mission as one of the twelve by his apostasy.

To claim that it conferred on him special privileges of rulership or authority over the other disciples, or in any unique manner constituted him the supreme shepherd of the Church, is utterly unfounded. All the disciples had the duty of tending the Lord's sheep. The one who had terribly fallen away is now reinstated in his former place among the rest.

St. Peter himself has shown that the charge did not mean some special monopoly of authority but the general rule for all pastors or presbyters—a reminder of a duty already imposed: "The elders therefore among you I exhort who am a fellow-elder . . . tend the flock of God which is among you" (1 Pet. v. 1, 2). St. Paul's words to the presbyters of Ephesus are a parallel. "Take heed unto yourselves, and to all the flock, in which the Holy Ghost hath

[1] chap. 1.

made you bishops, to feed the Church of God, which He purchased with His own blood" (Acts xx. 28). The feeding and tending the sheep is the common duty of all pastors. The telling St. Peter then to fulfil it is accounted for by his lamentable personal history. To find in the words a solemn investiture of Peter and the Bishops of Rome with full and supreme power of jurisdiction over the Church is to make Scripture mean whatever we desire.

The testimonies of the Fathers are as contrary to the papalist interpretation of this text as they are concerning the other two. It does not seem that any Father of the first six centuries understood it in the papalist sense. Some of them do from it exaggerate the office of St. Peter personally as Shepherd, but they understand his commission to be as representative of the whole body of the apostles and that the function of feeding the flock belongs to all who succeed him in the episcopal office. Their expositions show how far the Fathers were from consciousness of the papal view. The very fact that they varied about the sense of the text is a proof that they did not know the startling claims now founded on it. If they had regarded it as constituting for all time the Ruler of the Church they could not have been ambiguous or at variance in their interpretations; they could not have wholly omitted the momentous doctrine founded on the text.

St. Augustine wrote: "What was enjoined to Peter, not Peter alone, but also all the other apostles heard and held preserved, and, most of all, the partner of his death and of his day, the Apostle Paul. They heard that and transmitted it for our hearing; we feed you, we are together with you."[1] "When it is said unto him, it is said unto all, 'Lovest thou Me? Feed My sheep'."[2]

St. Gregory Nazianzen: "But Jesus received him and by a triple question and confession healed the triple denial."[3]

St. Cyril of Alexandria: "Wherefore did He ask the question of Simon only, although the other disciples were standing by? And what is the meaning of 'Feed My sheep' and the like? . . . Peter, overwhelmed with excessive terror, thrice denied the Lord—Christ heals the ill effects of what had happened and demands in various terms the triple confession, setting this, as it were, against that, and providing a corrective equivalent to the faults. . . . Therefore by

[1] Sermo 296, chap. 4. P. L. 38: 1354. See also p. 140.
[2] De Agone Christ. c. 30. P. L. 40: 308.
[3] Oratio 39, c. 18. P. G. 36: 556.

D

the triple confession of blessed Peter the offence of triple denial was abolished. But by the Lord saying 'Feed My sheep' a renewal, as it were, of the apostolate already conferred upon him is understood to have taken place, wiping away the intervening reproach of his falls and destroying utterly the littleness of soul arising from human infirmity."[1]

Immediately after the speaking of the Lord's words authorising Peter to resume his apostolic functions an incident occurred that illustrated the impulsive nature of the apostle and also gave occasion for our Lord to rebuke him. Peter asked concerning John: "Lord, and what shall this man do?" (or "what about him?"). If, as is claimed, Peter had been given the oversight of the other disciples it was a quite appropriate question. But the Lord's reply showed sharply it was none of Peter's business: "If I will that he tarry till I come, what is that to thee? You, yourself, follow Me" (John xxi. 21, 22).

The inevitable conclusion to be drawn from a candid consideration of these three Petrine texts was well stated by Archbishop Kenrick: "We have in Holy Scripture the clearest testimonies of the mission given to all the apostles and of the divine assistance promised to them all. These places are clear and admit no variety of interpretation. We have not one place of Scripture whose true sense is not in dispute in which anything of this sort is promised to Peter apart from the others. And yet the authors of the schema [submitted to the Vatican Council] wish that we attribute to the Roman Pontiff, as the successor of Peter, the power which by no certain testimony of Holy Scripture can be proved to have been given to Peter, unless in so far as he received it with the other apostles."[2]

It is the custom of Roman apologists to stress unfairly the enconiums on, or titles given to, St. Peter by some of the Fathers. It is well to remember that similar high-flown titles are given to other apostles and prelates.

Thus St. Cyril in an authoritative letter to Nestorius wrote that Peter and James "were of equal rank with each other as apostles".[3] St. Chrysostom calls Paul "the teacher of the world . . . the planter of the Church. . . . If therefore he receives a greater crown

---

[1] Hom. xxi, in Joan. xxi. P. G. 74: 749, 752.
[2] Friedrich, Documenta, i, 201.
[3] Ad. Nest. P. G. 77: 112.

than the apostles and be greater than they, it is manifest that he shall enjoy the highest honour and pre-eminences";[1] "Where Paul was, there also was Christ. . . . He is the light of the Church, the foundation of the faith, the pillar and ground of the truth";[2] "the apostle of the world";[3] "he had the care not of one household but also of cities and of peoples and of nations and of the whole world";[4] "the chief and leader of the choir of the saints".[5] Of St. John, Chrysostom says he is "the pillar of the Churches throughout the world, who hath the keys of the kingdom of heaven",[6] and couples with him St. Peter as receiving "the charge of the world".[7] St. Cyril of Jerusalem calls St. Peter and St. Paul "the presidents of the Churches".[8] Hesychius, presbyter of Jerusalem, calls St. James "the chief captain of the new Jerusalem, the chief of the priests, the prince of the apostles, the leader amongst the heads, the one who surpasses in splendour the lights, who is superior among the stars".[9] Pope Gregory I says St. Paul "obtained the principate of the whole Church".[10] According to St. Augustine, "when apostle is said, if it be not expressed what apostle, none is understood save Paul".[11]

Barrow warns that "we are not accountable to every hyperbolical flash or flourish occurring in the Fathers".[12]

The above instances show how futile are arguments adduced from rhetorical titles given to St. Peter to prove his supremacy of jurisdiction.

Boniface VIII, in his bull *Unam Sanctam*, cites John xxi. 17 as authorising his supremacy not only over the Church but over kings. This is only one example of how Papalism can distort the Scriptures.

[1] Hom. viii. P. G. 48: 772.
[2] Hom. i *in Rom.* xvi. P. G. 51: 191.
[3] Hom. xxi *in Ep. i ad Cor.* P. G. 61: 171.
[4] Hom. xxv *in Ep. ii ad Cor.* P. G. 61: 571.
[5] Hom. xxxii *in Rom.* xvi. P. G. 60: 678.
[6] Hom. i *in Joan.* P. G. 59:25.
[7] Hom. lxxxviii *in Joan.* P. G. 59: 480.
[8] Catech. vi, 15. P. G. 33: 561.
[9] *In Jacobum Fratrem Dom.*, viii. P. G. 93: 1480.
[10] In 1 Reg., lib. iv, c.v. 28. P. L. 79: 303.
[11] *Contra duas Ep. Pelag.*, iii, 3. P. L. 44: 589.
[12] *Treatise of the Pope's Supremacy*, (Oxford edition, 1852) p. 104.

CHAPTER XI

THE ACTS OF THE APOSTLES

The Roman claim that Peter was appointed by Christ to be His vicegerent, who would exercise on earth "the power which Christ Himself exercised in His mortal life", who was the "Master" of the apostolic college, the "Pastor of pastors",[1] can be tested by the record of the first days of the Church as given in the Acts of the Apostles. Then when Christ's visible presence was removed His Vicar and representative would have assumed the rulership in His stead. We never find St. Peter exercising such supreme authority. On no occasion does he act as Head and Governor of the Church. No doctrinal question is entrusted to his final judgment. At first it is the apostolate in common who exercise control. Afterwards the elders were associated with the apostles. The idea that Peter was the master of the apostolic council is a baseless delusion. No authority in the Church superior to that of the apostolate is found in the New Testament.

In the first chapter of the Acts we have Peter taking the lead, as he was accustomed to do, in proposing that one be appointed in the room of the traitor Judas. He does not attempt to fill the vacant place on his own authority as the Pope does in appointing a cardinal. His suggestion is followed and two are chosen by the company of believers. The final selection was made by lot. St. Peter's part in it displayed no supremacy of jurisdiction.

Acts vi gives an account of the appointment of the seven (traditionally called deacons), the first permanent officials in the Church other than the apostles. St. Peter takes no distinctive part in this important act of organisation. His name is not even mentioned. It is the apostolate as a whole that is responsible. The twelve call the multitude and explain the need of new officials, and issue directions. The choice is made by the company of believers.

In the first missionary extension of the Church outside Jerusalem we find Peter being given a subordinate part, acting under the

[1] Leo XIII in *Satis Cognitum*.

direction of the whole apostolate. "When the apostles which were at Jerusalem heard that Samaria had received the word of God they sent unto them Peter and John" (Acts viii. 14). "Can the apostolic college be said to have been above its Master in authority?" demands the *Satis Cognitum* of Pope Leo XIII. This fact shows the apostolic college was certainly above Peter. The sender is higher in authority than the sent. The Greek word used can be translated "to order (one) to go to a place appointed".[1] Subjects might be imagined humbly petitioning their king to go away on a mission with a fellow subject as a member of his suite, but we cannot conceive them dispatching their king and sending with him a subject with equal authority as their delegates. It is plain that the apostles regarded Peter as having no prerogative above themselves and as being on an equality with John who was joined with him on the mission.

When Peter admitted Gentiles into the Church his action was disapproved of by some members. If he was the supreme Pastor their opposition would have been shocking rebellion. "When Peter was come up to Jerusalem they that were of the circumcision contended with him, saying, Thou wentest in to men uncircumcised, and didst eat with them" (Acts xi. 2, 3). Peter, far from claiming sovereign authority as holding the place of our Lord in the Church, admitted their right to question his proceedings and submitted a defence.

The question of compelling Gentile converts to observe the law of Moses was one of the most pressing and vital that confronted the apostolic Church. The future of Christianity depended on freedom from the regulations of the Mosaic law. Here if ever an authoritative decision was required if there was a supreme ruler and infallible teacher in the Church. The course of the controversy showed there was no such personal source of authority to appeal to.

The trouble came to a head at Antioch. After "no small dissension and debate" (Acts xv. 2) the Christians there arranged that Paul and certain others should go to Jerusalem to obtain an authoritative decision. To whom were they to apply for this? On the Roman theory there could be but one answer—to the Representative of Christ who exercised His power on earth, to the "supreme Judge of the faithful". The action of the Antiochene Church repudiates such a claim. The delegates were sent "to the apostles and elders about the question". It was an outstanding occasion

[1] Grimm-Thayer, *Lexicon.*

for the preserving of unity and the securing of vital guidance. Nothing was known then in the Church that these could be had from St. Peter.

The council which followed at Jerusalem was in itself an absolute confutation of the papal dogmas. "If there were no other decisive passages in the New Testament against the papal claims, this chapter would be quite enough to prove that they were unknown to the apostles, and that St. Peter was only the foremost leader of the apostles for a time, but with no pretensions whatever to absolute supremacy and infallibility as head of the Church."[1]

When "the apostles and elders were gathered together to consider of this matter" there was "much disputation" (Acts xv. 6, 7). Peter made a speech arguing for liberty. Then Paul and Barnabas spoke. Then finally St. James as president summed up the discussion and gave the decision. "Wherefore my judgment is" ($\dot{\varepsilon}\gamma\dot{\omega}$ $\varkappa\varrho\dot{\iota}\nu\omega$). The council's determination followed the lines of St. James's pronouncement. St. Peter took part as an ordinary member. St. James had the office of president. "Peter orates, but James legislates."[2] St. Chrysostom writes: "There was no arrogance in the Church. After Peter, Paul speaks and none silences him; James waits patiently and does not start up. Great is the orderliness. Nothing [speaks] John here; nothing the other apostles, but held their peace, for he [James] was invested with the chief rule and they think it no hardship. . . . Peter indeed spoke more strongly, but James here more mildly, for thus it behoves the one high in authority to leave what is unpleasant for others to say . . . and he says well with authority, my sentence is . . ."[3]

The further records of the council make clear that the decision was the common act of the whole body. "It seemed good to the apostles and the elders with the whole Church." The decree began: "The apostles and the elder brethren unto the brethren. . . . It seemed good unto us, having come to one accord. . . . For it seemed good to the Holy Ghost and to us to lay upon you no greater burden than these necessary things" (Acts xv. 22 ff.). Paul and Silas went through the Churches and "delivered them the decrees for to keep which had been ordained of the apostles and elders that were at Jerusalem" (Acts xvi. 4).

---

[1] Brinckman, *Notes on the Papal Claims*, p. 72.
[2] St. Hesychius, *In Jacobum Fratrem Dom.*, viii. P. G. 93: 1480.
[3] Hom. xxxiii *in Act. App.*, c. 2. P. G. 60: 240.

Now when a matter is to be decided in the Roman Church the Pope issues a decree relying on his own sole authority. Thus Pius IX, when formulating the dogma of the Immaculate Conception in 1854, wrote: "We by the authority of our Lord Jesus Christ, of the blessed apostles Peter and Paul, and by that invested in us . . . declare and pronounce and define, etc." The Pope assumes to act as successor to St. Peter. He takes to himself powers St. Peter never possessed or attempted to wield. The papal claim is built on theories that Holy Scripture shows to be quite fictitious.

After the fifteenth chapter St. Peter's name does not again occur in the Acts. He fades out of the picture. In the great ensuing development of Christianity he is not recorded as taking part.

If the Roman theory was true we should have expected often to find Peter's authority and position invoked. The authority of the visible Head must have been resorted to in all great disputes and problems of discipline. Why did not St. Paul mention anywhere in his instructions the fundamental constitution of the Church—its divinely ordained centre of unity? For instance St. Paul in his farewell address to the Ephesian elders warns them of the coming dangers of disunion and heresy (Acts xx. 28 ff.). But he omits to tell them of the supreme Pastor and infallible Guide by cleaving to whom they would be safeguarded.

The journey of St. Paul to Rome is described in detail. No inspired writer tells a word of St. Peter ever arriving there.

CHAPTER XII

THE EPISTLES

There are twenty-two books in the New Testament besides the four Gospels and the Acts. Thirteen of these are written by St. Paul. There is only one that can be assuredly attributed to St. Peter. The other that bears his name is considered by most scholars not to be the composition of the apostle. St. Paul's epistles contain 87 chapters comprising 2,023 verses. St. Peter's epistle contains 5 chapters comprising 105 verses. If 2 Peter be added, this means an additional 3 chapters or 61 verses.

If St. Peter were the infallible Teacher and supreme Pastor surely this is an extraordinary state of things. Why was St. Paul so much more than he inspired for the feeding, ruling and governing of the Church? "Why all these letters from the unimportant Paul, instead of a collection of bulls issued *ex cathedra* from the chair of Peter at Rome?"[1]

When we examine the contents of the books we find that St. Peter gives, in general, exhortations to Christian living with practically no doctrinal instruction or directions for discipline. On the other hand, St. Paul deals authoritatively and at length with important questions of doctrine, problems of conduct, and ecclesiastical affairs. The influence of Paul in the formation of Christian doctrine is incalculable. His teaching—e.g. on grace, justification, free-will, the relation of Christians to the Jewish law, and to heathen environment, the unity of the Church, schism, the nature and obligations of love, the meaning of the resurrection, conscience, the Church, the indwelling of Christ—has had unparalleled power in moulding the thoughts and lives of men. Innumerable treatises are written on the theological teaching of St. Paul. It would be hard to find many on the doctrinal implications of St. Peter.

Further, we find that St. Paul issued his teaching, without trace of knowledge of any superior authority. His tone in directing his followers is incompatible with the existence of a divinely appointed

[1] Milner-White and Knox, *One God and Father of All*, p. 49.

chief ruler and teacher whom he was bound to obey. Nay, he insists on his absolute authority as an apostle who is not dependent on any human superior. "Paul an apostle, not from men, nor through man, but through Jesus Christ and God the Father" (Gal. i. 1). "For I make known to you, brethren, as touching the gospel which was preached by me, that it is not after man. For neither did I receive it from man, nor was I taught it, but through revelation of Jesus Christ" (Gal. i. 11, 12). When we remember the circumstances of St. Paul's entrance to the Church, and the leading position of Peter in the Church before that time, we see that there is no possibility of imagining any sovereign authority attached to Peter's position. Paul writes in other places in a way that shows also he was very far from recognising his own rank to be inferior to Peter's. "For I reckon I am not a whit behind the very chiefest apostles" (2 Cor. xi. 5). "For in nothing am I behind the very chiefest apostles" (2 Cor. xii. 11). The word used seems to imply an almost sarcastic reference.[1] A similar robust assertion of equality and independence is very evident when he writes: "But from those who were reputed to be somewhat (whatsoever they were, it maketh no matter to me: God accepteth not man's person) —they, I say, who were of repute imparted nothing to me: but contrariwise, when they saw that I had been intrusted with the gospel of the uncircumcision, even as Peter with the gospel of the circumcision . . . and when they perceived the grace that was given unto me, James and Cephas and John, they who were reputed to be pillars, gave to me and Barnabas the right hands of fellowship, that we should go unto the Gentiles, and they unto the circumcision" (Gal. ii. 6–9).

Had St. Peter really held *jure divino* the office alleged, then St. Paul's language is quite impossible. He could not have referred to him as one of those "reputed to be pillars". Nor could he have placed the name of James before that of Peter. Dr. Puller imagines a parallel case during the Vatican Council. Suppose the conduct of two missionary bishops had been called in question. Can we imagine one of them writing afterwards and saying: "When they perceived the grace that was given unto me, Archbishop Darboy, Pope Pius IX, and Archbishop Manning, who are recognised as pillars, gave to me and my companion the right hand of fellowship"? Why was it then possible for St. Paul to use such language when writing to his

---

[1] "Those superlatively great apostles"—Dr. Weymouth.

Galatian converts? "Because it never entered their minds that such a doctrine [that of the Vatican Decrees] would ever be devised and propagated by Christian men."[1] The limitation of Peter's mission to the Jews is another conclusive contradiction of the Roman claims.

But the incident when St. Paul had to oppose and sternly denounce Peter's mistaken policy is in itself quite destructive of such claims. "But when Cephas came to Antioch, I resisted him to the face, because he stood condemned. For before that certain came from James, he did eat with the Gentiles: but when they came, he drew back and separated himself, fearing them that were of the circumcision. And the rest of the Jews dissembled likewise with him. . . . But when I saw that they walked not uprightly according to the truth of the gospel, I said unto Cephas before them all, If thou, being a Jew, livest as do the Gentiles, and not as do the Jews, how compellest thou the Gentiles to live as do the Jews?" (Gal. ii. 11–14).

In the most explicit way St. Paul here condemns the action of St. Peter—the supposed representative of Christ in the Church. He shrank not from exposing his defection from "the truth of the gospel". He repudiated Peter's attitude to his face and "before them all". Instead of Paul being conscious that he was guilty of outrageous rebellion—imperilling his own salvation—he is proud of his stand, and the whole Christian Church ever since has followed the line taken by Paul and rejected that by Peter.

The clash at Antioch between the two apostles and their followers is not only a demonstration that Peter was not recognised to have supreme authority. It means something more. It shows that Peter had gone wrong again as he did when he opposed the teaching of the atonement ("Get thee behind Me, Satan"). He again errs by minding "not the things of God but the things of men". It shows that our Lord's prayer for him (Luke xxii. 32) cannot be taken as securing his doctrinal infallibility. His policy would have been fatal to the whole future of Christianity. It would have reduced the Church to a Jewish sect. In this supreme crisis Peter has reverted to the wrong side. The issues at stake were rightly seen by Paul to be vital. It was a challenge to the universal efficacy of the Cross of Christ. "Behold, I Paul say unto you, that, if ye receive circumcision, Christ will profit you nothing. . . . Ye are severed from Christ ye who would be justified by the law" (Gal. v. 2, 4). In the event, the Church was saved from imminent peril by St. Paul being able

[1] *Primitive Saints and the See of Rome*, pp. 111, 112.

to counteract the gravely misleading attitude of St. Peter. If Peter's leadership had prevailed, the council of Jerusalem was nullified and the Mosaic law compulsory on all Christians.

Throughout the writings of St. Paul there are many other passages directly in conflict with papal theories. He treats at length of the Church as the Body of Christ. This body has Christ as its Head (Eph. i. 22, 23; iv. 15). In that union with Christ the unity of the Church consists. He never refers to the need for unity with a visible Head. Had there been such a visible Head, St. Paul was bound to mention him when teaching unity and describing the constitution of the Church. "Now ye are the body of Christ, and severally members thereof. And God hath set some in the Church, first apostles, secondly prophets, thirdly teachers, etc." (1 Cor. xii. 27, 28). Similarly, when exhorting the Ephesian Christians to "keep the unity of the Spirit in the bond of peace" (iv. 3) he stresses the nature of Church unity. There is no consciousness of any Vicar of Christ; any "Head of the whole Church militant"; any divine appointment "that the Church of Christ may be one flock under one supreme Pastor". Then he again enumerates the authorities in the Church: "He gave some (to be) apostles, and some prophets, and some evangelists, and some pastors and teachers" (Eph. iv. 11). In both lists the apostles come first; in one list it is said they are "first". This would be improper if there was a vicegerent of Christ, Head and Sovereign of all. "It is obvious that if one of the apostolic college had been appointed visible head of the Church on earth St. Paul must have named him in this connection, so that the vital distinction between the apostolate and their 'Master' should not be in effect denied and thus the people misled with regard to a doctrine of Catholic truth from which no one can deviate without loss of faith and salvation."[1]

St. Paul often uses language that, if written by St. Peter, would have been proclaimed as proving his sovereignty. "Besides those things that are without [or, things that I omit], there is that which presseth upon me daily, anxiety for all the churches" (2 Cor. xi. 28). "And so ordain I in all the churches" (1 Cor. vii. 17). "According to the authority which the Lord gave me for building up and not for casting down" (2 Cor. xiii. 10). "In the day when God shall judge the secrets of men according to my gospel by Jesus Christ" (Rom. ii. 16).

[1] Denny, *Papalism*, p. 15.

If anyone were to put forward a theory of the supremacy of St. Paul as the chief lawgiver and teacher of the Church he would have far more plausible Scriptural grounds for it than can be urged for St. Peter. St. Paul writes to the Church of Rome, and from Rome, without mentioning St. Peter having any connection therewith. He writes to this Church, as to any other, without mention of any peculiar prerogatives belonging to it. He writes in a tone of full apostolic authority. Such a phrase as "For all things are yours; whether Paul, or Apollos, or Cephas" (1 Cor. iii. 22) illustrates his unawareness of Peter having special authority.

The epistles of St. Peter are completely destitute of any consciousness of his supposed supreme position. There is no inkling of any feeling that obedience or deference being due to him as Vicar of Christ. When he urges to the performance of duty he writes as on a level with those he addresses. "The elders therefore among you I exhort, who am a fellow-elder, and a witness of the sufferings of Christ" (1 Pet. v. 1). He does not even assume the authoritative laying-down-the-law tone of St. Paul. It is not sufficient to plead that humility restrained him. If he were commissioned to be Christ's vicegerent then it was his duty to make known that the Church possessed in him its divinely appointed Ruler and Teacher. He was not justified in concealing the charter of the Church's constitution. Why should he disguise what has been so stridently proclaimed by his "successors" as an essential part of God's plan for the salvation of the world? If, according to Pope Pius XI, "in this one Church of Christ no man can be or remain who does not accept, recognise and obey the authority and supremacy of Peter and his legitimate successors",[1] then how can St. Peter be excused for not divulging this? His epistles are not only silent but are incompatible with such a doctrine. As Barrow puts it, there is "no tang of such authority" in them; "no critic perusing these epistles would smell a Pope in them".[2] Surely St. Peter was as conscious of his infallibility as modern Popes can be, and the need for his exercising and teaching it was at least as great in his times as in 1870.

There is a remarkable passage in this epistle in which some reference to himself as the rock on which the Church is built might naturally have been expected. "If ye have tasted that the Lord is gracious: unto whom coming, a living stone, rejected indeed of men,

[1] Encyclical on *Fostering True Religious Union*, p. 13.
[2] *Treatise on the Pope's Supremacy* (1852 edition), p. 62.

but with God elect, precious, ye also, as living stones, are built up a spiritual house, to be a holy priesthood, to offer up spiritual sacrifices, acceptable to God through Jesus Christ. Because it is contained in Scripture, Behold, I lay in Zion a chief corner stone, elect, precious: and he that believeth on Him shall not be put to shame. For you therefore which believe is the preciousness: but for such as disbelieve, the stone which the builders rejected, the same was made the head of the corner; and, a stone of stumbling, and a rock of offence" (1 Pet. ii. 3–8).

In all this instruction it is Christ who is the foundation living stone, and the spiritual house is composed of living stones united with Him. St. Peter is completely unconscious of his own supposed sublime function as the rock on which the Church is built. In fact, the only place in the passage he mentions "rock" is in the phrase "rock of offence" (πέτρα σκανδάλου). His words exclude the tremendous prerogatives read into the text in Matthew xvi. 18.

In chapter v, verse 2 St. Peter tells his fellow-elders to "tend the flock of God". It is highly significant that the word used (ποιμάνατε) is the same as that which Christ used to him in John xxi. 16. Why interpret it in the one verse as imparting an exclusive sovereignty of jurisdiction and not in the other?

The next verse contains a warning that is a piquant condemnation of the habits of many of those who claim to be St. Peter's successors. "Neither as lording it over the charge allotted to you, but making yourselves ensamples to the flock."

The second epistle, claiming to be by St. Peter, is written in view of his approaching death. The writer is distressed about the dangers to fall on the flock, the false teachers who shall privily introduce heresies, the moral corruptions that will prevail whereby "the way of truth shall be evil spoken of" (2 Pet. ii. 1, 2). A lurid forecast is given of the Church's difficulties, but the one great security, *ex hypothesi*, of a supreme Pastor and infallible Guide is never once mentioned. The flock are told nothing of the legitimate successor whom they are to follow when the writer has passed away. Such a silence is not only inexplicable but inexcusable from the Roman point of view. If Christ had appointed a visible Head for the safeguarding of the flock, whom they were bound to reverence and obey, the writer must have disclosed it here.

His anxiety is that they remember the principles of the faith—loyalty to a living infallible Voice is omitted. "I think it right, as long as I am in this tabernacle, to stir you up by putting you in remembrance; knowing that the putting off of my tabernacle cometh swiftly, as our Lord Jesus Christ signified unto me. Yea, I will give diligence that at every time ye may be able after my decease to call these things to remembrance" (2 Pet. i. 13–15). "This is now, beloved, the second epistle that I write unto you; and in both of them I stir up your sincere mind by putting you in remembrance; that ye should remember the words which were spoken before by the holy prophets, and the commandment of the Lord and Saviour through your apostles" (2 Pet. iii. 1, 2). The writer plainly regards the apostles (without distinction) as, with the prophets, the sources of the truth. He has no other external security to exalt; nothing of the appointment of a successor; nothing of obedience to him. If the epistle is not authentic, still it is a witness to what its composer believed would be attributable to St. Peter and what the Church of the early centuries accepted as appropriate to him.

In all the remaining books of the New Testament we find a similar ignorance of the existence of a visible Head of the Church. There are constant warnings against wrong teachings and fallings away, but no exhortation to heed him who is set for the "feeding, ruling and governing of the whole Church". In the Apocalypse the messages to the seven Churches reveal a sad declension. The way of recovery is proclaimed, but there is never a direction to hearken to the Bishop of Rome. The future of the Church is sketched through fierce persecutions up to the coming of the new Jerusalem. Rome is denounced as Babylon. One looks in vain for any reference to the vicegerent of Christ having his seat there. On the contrary, her final destruction is exulted in: "Fallen, fallen is Babylon the great, and is become a habitation of devils. . . . Come forth, my people, out of her, that ye have no fellowship with her sins, and that ye receive not of her plagues: for her sins have reached even unto heaven. . . . Rejoice over her, thou heaven, and ye saints, and ye apostles, and ye prophets; for God hath judged your judgment on her" (Rev. xviii. 2, 4, 5, 20).

CHAPTER XIII

WAS ST. PETER AT ROME?

There is considerable traditional authority for the stay of Peter at Rome. The evidence is far from conclusive. On the other hand, there are impressive reasons for disbelieving in it. The standard Roman theory is that Peter arrived in Rome in the second year of the Emperor Claudius (42) and was bishop there for twenty-five years, until the last year of Nero (67). This is according to Jerome and Eusebius. Jerome was secretary to Pope Damasus. It is significant that the Liberian Catalogue, the basis of the Roman *Liber Pontificalis*, places the twenty-five years' residence between the years 30 and 55. This inexplicable divergence between chief authorities casts doubts on the story. Both sets of dates are irreconcilable with known facts. Roman Catholic scholars are now content to bring Peter to Rome in 63 and to fix his death in the following year.[1]

There is no Biblical evidence for Peter ever visiting Rome. There is much that is unfavourable. He was not in Rome when St. Paul wrote his Epistle to the Romans in 57 or 58. If he were he would have been mentioned among the salutations. Nor had he been there previous to that date. For in this epistle St. Paul "lays it down as a principle governing all his missionary labours that he will not build on another man's foundation".[2] "Making it my aim so to preach the gospel, not where Christ was already named, that I might not build upon another man's foundation" (Rom. xv. 20). "It seems impossible to suppose that St. Peter had already worked in Rome when St. Paul wrote the Epistle to the Romans."[3]

St. Paul arrived as a prisoner in Rome in 60 (Findlay) or the spring of 61 (Lightfoot). He spent at least two years there. How much longer we cannot tell. During that time he wrote four epistles. St. Peter was not there then. To the Colossians we find St. Paul

[1] e.g. Duchesne, *Early History of the Christian Church*, vol. i, pp. 45, 47 (E. T.).

[2] Sanday and Headlam, *Romans* xxvi.

[3] F. H. Chase, *Hastings' Dictionary of the Bible*, vol. iii, p. 778.

referring to several of his friends in Rome. "These only are my fellow-workers unto the kingdom of God, men that have been a comfort unto me" (Col. iv. 11).

It is probable that St. Paul after 63 may have been absent from Rome. On his return, shortly before his death, he wrote the Second Epistle to Timothy. Of his notable friends, "Only Luke is with me. . . . At my first defence no one took my part, but all forsook me" (2 Tim. iv. 11, 16). What space is left for Peter to have been at Rome? What becomes of his episcopate there? How can he be said to have planted the Church there? There was evidently an important body of Christians there when Paul addressed his long and closely reasoned epistle to them. Are we not forced to the conclusion that doctrinal and not historical reasons have been accountable for the insistence of the Petrine visit?

St. Luke in the Acts of the Apostles makes no reference to Peter's work at Rome. In the first twelve chapters of his book he gives chief place to the activities and leadership of Peter.

An argument against the Roman theory is derived from St. Peter's first epistle. He gives Babylon as the place where it is written (1 Pet. v. 13). It was natural that he to whom the evangelising of the Jews was chiefly committed should make his way to that centre where there was a very large and important settlement of Jews. At the day of Pentecost the first places in the list of foreign Jews are given to "Parthians and Medes and Elamites, and the dwellers in Mesopotamia" (Acts ii. 9). The order of the districts to which the epistle is directed is such as accords with it being written from Babylon. Those nearest that city are mentioned first.

It is doing unreasonable violence to Peter's words to eliminate the plain natural meaning of Babylon and say that he must have intended a metaphorical reference to Rome. Why should he? All the rest of the epistle is written in direct non-mystical language. There is no force in the argument that in the Apocalypse (written afterwards) Rome is named Babylon. "It is surely very strange," writes Dr. Streeter, "that anyone writing an actual letter from Rome itself should date it as from Babylon. To call Rome Babylon is entirely consonant with the fiery symbolism of the Apocalypse; it is appropriate in a work like the *Sibylline Oracles*, which is not only apocalyptic in spirit but metrical in form. But in the sober prose of a letter it seems out of place, and quite extraordinarily so in this particular letter. Not only the style of 1 Peter, but its whole attitude towards the Roman power is the very antithesis of that of the author of Revelation, awaiting with exultation the fall of 'The great city, the woman on whose forehead a name is written, MYSTERY, BABYLON THE GREAT, THE MOTHER OF THE HARLOTS AND OF THE ABOMINATIONS OF THE EARTH . . . drunken with the blood of the saints, and with the blood of the martyrs of Jesus' (Rev. xvii. 5 ff.)".[1]

In the epistle the readers are enjoined: "Be subject to every ordinance of man for the Lord's sake: whether it be to the king, as supreme; or unto governors, as sent by him for vengeance on evildoers and for praise to them that do well. . . . Fear God. Honour the king" (1 Pet. ii. 13, 17). This is not the language of a man who regarded the kingly power and its representatives with the abhorrence that the Apocalyptic writer felt.

Corroboration of the Babylonian origin is forthcoming from the fact that there are very scanty references to the epistle in early Latin writers. It is not mentioned in the (Roman) Muratorian Fragment which enumerates the canonical Scriptures. There is evidence of its early use in the East, as by Papias and Polycarp. If it had been written from Rome by St. Peter, and if he had been martyred there, a very different reception for the epistle was to be expected.

Professor E. T. Merrill rejects the theory of the Roman place of authorship. He writes: "When a simple, straightforward and otherwise unimpeachable interpretation is discarded in favour of one that lacks these qualities, the probability is that something has gone wrong in the valuation of evidence. The interpretation of St. Peter's epistle as dated from an actual Babylon is perfectly natural, and in itself unobjectionable. It is safe to affirm that no doubt about it would ever have been raised unless the later story of St. Peter's Roman ministry had been created and sadly needed the clothing of substantiation. Moreover the attribution of a mystical meaning to the place named Babylon in the letter appears in itself unreasonable. The apostle has not been talking in apocalyptic language anywhere else; why should he interpolate here a single enigmatic word? What possible purpose could it serve? And how could a simple-minded Cappadocian, let us say, be expected to understand it in any other than its literal sense?"[2]

The patristic support for St. Peter having been at Rome has been exaggerated.

[1] *The Primitive Church*, p. 117.
[2] *Essays in Early Christian History*, p. 282.

E

(1) The first post-apostolic document from the Church of Rome is that which is called the Epistle of Clement. The circumstances in which it was written would naturally have evoked a mention of the connection of St. Peter with Rome. No such claim is made. Much stress is laid on a phrase in chapter v as if it were a proof of his martyrdom there. "Through jealousy and envy the greatest and most righteous pillars (of the Church) were persecuted and condemned unto death. Let us set before our eyes the good apostles. Peter, who through unrighteous jealousy endured not one or two but many labours, and so having borne witness, proceeded to his due place of glory. Through jealousy and strife Paul displayed the price of endurance." This does not definitely connect St. Peter with Rome. The arguments derived from the citing his name prove nothing. In the preceding paragraph Clement had commemorated Abel, Jacob, Joseph, Moses, etc., as men who suffered through jealousy and envy.

(2) Next the name of Ignatius is appealed to. The phrase relied on is often quoted as: "I do not give you orders as Peter and Paul did."[1] This is not correct. The words are "Not as Peter and Paul do I give you orders. They were apostles, I am a convict" (iv). This only means that he does not assume apostolic authority to command. It is a favourite form of speech with him. To the Ephesians he says (iii): "I do not give you orders as being somewhat" or "some one important". To the Trallians (iii): "I did not consider myself qualified to give you orders as an apostle, being a convict."

(3) The next important writer having association with Rome is Justin Martyr. His silence about Peter is "noteworthy".[2] In his *Apology* (150), addressed to the Emperor Antoninus Pius, he tells a queer story, of the heretic Simon of Gitto who, he says, at Rome worked magic by the aid of demons in the days of Claudius and was honoured by a statue. Justin's error about the statue has been exposed. It is strange that in referring to Simon he does not mention Peter, for from the Simonian legends the real development of Peter's connection with Rome arose. The silence over so long a period of the early writers is remarkable.

(4) The first definite reference to Peter having been at Rome comes a century after the supposed visit and is in the quotation given by

---

[1] Cf. Dom Chapman, *The Papacy*, p. 27; Duchesne, *Early History of the Christian Church*, English translation, vol. i, p. 154.
[2] Foakes-Jackson, *Peter: Prince of Apostles*, p. 154.

Eusebius (ii, 25) from Dionysius of Corinth (170). Dionysius, writing to the Romans, said that Peter and Paul had planted the Church at Rome and Corinth. He is manifestly wrong about Peter planting the Church in either place. He adds: "Both of these having planted us in Corinth, and having in like manner taught in Italy, suffered martyrdom about the same time."

(5) After this the testimonies to St. Peter at Rome are general. Irenaeus (c. 180) tells of the Roman Church "being founded and established by the two most glorious apostles Peter and Paul. . . ."[1] Irenaeus makes the same inadmissible claim as Dionysius for the founding of the Church of Rome. He also copies the erroneous statement of Justin about a statue to Simon of Gitto (whom he identifies with Simon Magus of the Acts) at Rome.[2] Eusebius quoted Gaius (c. 200): "I can show you the trophies of the apostles. For if thou wilt go to the Vatican or to the Ostian road, thou wilt find the trophies of those who founded this Church."[3] Tertullian is the first to state Peter was crucified,[4] and Origen adds the detail that it was head downwards.[5]

The conclusion of Foakes-Jackson represents a favourable estimate of the evidence for the traditional view. "Despite the great names by which it is supported, the literary argument for Peter's visit to Rome is certainly unsatisfactory, although the probability that he visited the city is strong."[6]

One thing is clear: an essential part of the papal claim is unproven. A probability is not sufficient basis for infallibility.

[1] *Adv. Haeres*, iii, 3.
[2] Ibid., i, 23.
[3] *Historia Ecclesiastica*, ii, 25.
[4] *Praescrip.*, 36.
[5] *Apud*, Eusebius, iii, 1.
[6] *Peter: Prince of Apostles*, p. 161.

CHAPTER XIV

WAS ST. PETER BISHOP OF ROME?

We have seen that there are considerable reasons for questioning the residence of St. Peter at Rome. All the tremendous claims based on his episcopate there collapse if his residence in the city be unproven. There are many scholars who admit the residence but wholly reject the episcopate.

It is instructive to note how the Vatican Decrees glide over any proof that Peter was Bishop of Rome. No evidence is offered.

1

It is erroneous to attribute a local episcopate to the missionary apostles. Their work in founding Churches in many countries was entirely different from diocesan episcopacy. Is it to be supposed that Paul was Bishop of Corinth and of Ephesus and of Rome, etc.? The work of an apostle was of another order than oversight of a particular district. "The functions of a king and a lord mayor are not more distinct than those of an apostle and a local bishop."[1]

The traditional story of a twenty-five years' episcopate for Peter has now been exploded. Modern Roman controversialists fall back on the ingenious expedient of suggesting that he came to Rome after St. Paul's first captivity. But he was not there just before St. Paul's death, and yet the tradition is that both apostles died about the same time under Nero. His episcopate must have been an exceedingly brief and elusive one unless we have to consider St. Peter to have been the first of absentee bishops.

The attempt to change the apostle's normal work of founding Churches with assuming a fixed habitation and office as a local bishop breaks down in other ways. In the time of Jerome (d. 420) the belief in the Roman episcopate was unquestioned. He chronicles St. Peter's Roman episcopate, but fixes it after his being bishop in Antioch and his preaching in Pontus, Galatia, Cappadocia, Asia

[1] Salmon, *Infallibility of the Church*, p. 355.

72

and Bithynia.[1] Here we have St. Peter bishop of another city. Surely the Bishops of Antioch have a prior claim to be successors of St. Peter. Chrysostom reflects the claims of Antioch. A Bishop of Antioch, he declares, received Peter's Chair. "This is a mark of the dignity of our city because it had the first of the apostles as teacher. We received him as teacher, but we did not permanently keep him but conceded him to the royal city of Rome. But truly we did permanently keep him. We did not retain the body of Peter, but whilst . . . we retain the faith of Peter we have Peter himself."[2] If the office of the apostolate be confounded with the office of a diocesan bishop such anomalies naturally ensue.

2

If Peter was Bishop of Rome, so was Paul. The earliest writers who connect Peter with Rome attribute equal functions to Paul. As a matter of fact they are careful to show that neither was bishop. The first of these, as we have seen, was Dionysius of Corinth. His account is that both Peter and Paul planted the Corinthian Church and "in like manner taught in Italy". By the papal methods of argument Peter was therefore bishop in Corinth, too. Irenaeus likewise tells of the Roman Church being planted by Peter and Paul, and adds that the blessed apostles, having founded and established the Church, committed the office of the episcopate to Linus. Eusebius in the fourth century is careful to associate the two apostles but keeps them separate from the episcopal succession. "After the martyrdom of Paul and Peter, Linus was the first that received the episcopate at Rome."[3] The order of the names is worthy of note. In another sentence he writes that "Clement occupied the third place of those who were bishops after Paul and Peter".[4]

The witness of Epiphanius (375) is striking. His list of the succession of the Bishops of Rome is important. In his account, in a short paragraph, he records the joint work of Peter and Paul in Rome five times and also speaks of the succession from the apostles.[5] He strives to solve one part of the difficulty by telling that Peter and Paul were "apostles and bishops".

[1] *De Viris Illustribus*, i, 1 (Migne). P. L. 23: 638.
[2] Hom. ii, *in Inscript.* (Migne). P. G. 51: 86.
[3] *Historia Ecclesiastica*, iii, 2.
[4] Ibid., iii, 21.
[5] *Adv. Haeres*, xxvii, 6. P. G. 41: 372.

Are we to conclude, then, that Rome began with a double episcopate? If so, it is strange that Paul never notices his fellow-bishop! For the same reason Corinth must have enjoyed a twin episcopate also. "I cannot find," writes Bishop Lightfoot, "that any writers of the first two centuries and more speak of St. Peter as Bishop of Rome. Indeed their language is inconsistent with the assignment of this position to him."[1] "The earliest documents and traditions connected with the Roman Church bear constant reference to 'Peter and Paul'; never before the third century is the name of one mentioned without corresponding mention of the other." "It is clear beyond any possibility of cavil that in primitive times neither the Roman Church itself, nor Christians from outside who visited Rome or wrote about the history of its Church, ever thought of suppressing the name of St. Paul. But in the course of the third century a significant change came about, and the name of Peter began to be used alone."[2]

These facts are so devastating to the Roman claims that an apologist of Cardinal Wiseman's standing can only attempt to meet them by mutilating the text. He coolly writes: "To Peter, as Irenaeus observes, succeeded Linus."[3]

The single episcopate did not develop in Rome until some time in the second century. The evidence is convincing for this. Therefore St. Peter did not institute a monarchical episcopacy there and so had no "successors" in the office. The Church for a time of unknown extent was governed by a body of presbyter-bishops.

Two documents were written from within the Roman Church and one addressed to it at the end of the first century and the beginning of the second.

(a) The so-called Epistle of Clement (96) is one from the whole Church of Rome to the Church of Corinth. It gives no indication of a single authority there. It makes it clear there was no such ruling functionary above the presbyters in Corinth. In it the titles "bishop" and "presbyter" are interchangeable. The whole picture is of a time prior to the development of the episcopate out of the presbyterate. It is in keeping with the conditions that prevailed earlier, when Polycarp wrote to Philippi.

It is inconceivable that this remonstrance on terms of equality

[1] *Clement*, vol. ii, p. 501.
[2] C. H. Turner, *Catholic and Apostolic*, pp. 219, 224.
[3] *Lectures on the Principal Doctrines and Practices of the Catholic Church*, p. 278.

of the Christian community of Rome with that of Corinth could ignore the fact that in Rome there was placed the Vicar of Christ, the supreme ruler of the Church. As Dr. Bright has written: "On the papal hypothesis, it would not be 'lowliness' but unfaithfulness to a trust, which would make a supreme Pontiff thus keep his own name and personality in the background. For it was to him, not to his Church, that the spiritual sovereignty on that supposition had been committed by our Lord; and it was the part of true charity to enforce a much-needed admonition by the full sanction of the supposed Petrine 'Charter'."[1] It is pointed out that the modesty imputed to Clement has not been imitated by his successors.

(b) *The Shepherd of Hermas* was written in Rome in the time of Clement. This is plain from Hermas's own words. He tells how he was instructed in a vision to send his books "one to Clement and one to Grapte. So Clement shall send it to the cities abroad, for this charge is committed unto him, and Grapte shall instruct the widows and the orphans; while thou shalt read it to this city together with the presbyters who preside over the Church".[2]

Clement may have lived into the second century. The not always reliable Muratorian Fragment states Hermas was brother of Pius who was Bishop of Rome (c. 140). At any rate, *The Shepherd* was quoted as Scripture by Irenaeus and was highly valued by Origen, who suggests it may have been written by the Hermas of Romans xvi. 14.

As is evident from the extract given, the Church of Rome in Hermas's time was still in charge of a body of presbyters. This is the account given all through: "Now therefore I say unto you, that are rulers and that occupy the chief seats".[3] Hermas makes no allusion whatever to St. Peter at Rome. "Government is by a body of presbyters or bishops, to whom everything is to be referred."[4]

(c) Ignatius (c. 110) in six of his letters stresses strongly the importance of the bishop's position. In his letter to the Church of Rome ("to her that has the chief place in the district of the region of the Romans") he makes no allusion whatever to the episcopal office there. From one who was an extreme enthusiast for obedience to the bishop this is an extraordinary omission. Its natural explanation is that, as we have seen from Clement and Hermas, the single

---

[1] *The Roman See in the Early Church*, p. 24.
[2] *Vision*, ii, 4.
[3] Ibid., iii, 9.
[4] Bishop John Wordsworth, *Ministry of Grace*, p. 126.

episcopate had not developed in Rome at that period when it was well established in the East. "In this epistle alone there is no allusion to the episcopal office as existing among his correspondents."[1]

But, on the papal hypothesis, Ignatius was writing to the place where the divinely instituted ruler of the whole Church had his seat—the ruler who had jurisdiction over him, the Bishop of Antioch. Why does Ignatius send no respectful salutations to his ecclesiastical sovereign? Why does he not recommend to his care the Church of Antioch now being left without its head?

The witness of Irenaeus is positive against Peter being in any sense the first Bishop of Rome. The historic value of his list is another question. It, like others, is polemical, that is, directed against the heretics, in order to show the apostolic succession of right doctrine. We may assume that the leading presbyter of each period was singled out for a pre-eminence that accorded with the ecclesiastical conceptions prevailing at the end of the second century.

Lightfoot makes the cautious statement that "the reason for supposing Clement to have been a bishop is as strong as the universal tradition of the next ages can make it"; but he considers that we need not suppose him to have attained the same distinct isolated position of authority which his successors had at the close of the second century or which his contemporaries, Ignatius and Polycarp, had. "He was rather the chief of the presbyters." "No more can safely be assumed of Linus and Anacletus than that they held some prominent position in the Roman Church."[2]

3

Hegesippus (c. 165) wrote: "When I came to Rome I made a succession list as far as Anicetus."[3] This language makes it probable that no such list existed until he set to work on it. His purpose was to controvert heretics by showing the continuity of teaching through a chain of office-bearers. His statement "implies in some degree individual research".[4]

It is now generally accepted that the lists of Irenaeus and Epiphanius are copied from that of Hegesippus.

Soon after the formation of the succession lists for the Roman

[1] Lightfoot, *Philippians*, p. 218.
[2] Ibid., p. 221.
[3] Eusebius, *Historia Ecclesiastica*, iv, 22.
[4] Streeter, *The Primitive Church*, p. 294.

Church began we find confusion appearing in the order of names. How could this occur if the Roman bishop was regarded as the head of the whole Church, to whom obedience was due on peril of forfeiting salvation? Tertullian, a younger contemporary of Irenaeus, challenging heretics to "unfold the roll of their bishops", tells that "Clement was ordained by Peter".[1] Here the order of Irenaeus is upset and his statements contradicted. Tertullian makes it plain that he had no idea of apostles being themselves local bishops. Here he is at one with Irenaeus. His challenge is for the unfolding of the roll of bishops "in such a manner that their first bishop had for his ordainer and predecessor one of the apostles or of those apostolic men who never deserted the apostles". It is significant that the first instance he gives is not Rome but Smyrna, where the local Church "records that Polycarp was placed there by John". He not only separates the apostolic founder from the line of bishops but puts Rome on an equality with other Churches as guardians of truth.

When we come to the earliest lists originating from the Church of Rome itself we find the confusion becoming worse. The Liberian catalogue (Rome, 354) is incorporated in the *Liber Pontificalis*. By this time Peter is counted in as the first bishop. Then follow Linus, Clement, Cletus and Anacletus. Thus Clement is third on one list; first according to Tertullian; second on another list. The extraordinary blunder of making Cletus a different bishop from Anacletus shows how little dependence can be placed on these lists. Yet the order, Peter, Linus, Clement, is followed by Optatus (370) and Augustine (*c.* 400). The order in the canon of the Mass is Linus, Cletus, Clement.

Another fundamental basis for the papal dogma is seen to be a fable. Unless compelled by theological interests, no one could maintain that Peter was Bishop of Rome.

4

The Vatican Decrees evade the proving that Peter was Bishop of Rome but have a chapter "on the perpetuity of the Primacy of the Blessed Peter in the Roman Pontiffs". Four patristic authorities are cited. One of them is from a fifth-century Bishop of Rome—Leo I. His claims marked a notable advance in papal pretensions.

[1] *De Praescr.*, 32.

The other three furnish startling instances of how the highest papal pronouncements misrepresent and manipulate the evidence. The arrogant words of a Roman priest-delegate at the Council of Ephesus are quoted as if it was a decision of the Council. Another is a shockingly mutilated sentence from Irenaeus, the context of which excludes the meaning attributed to it.[1]

The fourth is some words of the Council of Aquileia (381) that are strangely mixed up with the Irenaean quotation, and words are added that are not in either original. The Council of Aquileia was pleading with the Emperor Gratian to suppress the anti-Pope Ursicinus. It was afraid he might gain the ear of the emperor. After many accusations against Ursicinus, the Council wrote begging the emperor "not to suffer the Roman Church, the head of the whole Roman world, and that sacred faith of the apostles to be disturbed, for *thence spread out to all the rights of venerable communion*". It went on to plead that the emperor would, by the rejection of Ursicinus, "restore the security lost to us bishops and to the Roman people who since the report of the Prefect of the City are in suspense."[2]

The argument is plain. The Church of Rome, as the head of the Roman world, was the natural centre of communications among the Christian Churches. A disputed episcopate there would cause wide confusion. The quotation cannot bear the meaning imposed on it.

The failure of the Vatican Council to find Scriptural or patristic authority for the dogma that the primacy of Peter is perpetuated in the Roman Pontiffs is indisputable. The attempt to manufacture evidence is regrettable.

When such are the devices in the *Pastor Aeternus* of Pius IX, with the Vatican Council approving, it is not surprising that Cardinal Newman wrote, after nineteen years' experience of Romanism: "Unless one doctored all one's facts one should be thought a bad Catholic."[3]

---

[1] See pp. 90 ff.
[2] *Ep. inter Ambrosianas*, xi, 5. P. L. 16: 986.
[3] *The Month*, January 1903, p. 4.

CHAPTER XV

ST. PETER IN APOCRYPHAL LITERATURE

T he influence of the fictitious writings that abounded from a very early date can scarcely be exaggerated in originating and disseminating the tradition about St. Peter's connection with Rome. Salmon, a leading authority on the Clementine writings, goes so far as to state that the real inventor of the story of St. Peter's Roman episcopate was an editor of the *Clementine Romances*.[1] A rank crop of forged Acts of the various apostles was in circulation. Eusebius mentions the "Acts of Peter", the "Gospel according to Peter", the "Preaching" and the "Apocalypse" of Peter.[2] Lawlor dates the "Preaching" as not later than about 140. "If we could be sure that it was quoted by Ignatius it must be put back to *c*. 100."[3] He dates the "Apocalypse" as not later than about 150. Dr. James and Harnack placed it earlier. In that uncritical age these fictions were liable to be regarded as authentic. Clement of Alexandria often cited the "Preaching" and quoted the "Apocalypse" as "Scripture".

Another species of such writings are those associated with the name of Clement. They exist in two forms, known as the "Clementine Recognitions" and the "Clementine Homilies". Salmon fixes the date as about 200.[4] Lightfoot considers that they date from some time earlier.[5] They incorporate earlier sources.

These imaginative writings met a demand for more information about the apostles than is given in Scripture. They also were used to support the views of certain sects in the early Church. There existed different groups of Ebionites who maintained that Christians must observe the Mosaic law. By them St. James and St. Peter were exalted and St. Paul reviled as "the enemy". Although they

---

[1] *Infallibility of the Church*, p. 360.
[2] Eusebius, *Historia Ecclesiastica*, iii, 3.
[3] Cf. Lawlor, ibid., ii, 78.
[4] *Dict. Chr. Biog.*, vol. i, p. 577.
[5] *Clement*, vol. i, p. 16.

reflected the outlook of the time in not knowing anything of a supremacy in the Church of Rome, and in representing St. James as superior to St. Peter, yet the place given to Peter came afterwards to substantiate the Petrine–Rome assumptions.

The *Clementine Romances* tell of a struggle round various parts of the world between Peter and Simon Magus. Peter is the conquering hero always and Simon the thwarted villain. The accounts abound in orgies of puerile miracles. Simon personifies the spirit of heresy and diabolical alliance. Peter's work is to follow him everywhere and expose him.

They are written with a strong anti-Pauline motive. This has been toned down by later editors as Rufinus (d. 410). Though Simon Magus is not absolutely a disguise for Paul, there are clear indications that Paul is bitterly attacked in the censures ostensibly directed against Simon. Peter is represented as the real Apostle to the Gentiles, accomplishing great things in the cities that Paul's name was associated with. The last place of conflict is Antioch, with a forecast of Rome. Lightfoot describes the plan of the writer of the *Clementine Romances* as "transferring the achievement of St. Paul to St. Peter whom he makes the Apostle of the Gentiles".[1] Barnabas and Clement are Peter's friends and disciples, not Paul's. The whole tendency is to exalt Peter at the expense of Paul.

Letters from Peter and Clement are prefixed to the Homilies. Peter is made to declaim against "the lawless and foolish doctrine of the enemy". Clement tells James, "the bishop of bishops", of the death of Peter, "who was commanded to enlighten the darker part of the world, namely the west, and was enabled to accomplish it". At Rome Peter testified against the wicked one who withstood him (cf. Gal. ii. 11). Peter before his death nominated Clement, "who has journeyed with me from the beginning", to have his own chair of discourse. Then Peter ordained him and placed him in his chair and ordered him to report to James an account of his death and of Clement's succession as bishop. This is the first appearance of the legend that Peter was Bishop of Rome, if his "chair of discourse" is to be so understood.

It is quite clear how the original forms of such concoctions influenced subsequent orthodox writers. In these books are to be found the sources of much that later writers recorded. Tertullian probably derives from them the statement that Clement was ordained

[1] *Clement*, vol. ii, p. 30.

to the Roman Church by Peter.[1] Jerome states that Peter "in the second year of the Emperor Claudius [i.e. 42], went to Rome to expel Simon Magus and occupied there the sacerdotal seat for twenty-five years".[2] The visit itself is probably as little to be credited as the date or duration or cause.

Tertullian refers to the system of Simonian sorcery, serving angels, condemned by the Apostle Peter in the person of Simon himself.[3] The confuting of Simon at Rome was a traditional reason for Peter going there and fits in with the Ebionite effort to depreciate Paul. Eusebius tells of the success of Simon Magus at Rome, and how in the reign of Claudius, "by the benign and gracious providence of God", Peter was conducted to Rome against this pest of mankind.[4] Hippolytus (d. 236) tells of St. Peter's contests and triumph over Simon at Rome.[5] So does Augustine.[6]

The *Actus Petri cum Simoni* (c. 170) revel in grotesque supernatural marvels, including a speaking dog, and culminate with the final destruction of Simon, who, when giving a flying exhibition at Rome, is made to crash by Peter. Commodian (c. 250) retails that the dog said to Simon: "Peter is calling for thee."[7] The flying incident (in various forms) is recorded by the *Syriac Didascalia*[8] (third century), Ambrose,[9] Cyril of Jerusalem,[10] Arnobius,[11] Epiphanius,[12] Theoderet,[13] Sulphicuis Severus,[14] etc. Marvellous to relate, the Sixth General Council (680) repeats it.[15]

The Epistle of Clement to James in the Homilies was accepted and honoured until the Renaissance. It is quoted as a high authority to be received with reverence on account of its venerable antiquity at the Synod of Vaison (442).[16] With unconscious appropriateness the forgers of the False Decretals put it at the head of their pontifical

---

[1] *De Praescr.*, 32.
[2] *De Viris Illustribus*, i, 1. P. L. 23: 638.
[3] *De Praescr.*, 33.
[4] *Historia Ecclesiastica*, ii, 14.
[5] *Refutatio*, vi, 20. P. G. 16: 3226.
[6] *De Haeresibus*, i, 1. P. L. 42: 25, 26.
[7] *Carmen Apologeticum*. See Shotwell and Loomis, *The See of Peter*, p. 155.
[8] See Headlam, *Hastings' Dictionary of the Bible*, vol. iv, p. 521.
[9] *In Hexaemeron*, iv, 8. P. L. 14: 218.
[10] *Catecheses*, vi, 15. P. G. 33: 564.
[11] *Adv. Gentes*, ii, 12. P. L. 5: 828, 829.
[12] *Panarion*, xxi, 5. P. G. 41: 293.
[13] *Haeret. Fab.*, 1. P. G. 83: 344.
[14] *Chronicorum*, ii, 28. P. L. 20: 146.
[15] Mansi, xi, 666.
[16] *Labbe and Cossart*, iii, 1458.

letters (having judiciously altered it)—"A monstrous parent of a monstrous brood".[1]

If any exploits of Romanist controversialists could astonish us we might wonder at Mr. C. F. B. Allnatt more than once relying on it as patristic evidence concerning the position of the Papacy.[2] "The Simon Magus legends and the Clementine letter taken together made invaluable propaganda for the rising Papacy, at first appealing mainly to the uncritical and unlearned believer, but subsequently admitted, as a part of history, by the gravest Fathers of the Church."[3]

The credulity of even the best of patristic authorities about the egregious Simonian legends diminishes the regard attaching to such statements as that of Gaius about the tombs of the apostles at Rome. It would be strange if at the end of the second century localities had not been found for their tombs. This "narrative concerns the two greatest of all the apostles and came to be of the utmost importance as used to support the claim of the Roman Church to pre-eminence above all others".[4] Gregory of Tours (d. 594), who followed a more orthodox version of the legend which joined Paul with the triumph over Simon, tells there could be seen in Rome in his time two grooves in the rock made by the knees of the blessed apostles when they prayed for the collapse of the flying Simon.[5]

[1] Lightfoot, *Clement*, vol. i, p. 102.
[2] *Cathedra Petri* (2nd edition), pp. 16, 49.
[3] Shotwell and Loomis, *The See of Peter*, p. 127.
[4] E. T. Merrill, *Essays in Early Christian History*, p. 320.
[5] *De Gloria Martyr*, i, 28. P. L. 71: 728.

CHAPTER XVI

EPISTLE OF ST. CLEMENT

The document that is commonly called the Epistle of Clement is probably the earliest piece of Christian literature outside the New Testament. Its date is 95 or 96. Here we have a witness of prime authority.

Do we find the supposed bishop exercising power of jurisdiction as successor to St. Peter? The occasion called for such an oversight. The Corinthians had irregularly set aside some of their presbyters. The epistle is an effort to restore elementary Church order in Corinth.

It affords striking evidence against the papal theory. It is not even written in the name of the Bishop of Rome. No reference is made in it to any bishop, either in Rome or Corinth. Clement's own name is not once mentioned. We only know of his authorship by tradition. It is addressed from the Church of Rome to the Church of Corinth. Later writers refer to it as the Epistle of the Church. Dionysius of Corinth writes to the Roman Church of the "epistle written unto us through Clement".[1] Irenaeus tells how in the time of Clement "the Church in Rome sent a very adequate letter to the Corinthians".[2] Clement of Alexandria calls it in one place the Epistle of the Romans to the Corinthians.[3] It is a brotherly, strongly expressed remonstrance against grave misconduct, from one Church to another. As Lightfoot writes: "The later Roman theory supposes that the Church of Rome derives all its authority from the Bishop of Rome, as the successor of St. Peter. History inverts this relation and shows that, as a matter of fact, the power of the Bishop of Rome was built upon the power of the Church of Rome. It was originally a primacy, not of the episcopate but of the Church."[4] Even in the latter half of the second century Dionysius of Corinth, writing to Soter of Rome, refers to another

---

[1] Eusebius, *Historia Ecclesiastica*, iv, 23.
[2] *Adv. Haeres*, iii, 3.
[3] See Lightfoot, *Apostolic Fathers*, vol. i, p. 69.
[4] Ibid., vol. i, p. 70.

letter as from the Roman Church. "We read your epistle." "Your" is in the plural.[1]

There is no reference in the epistle to Peter having been Bishop of Rome. In fact it is not distinctly stated that Peter had visited Rome.[2]

St. Paul in the epistle is coupled with St. Peter and receives even more extended eulogy. It is also remarkable how St. Paul's work in the West is mentioned without any similar reference to that of Peter there.

The advocates of the papal claims magnify strangely the fact that the Church of Rome wrote such a letter to the Church of Corinth. It was natural for one Church, or its bishop, to write fraternal messages to others. There are many instances of this laudable custom. There are the letters of Ignatius. Eusebius gives repeated instances. He tells, for instance, how Dionysius of Corinth "used to communicate without stint of his inspired industry" to those in foreign lands. He mentions seven of his "Catholic epistles".[3] Polycarp wrote an important letter to Philippi. According to Irenaeus he also wrote letters "to the neighbouring Churches confirming them".[4] Several of Cyprian's letters were addressed to the Roman clergy.

Clement's epistle, a communication from one Christian community to another, cannot be reconciled with modern Roman claims. "Nothing in the letter suggests subordination of Corinth to Rome. . . . The tone suggests Christian solidarity, not obedience of one Church to another."[5] It was natural for Roman Christians to write to their Corinthian brethren in a time of crisis, for Corinth had been refounded as a Roman colony in 44 B.C. "Corinth was a *pied-à-terre* of Rome on Greek soil."[6] The epistle is wholly destitute of even the rudiments of papal authority.

The efforts of Roman apologists to discover the Vatican theology in this letter are characteristic. T. W. Allies sees in this letter of the Roman Church an instance how the "Bishop of Rome and he alone claims a control over the Churches of the whole world".[7]

---

[1] Eusebius *Historia Ecclesiastica*, iv, 23.
[2] See p. 70.
[3] *Historia Ecclesiastica*, iv, 23.
[4] Ibid., v, 20.
[5] Dr. W. K. Lowther Clarke, *The First Epistle of Clement to the Corinthians*, p. 19.
[6] Ibid.
[7] *The See of Peter*, p. 84.

Dom. John Chapman considers that "a few centuries later we should have called this a papal decretal, sent by papal legates".[1] Mr. Adrian Fortescue sees in it "perhaps the clearest example of the Pope's universal jurisdiction before the year 100. . . . Rome sends her legates to settle the dispute and enforce her commands. . . . The Pope's writ carried and was obeyed in Greece within about sixty years from the death of our Lord".[2] Mr. Fortescue holds that "the Church of God at Rome" means the authority of its bishop.

[1] *The Papacy*, p. 26.   [2] *The Early Papacy*, pp. 34-6.

F

CHAPTER XVII

TERTULLIAN

Tertullian of Carthage (*c.* 160–235) was a voluminous and brilliant writer. He, like Irenaeus, Hippolytus, Athanasius, Augustine, etc., was concerned to defend the truth against heresies. Like them, he did not know that there was in Rome an infallible Authority and supreme Ruler by whose judgment all matters of faith must be decided. In all his controversies he never once makes appeal to the "Father and Teacher of all Christians". Contrariwise, his arguments are incompatible with such a belief.

Tertullian follows very closely the standpoint of Irenaeus—which is that of Protestantism today—in relying on the faith as guaranteed by Scripture and tradition. His attitude can be clearly seen, for example, in his little book, *De Praescriptione Haereticorum*, a Demurrer against Heretics. Where is the rule of faith to be found? "Where the end of seeking? Where the resting place of belief?"[1] His answer is, What Christ and His apostles preached, and this ought to be found "through the same Churches which the apostles themselves founded by preaching. . . . All doctrine which agrees with those apostolic Churches, wombs and origins of the faith, must be reckoned for truth as preserving unquestionably that which the Churches received from the apostles, and the apostles from Christ, and Christ from God; and on the other hand, all doctrine which savours contrary to the truth of the Churches and of the apostles of Christ and of God must be condemned at once as having its origin in falsehood. . . . We are in communion with the apostolic Churches, a privilege which no diverse doctrine enjoys. This is evidence of truth".[2] This is misleading and reprehensible if all that is required is to be in communion with the infallible Teacher. Yet the Papacy claims to be "faithfully adhering to the tradition received from the beginning of the Christian faith".[3]

Tertullian announces how truth is to be investigated. He challenges the heretics. "Let them set forth the earliest beginnings of

[1] *De Praescr.*, 10. [2] Ibid., 21. [3] Vatican Decrees, chap. 4.

86

their Churches; let them unfold the roll of their bishops coming down by succession from the beginning in such a manner that their first bishop had for his ordainer and predecessor one of the apostles or of those apostolic men who never deserted the apostles. For in this way apostolic Churches declare their origins: as for instance the Church of the Smyrneans records that Polycarp was placed there by John; and the Roman Church that Clement was ordained thereto by Peter and exactly in the same way the rest of the Churches can produce persons who, ordained to the episcopate by apostles, became transmitters of the apostolic seed."[1]

Further on he adduces against his opponents the apostolic Churches "where the very chairs of the apostles at this day preside in their own places and where their own genuine letters are read. . . . If Achaia is nearest to thee thou hast Corinth. If thou art not far from Macedonia thou hast Philippi. If thou canst travel into Asia thou hast Ephesus. Or if thou art near to Italy thou hast Rome, where we, too, have an authority close at hand".[2]

Tertullian's argument is that of a man who had never heard of any unique *jure divino* fount of teaching in Rome. To him Rome has no more intrinsic superiority as a court of appeal than any other apostolic Church. In one of his lists the order is Smyrna, Rome; in the other Corinth, Philippi, Ephesus, Rome.

Some of the false teachers of the period took the line that the knowledge of the apostles was imperfect and that fuller revelations came later. They urged that Paul with this later knowledge rebuked Peter. Tertullian in his reply does not make any claim that Peter ruled on earth in Christ's stead.

He is ignorant of the supreme position claimed for him. He defends the reputation of Peter as compared with that of Paul "and declines to pit apostle against apostle". "It is fortunate that Peter is on a level with Paul in martyrdom".[3] Likewise, he is ignorant of the supreme authority of the Church of Rome. When he eulogises the happiness of that Church the reasons he cites are that the Apostles Peter and Paul poured out their whole doctrine with their blood there. (Under the influence of apocryphal acts, he believes that John was plunged into boiling oil there.) To him all apostolic Churches are on an equality. "Therefore the Churches, whatever their number or size, are one primitive Church coming from the apostles, from which they all are. So all are primitive and all

[1] *De Praescr.*, 32.   [2] Ibid., 36.   [3] *De Praescr.*, 24.

apostolic, since they are all approved in the unity of the communion
of peace, the title of brotherhood and the interchange of hospitality
—rights which nothing governs but the one tradition of the same
sacrament."[1] He uses the phrase that Cyprian afterwards made
familiar—"the apostolic Churches, wombs and origins of the faith".

In chapter 32 the challenge is that "their first bishop had for his
ordainer and predecessor one of the apostles". This marks off the
first bishop from the number of the apostles. Tertullian had no
thought of the apostle being himself the first bishop.

Tertullian was a prolific author. The one book we have been
concerned with is typical of the rest in its witness against papal
claims. The wide range of subjects he covered makes this witness
the more emphatic. Whenever the opportunity occurs for appeal
to the supreme authority of Rome, there is no consciousness shown
of this. For instance, when he is defending ceremonial usages for
which there is no Scriptural rule, he writes: the objector "will be
told tradition has originated, custom has confirmed, and faith
observes them."[2]

There is a significant passage in his *De Pudicitia*, written in his
Montanist days. "I hear also that an edict has been issued, and a
peremptory one, too. The Pontifex Maximus forsooth, the Bishop
of bishops, sets forth his edict—'I remit the sins of adultery and
fornication to those who have performed penance'."[3] It is probable that the rigorist Tertullian is protesting against a rule of the
lax Callistus, Bishop of Rome. In irony he affixes to him the title
Pontifex Maximus, then borne by the emperors. The Popes did
not assume that title until many centuries later.

[1] *De Praescr.*, 20.   [2] *De Corona*, 4.   [3] Chap., 1.

CHAPTER XVIII

ST. IRENAEUS

1

Irenaeus, Bishop of Lyons at the end of the second century, wrote a lengthy book against the Gnostic heresies. The whole tenor of this great work witnesses against papal claims. In all the five books of it he never once appeals to the duty of obeying the Bishop of Rome or of hearkening to his infallible teaching. He is wholly unconscious that God has given to the Church Sovereign Rulers endued with "the plenary power of feeding, ruling and governing the universal Church", by whom "the whole flock of Christ, kept away by them from the poisonous food of error, might be nourished with the pasture of heavenly doctrine".[1] He laboriously tries to counteract the heretics of his time in just the way a member of our Church would today—by appeal to Scripture, tradition, history and reason. He knew no other standards of orthodoxy than "the preaching of the apostles, the authoritative teaching of the Lord, the announcements of the prophets, the dictated utterances of the apostles and the ministration of the law".[2]

Against the heretics' pretensions that they possessed secret apostolic teaching outside the Scriptures, Irenaeus urged that the teaching of the apostles is to be discerned in the Churches which have a regular succession of bishops from the time of their apostolic founders. He stresses the apostolic succession of doctrine.

Since it would take too long, Irenaeus continues, to count up the series of bishops in all the Churches, he cites three: Rome, which received its faith from Peter and Paul; Smyrna, in which Polycarp was appointed by the apostles; and Ephesus, founded by Paul and where John resided. This line of argument is clearly inconsistent with the papal position. Had Irenaeus been at all aware of papal prerogatives he would have looked no further than Rome. He could

[1] Vatican Decrees, chap. 4.   [2] Adv. Haeres, ii, 35, 4.

89

not, even as a matter of convenience, have cited three apostolic
Churches as on an equality among themselves.

2

Yet it is in this connection that a sentence occurs which perhaps
more than any other one from the Fathers has been relied on to
enforce the Roman claims. In book after book of Roman apologists
we find it stressed. It is appealed to in the Vatican Decrees. The
Satis Cognitum of Leo XIII, when telling of the "shining testimonies"
that prove the *concensus antiquitatis*, puts it in the forefront as "very
remarkable". So great is the importance attached to it that it is
well to quote it in full[1] (we have only a Latin translation for it
instead of the original Greek).

"Ad hanc ecclesiam propter potentiorem principalitatem necesse
est omnem convenire ecclesiam, hoc est, eos qui sunt undique fideles,
in qua semper ab his qui sunt undique, conservata est ea quae est
ab apostolis traditio."[2]

This may be translated: "For to this Church, on account of its
more influential pre-eminence, it is necessary that every Church
should resort—that is to say, the faithful, who are from all quarters;
and in this Church the tradition which comes from the apostles has
ever been preserved by those who are from all quarters."

There is nothing here that causes surprise in a second-century
writer. How, then, do Romanists find it so valuable to them? One
has to answer: by mistranslation and mutilation.

Let us take the translation in Allnatt's *Cathedra Petri*:[3] "For
with this Church, on account of her more powerful headship (or
supremacy), it is necessary that every Church, that is, the faithful
everywhere dispersed, should agree (or be in communion); in which
(in communion with which) Church has always been preserved by
the faithful dispersed that tradition which is from the apostles."

(1) Now in the first place such an interpretation is rendered impossible by Irenaeus's line of reasoning, here and throughout the
whole work. If there was one Church with which all must agree
why does he appeal to the tradition of the apostles manifested "in

---

[1] "The most important testimony to the authority of Rome in the first ages
of the Church is that of Irenaeus." Addis and Arnold, *Catholic Dictionary*
(2nd edition), p. 672.

[2] iii, 3, 2.

[3] p. 85; the words are printed in capitals.

the whole world" (*in toto mundo*) and which may be clearly perceived "in every Church"? If Rome was the divinely appointed source of truth why does he explain his referring to her by the plea that it is "because it would be very long" (*quoniam valde longum*) in his book to "count up the series of bishops in all the Churches"? Irenaeus again and again makes his appeal to the consentient witness of all the apostolic Churches. "Wherefore we should hearken to those presbyters who are in the Church; those who have their succession from the apostles, as we have pointed out; who with their succession in the episcopate received a sure gift of the truth at the good pleasure of the Father; but the rest who withdraw from the primitive succession etc."[1]

If Irenaeus knew that the Roman bishop was Head of the whole Church, possessing the plenitude of power and that "if any questions regarding the faith shall arise they must be defined by its judgment", then how outrageous it was for him to make Smyrna and Ephesus and the other apostolic Churches joint sources of evidence with Rome? He had only to say to the Valentinians and the rest that their doctrines were not the same as those of Eleutherius, the Vicar of Christ.

(2) The words translated "agree" with or "be in communion" with—*ad . . . convenire*—do not bear that meaning. It is palpably a false rendering. The natural meaning of *convenire ad* is to "come together to" or "resort to". Puller states that in the twenty-six passages in the Vulgate where the words *convenire ad* occur the meaning in every instance is "to resort to" or "come together to". "It would perhaps be rash to lay down a universal negative, and to say that *convenire ad* never means 'agree with'; but as far as I am aware no such passage has ever yet been produced."[2]

(3) The "agree with" interpretation is completely ruled out by the following words of the sentence. Irenaeus adds the explanatory clause, "that is, the faithful who are from all quarters (*undique*)". This parenthesis would be out of place if he meant that every Church must agree with the Church of Rome, but they are very apposite with his words that every Church must resort to Rome. Agreement would not require such an explanation. But the idea of every Church resorting to it needs the explanation which he gives by stating that members from all quarters are under a necessity of visiting the city.

The position of Rome was such in the ancient world that there

[1] iv, 26: 2. [2] *Primitive Saints and the See of Rome*, p. 26.

was a continuous influx of people to it from all parts. A sentence from the ninth canon of the Council of Antioch (341) has been quoted in this connection: "All who have business come together from all quarters to the metropolis." Besides, if it were meant that every Church must agree with Rome the word to expect would be *ubique*, "everywhere". The word *undique* is more natural to the idea of a people journeying "from all sides" to a centre.[1]

(4) The question is put beyond all doubt by the concluding words of the sentence: "In this Church (*in qua*) the tradition which comes from the apostles has ever been preserved by those (*ab his*) who are from all quarters (*undique*)." The journeys of the faithful to Rome have the result of keeping alive there the true tradition of the various Churches. "If the point had been that the other Churches must needs teach just what the Roman Church taught . . . why go on to say that it was by members of these same Churches that the apostolic tradition was preserved in the Roman?"[2] Rome is not held up as having an infallible universal Teacher who announces the truth but as a place in which the truth is safeguarded by the constant communications of representatives from the orthodox apostolic churches. It is thus a reservoir of orthodoxy.[3] An apt simile is taken from what Gregory Nazianzen said at a later date of Constantinople, "to which the ends of earth resort from all quarters and from which they start afresh as from a common emporium of the faith".[4]

(5) We are now in a position to see the significance of the words *necesse est*. It is natural to say that "it is necessary" for people from all quarters to visit the metropolis of the world, but if agreement with the faith of Rome was meant some word implying duty or moral obligation like "ought (*oportet*) was to be expected.

It is extremely significant to find the Vatican Decree not venturing to quote the final part of the sentence. It mutilates it by omitting the crucial last phrase and stops its quotation at the word *fideles*. Leo XIII, in his *Satis Cognitum*, is even more economical, for he does not dare to go beyond the word *ecclesiam*—and this in spite of his heralding the testimony as *illud valde praeclarum Irenaei*. One

---

[1] Cf. Mark i, 45: "They came to Him from every quarter." Vulgate: "conveniebant ad eum undique." Is this to be translated, "they agreed with Him everywhere"?

[2] Bright, *Roman See in the Early Church*, p. 34.

[3] B. J. Kidd, "Christendom in Miniature," in *The Roman Primacy*, p. 15.

[4] Oratio xiii, 10 (Migne). P. G. 36: 469.

not familiar with the dubious ways of Roman controversialists might regard such distortions as scarcely credible. Yet from the papal throne itself we find this and similar misrepresentations. Cardinal Mercier was widely respected as a high-minded prelate, yet in his *Pastoral*, made famous by George Tyrrell, he translates Irenaeus thus: "For such is the superiority of the pre-eminence of the Church of Rome that all the Churches, that is to say, the faithful from all points of the universe, ought to be in accord with her and that the faithful, wherever they may be, find intact in her the apostolic tradition."

It can be noticed above how Allnatt destroys the meaning of *in qua* (i.e. "in this Church") by paraphrasing it as "in communion with which".

It may be thought a comparing of the small with the great to cite the appeal to this sentence of a recent convert, Mr. Arnold Lunn, but he may serve to show how even still Romanists are deceived and deceive. After retailing the translation that the whole Church "must needs agree with" Rome, he goes on to proclaim: "The old-fashioned Protestants' appeal to the Early Fathers and to the Primitive Church collapses as all instructed Protestants would now agree."[1] At all events, such a statement helps us to understand how converts to Rome are made.

A modern Anglican writer, who maintains that "there is better support for the papal case than has been hitherto acknowledged",[2] contorts the sentence almost out of recognition. Here is his translation: "For every Church, that is, the faithful in each place, in which the identical *paradosis* given by the apostles is always preserved by those who preside in each place, is necessarily in agreement with this Church because of its superior origin."[3] Since each orthodox Church obviously agrees with another orthodox Church, what is the force of the reason given "because of its superior origin"? Dr. Jalland seems to recognise that in his version the twice-repeated phrase about "those who are from all quarters" (*sunt undique*) does not, as the Americans say, "add up". So he takes *undique* to mean "in each place". When that is not sufficient for his argument he coolly changes (without a vestige of authority) the latter *sunt undique* to *praesunt undique*!

[1] *Now I See*, pp. 217, 218.
[2] T. G. Jalland, *The Church and the Papacy*, p. viii.
[3] p. 111.

If Irenaeus meant to teach the supreme authority of the Roman See in disputes about the faith, he could have said so in plainer and less unmeaning verbiage than the sentence attributed to him. Besides, he would then not have found it necessary to appeal to the tradition of Smyrna and Ephesus or to write in the next paragraph: "Suppose there arise a dispute about some ordinary question among us should we not have recourse to the most ancient Churches with which the apostles held constant intercourse, and learn from them what is certain and clear in regard to the present question. For how should it be if the apostles themselves had not left us writings? Would it not be necessary to follow the course of the tradition which they handed down to those to whom they committed the Churches."[1]

An illuminative discussion of the passage by Dr. W. L. Knox is to be found in the *Journal of Theological Studies*, vol. xlvii (July-October 1946, pp. 180–4). He quotes many authorities, showing that "if we look at the historians of the hellenistic age we shall find that the argument from the position of the city of Rome is a commonplace with them". The *potior principalitas* refers to the fact that the city or Church of Rome "is the centre of the empire, is bound to be visited by people from all parts of the world and is best able to acquire accurate information". The final clause means "in it the tradition which is from the apostles is preserved by those who come from all parts of the world". He arrives at the conclusion that the evidence leads us to an excellent sense for the passage: "To Rome, as the centre of the empire, all Churches, that is, the faithful everywhere, must come together, and in it, by the faithful who are everywhere (i.e. the faithful from every city of the οἰκουμένη settled in Rome, its ἐπιτόμη), preserve the apostolic tradition. The point is that not only does Rome preserve the tradition of SS. Peter and Paul but that this tradition is reinforced by the tradition of every Church in the world, since every Church in the world is represented there."

He cites from Galen a reference to Rome as the "epitome of the world", and from Athenaeus "the populace of the world", "an epitome of the civilised world".

Dr. Knox easily disposes of the "rather dubious" translations of Dr. Jalland: "To amend a reading merely because it does not suit the sense you think it ought to bear savours of temerity." The

[1] *Adv. Haeres*, iii, 4, 1.

meaning of Irenaeus' words as they stand is a "perfectly good one".

It is gratifying to know that scholarly Roman Catholics now see that their Church's interpretation of Irenaeus cannot be maintained. Dom Chapman's admission is disingenuous: "You may translate *convenire* 'agree' or 'resort to' as you please."[1] Puller quotes the eminent historian Dr. F. X. Funk as stating that the translation "resort to" has begun "to meet with more acceptance even in Catholic circles", and that he, after pointing out the absurdity the Roman interpretation leads to, writes: "Under these circumstances there remains no other course than to abandon the traditional translation of *convenire*, which is the sole cause of the above-cited absurdity."[2] Wilhelm and Scannell, in their *Manual of Catholic Theology*, adopt the translation "resort to".[3]

(6) What is meant by the words *propter potentiorem principalitatem*? *Principalitis* may be taken in either of two senses: (*a*) priority, as regards time; or (*b*) priority, as regards rank. Its primary meaning is, priority of time. In that sense it is used several times by Irenaeus in this book. It is in that sense it occurs frequently in Tertullian. He writes of *principalitatem veritatis et posteritatem mendacitatis*".[4]

The words might well mean "a more impressive priority". But the general opinion is that they should be understood as referring to the superior pre-eminence in rank of the Church of the city of Rome. The root word *princeps* did not originally imply rulership. Any Latin lexicon (as Lewis and Short's) gives many instances of its use in quite a different sense—for example, *princeps senatus*, the first senator on the censors' list; *princeps juventatis*, a title of honour that many might have.

Irenaeus makes plain in what the pre-eminence of the Roman Church consisted. It was, he writes, great and very ancient and universally known and founded by the two glorious apostles, Peter and Paul. There is no basis here for sovereignty or supremacy. Irenaeus in this passage does not even mention the Bishop of Rome. He is a witness to the truth of Bishop Lightfoot's statement that history "shows that as a matter of fact the power of the Bishop of Rome was built upon the power of the Church of Rome".[5]

[1] *The Papacy*, p. 28.
[2] *Primitive Saints and the See of Rome*, p. 25.
[3] 1: 28 (1890 edition).
[4] *Praescr.*, 31.
[5] *Apostolic Fathers*, vol. i, p. 70.

3

I have already called attention to Irenaeus's witness against Peter being the first Bishop of Rome. He never separates Peter from Paul in the founding of that Church. Both, according to him, were joined in its establishment. He never refers to Peter as the first bishop but consistently excludes him from the episcopal line. By no forcing of his words can he be made to subscribe to the teaching that Peter, the prince of the apostles, "lives, presides and judges to this day and always in his successors the bishops of the holy See of Rome which was founded by him and consecrated by his blood."[1] Such a theory is repugnant to his whole position. Yet the papal dogmas are gravely paraded as "faithfully adhering to the tradition received from the beginning of the Christian faith";[2] and Irenaeus is cited as a witness by both Pius IX and Leo XIII. We cannot receive this unless we are prepared to believe that black is white, that the simplest language of the Fathers means the reverse of what our intellects inform us.

In the next chapter we will find Irenaeus condemning the action of a Pope and showing that he was unaware that none can lawfully review a papal decision.

[1] Vatican Decrees, chap. 2.
[2] Ibid., chap. 4.

CHAPTER XIX

POPF VICTOR

The history of Victor, Bishop of Rome (*c.* 188–98), is memorable as that of the first Pope to attempt to influence the ecclesiastical policy of the other Churches. The practice prevailed in Asia Minor of keeping Easter on the day of the paschal full moon, whether it fell on a Sunday or not. The other Churches kept it on a Sunday. There had long been differences about this, but both ways were tolerated until the time of Victor. He sent out letters from his Church asking synods to be called on the matter. Most of them agreed against the Asian custom, which was called Quartodecimanism. Victor sought to enforce the rule of Easter being kept on a Sunday.

Here is a definite case of the exercise of leadership by a Bishop of Rome. According to the Vatican Decrees Victor, as Pope, had "full and supreme power of jurisdiction over the universal Church", and all, of whatever rite and dignity, were bound to render true obedience. The event showed that neither in East nor West was such a conception of his authority recognised. Any bishop could, of course, cut off Churches from communion with his own Church. It was quite a different thing to compel other bishops to excommunicate them. Victor excommunicated the Asian ones, but failed in a striking manner to make his excommunication general. His action was condemned and resisted.

Polycrates was then Bishop of Ephesus. He wrote "to Victor and the Church of Rome", stoutly refusing to alter his custom. He tells how a great number of bishops with him in synod also refused. He mentions that he was the eighth of his family to be a bishop. His letter shows no trace of knowledge that by not submitting to the one supreme Pastor he was losing faith and salvation.

The terms of his reply show how little he regarded the authority of Victor. "Therefore I for my part, brethren, who number sixty-five years in the Lord, and have conversed with the brethren from all parts of the world and traversed the entire range of holy

Scripture, am not affrighted by threats. For those better than I have said 'we must obey God rather than man'."[1]

The sequel to this, as told by Eusebius, is instructive. Polycrates had unceremoniously rebuffed the demands of Victor. Did Victor succeed in disciplining him and bishops who acted with him? He tried to do so, but failed, and only drew on himself the censure of the Church. Eusebius significantly states that he "endeavoured" to cut off the Churches of Asia and the neighbouring ones from the communion and denounced them in letters as utterly excommunicate. But "this did not please all the bishops. On the contrary, they exhorted him in reply to have a mind for the things which make for peace and neighbourly union and charity. And their words are extant, also, in which they censure Victor with unusual severity". All these bishops were lacking in understanding that the Bishop of Rome had supreme authority in the Church. They not only withstood him but joined in rebuking him.

Irenaeus is specially mentioned as one who in the name of the "brethren" in Gaul "becomingly admonished Victor not to cut off whole Churches of God for observing an ancient custom handed down to them". The historian Socrates says that Irenaeus "nobly attacked"[2] Victor, "reproaching his hot-headedness". Socrates considers that Victor showed "immoderate heat" in his action.

The Church in the second century was not disposed to follow the lead of Rome. They displayed natural resentment at the bishop there acting in an overbearing manner. Jerome refers with approbation to Polycrates' stand. He tells how Polycrates "wrote against Victor, Bishop of Rome, a synodical epistle" and sees in it his "ability and authority".[3]

"From the point of view of the Vatican Council, Polycrates' letter was a wicked act of rebellion, and all the bishops of Asia, by consenting to that act of rebellion, became partakers in their metropolitan's guilt."[4]

---

[1] Eusebius, *Historia Ecclesiastica*, v, 24.
[2] *Ecclesiastical History*, vol. v, p. 22.
[3] *De Viris Illustribus*. P. L. 23: 695.
[4] Puller, *Primitive Saints and the See of Rome*, p. 17.

CHAPTER XX

ST. CYPRIAN

Cyprian became Bishop of Carthage in 248, and suffered martyrdom in 258. He was the foremost ecclesiastical personality of his time in the Western Church. St. Gregory Nazianzen wrote that he " presided not only over the Church of Carthage and over Africa, but also over all the countries of the West and over nearly all the regions of the East and of the South and of the North".[1] The life and teaching of this illustrious saint are irreconcilable with the papal claims.

1

When there was a schism and an anti-pope in the Church of Rome Cyprian wrote his famous treatise *On the Unity of the Church*. In it there is not a trace of consciousness that the Bishop of Rome is the centre of unity, the true Vicar of Christ. To Cyprian he was the bishop of the "principal Church", but had no more authority than any other bishop. Cyprian is the first of the Fathers to recognise him as succeeding to St. Peter's episcopal chair. This recognition makes his unconsciousness of any jurisdiction over the Church, or special prerogatives, the more remarkable. As the Rev. F. W. Puller writes: "In the whole treatise there is not a word about any peculiar authority either in St. Peter or in the Roman See." "You may read the whole treatise on *Unity* from beginning to end, and you will not find one single word about Rome or about the Pope, or about any papal jurisdiction derived from St. Peter."[2]

The views that Cyprian emphatically taught exclude the Roman claims. For him no bishop had jurisdiction over another bishop. "The episcopate is one, of which each singly holds a part *in solidum*."

---

[1] Oratio xxiv, 12. P. G. 35: 1184. The priests and deacons of Rome were accustomed to address him as "most blessed and glorious Pope" (Ep. 30: 8). (The numbering of the letters is that of the Ante-Nicene Chr. Lib. edition. This order is in general one figure lower than that of Migne, P. L.)

[2] *Primitive Saints and the See of Rome*, pp. 84 n, 88.

"This unity we ought to hold and maintain, especially we, the bishops, who preside over the Church, that we may prove the episcopate itself one and indivisible."[1] The phrase *in solidum* is a legal one, and Cyprian was a lawyer before his conversion. Its meaning is akin to our commercial terms "jointly and severally responsible".

Each bishop has an independent status, but all are preserved in the unity of the Church by mutual concord. "There is one God and one Christ and one Church of Christ and one faith and a people bound together in a firm unity of body by the glue of concord."[2] Writing later to Bishop Stephen of Rome, he states: "For therefore, dearest brother, is the body of bishops so large, bound together by the glue of concord as the bond of unity, that if any one of our college should attempt to introduce heresy and to rend and lay waste the flock of Christ the rest may come in and aid, and as good and merciful shepherds gather the Lord's sheep into the flock."[3]

Cyprian held peculiar views about the force of our Lord's words to St. Peter in Matthew xvi. He regarded the promise to St. Peter as the institution of the episcopate and the manifesting of episcopal unity. After quoting our Lord's words to St. Peter, he goes on: "Though to all the apostles after this resurrection He gives equal power . . . yet in order that He might manifest unity, by His own authority, He arranged for that same unity a beginning from one. Certainly the other apostles were what Peter was, endued with an equal fellowship both of honour and power; but the beginning [*exordium*] starts from unity that the Church of Christ may be demonstrated as one."[4]

Here one of the greatest Church leaders of the third century is writing a treatise specifically on the grounds of the Church's unity. He never once mentions the prerogatives of the Bishop of Rome—the assumed "visible Head of the whole Church militant". According to Roman dogma it is the Bishop of Rome who assures unity. He possesses truly episcopal and immediate jurisdiction over all Churches. All must obey him in matters of discipline as well as of faith.

The principles and (as we shall see) the practice of Cyprian are so directly contrary to this doctrine that, according to it, he is

[1] *De Unitate*, 5.
[2] Ibid., 23.
[3] Ep. 66: 3.
[4] *De Unitate*, 4.

destitute of faith and salvation. Yet whenever the Roman Mass is celebrated he is venerated, and his merits and prayers invoked.

The absolute contradiction between the teaching of Cyprian and that of Rome has been forcibly and properly expressed by Archbishop Benson: "The very mention of the supremacy of one Pontiff or the universality of one jurisdiction is the precise contrary of the Cyprianic statements."[1] "Peter's successors are nowhere mentioned or hinted at by Cyprian as necessary to the Church's unity. But the successors of the other apostles are. . . . A headship attributed to the successors of one among them would simply ruin at once the whole theory of the unity." Cyprian's theory "could not even coexist with the theory of a dominant centre. The two views are mutually exclusive."[2]

That Cyprian did not understand our Lord's commissions to St. Peter as involving any exclusive jurisdiction to the apostle or his successors is recognised by scholars of all the Churches. Dr. B. J. Kidd writes that Cyprian "takes the *Tu es Petrus* as the charter not of the Papacy but of the episcopate".[3] Dom. Chapman—most capable of modern Roman apologists—interprets Cyprian's line of thought thus: "The text Matthew xvi. 18 is the charter of monepiscopacy. . . . The power given to Peter of binding and loosing is the episcopal power. What is more important is that the founding of the Church upon Peter is identified with the founding of the Church upon bishops. . . . Bishops are successors of the apostles."[4]

Professor Bartoli, D.D., has told that while a member of the Society of Jesus he wrote an article against an Anglican. "In the course of my article I quoted against him certain words by St. Cyprian in his treatise *De Unitate Ecclesiae* which as it seemed to me settled once for all the lawfulness of the claims of the Papacy to universal domination." His friend, a German Jesuit, read the article, smiled, stared at him and amazed him by stating that the words he relied on were a later interpolation.[5]

This famous corruption of Cyprian's treatise has been forced by Roman ecclesiastics to be continued in printed editions against the

[1] *Cyprian*, p. 193.
[2] Ibid., pp. 196, 197.
[3] *The Roman Primacy*, p. 24.
[4] *Studies on the Early Papacy*, p. 32. Chapman considers Cyprian's theory of the episcopate an "absurd doctrine" (p. 40), and that his doctrine of church unity "has led him into heresy and into schism" (ibid.).
[5] *The Primitive Church and the Primacy of Rome*, pp. xiii, xiv.

impressive evidence and the protests of foremost Romanist scholars. Archbishop Benson calls it "the grossest forgery in literature".[1] The interpolations include such words as "Primacy is given to Peter".

2

It is disconcerting to find Pope Leo XIII, in his *Satis Cognitum*, repeatedly citing Cyprian in a most misleading way. He links Cyprian with Irenaeus as luminous examples of the consent of antiquity. He instances three passages. (1) One is (Ep. 44) where he states Cyprian affirms the Roman Church to be the "root and womb of the Catholic Church".[2] This sounds impressive to one who is not familiar with the context or Cyprian's usual vocabulary. To Cyprian it is the Church Catholic and Apostolic that is the root and womb of all local Churches and members. The figure is of constant recurrence where Rome is not meant. "He cannot have God for his father who has not the Church for his mother."[3] The Church is the "one mother abundant in issues of births. It is of her bringing forth (*foetu*) we are born, by her milk that we are nourished".[4] "There is one God and one Christ and one Church of His, and one faith. . . . Unity cannot be sundered . . . whatever has been parted from the womb cannot live and breathe of itself."[5] When in violent dispute with Rome he wrote: "We who hold to the head and root of the one Church."[6]

Owing to the schism in the Roman Church, the African Christians did not know which of the rival bishops they should communicate with. They sent two envoys to find out and report who was the rightful bishop. They were anxious, as Cyprian explains in this letter to Cornelius, to maintain the harmony of the Church. "Now we, furnishing all those who sail hence with a rule lest in their voyage they in any way offend, know well that we have exhorted them to acknowledge and hold fast to the womb and root of the Catholic Church." As soon as they obtained definite information that Cornelius and not Novatian was the regularly appointed bishop, then "all scruples being removed", they determined to adhere to him, "that is, as well, to the unity as the charity of the Christian Church".

---

[1] *Cyprian*, p. 193.
[2] Cf. *Tertullian*, p. 86.
[3] *De Unitate*, 6.
[4] Ibid, 5.
[5] Ibid., 23.
[6] Ep. 72: 2.

There is not here the least suggestion of any special authority belonging to the Roman bishop. Anything Cyprian writes would apply with just the same force to any other Church where there was a disputed succession. All he means is that by communicating with the legitimate local Catholic bishop they were preserving Church unity.

(2) Just the same explanation is to be given of another phrase that Pope Leo XIII made use of. Cyprian is cited as telling his correspondent, Antonianus, that to communicate with Cornelius is to communicate with the Catholic Church.[1] Antonianus, who lived at Rome, was wavering between the claims of Cornelius and Novatian. Cyprian explains to him how Cornelius was the legitimately chosen bishop, how any usurping bishop is "outside the Church . . . because he does not preserve the unity of the Church". So by adhering to Cornelius Antonianus will be in communion with the Catholic Church.

(3) The other phrase laid stress on in the *Satis Cognitum* is where in Cyprian's Epistle 54 he refers to "the chair of Peter and the principal Church whence episcopal unity has sprung".

We have seen how Cyprian held that the prerogatives of Peter were the assurance of the prerogatives of the whole episcopate. So it is quite consistent with his views to find him referring to Rome as the chair of Peter from which episcopal unity has sprung. The past tense is to be noted, *exorta est*. Neither does any papal argument lie from Cyprian's describing Rome as the "principal Church". It was the apostolic Mother Church of the West—the Church of the world's metropolis. To Cyprian, as to his generation, Rome was "the city".[2] He writes elsewhere: "Rome by her greatness ought to have precedence of Carthage."[3]

It is more likely that Cyprian uses the word "principal" in the sense of first in time or original. Mgr. Battifol[4] has a long disquisition giving his reasons for this interpretation. He cites numerous occurrences of the word in ecclesiastical writers as Tertullian.[5] Ambrose's *principalis . . . substantia* at the creation; the term *litterae principales* for initial letters of words. Battifol's conclusion is that here *ecclesia principalis* means the inaugural Church, "the Church anterior to all the others, the oldest, of which all the others

---

[1] Ep. 51: 1.
[2] Ep. 44: 3.
[3] Ep. 48: 2.
[4] *Cathedra Petri*, chap. v, p. 135 ff.
[5] See p. 95.

are scions and cadets, the Church established by Christ in the person of St. Peter on the day of the *Tu es Petrus*".[1]

Battifol condemns the translation here of *principalis* by "sovereign" and notes that Duchesne has abandoned it. He calls special attention to the past tense of the verb "has sprung". "The unity does not spring forth, it has sprung"[2]—thus referring to date in the past.

The very same section of this epistle (54) of Cyprian contains statements that are in absolute, direct opposition to Roman claims. It is an instance of how detached words or phrases are unfairly seized on by Roman controversialists from authors whose whole standpoint is opposed to such pretensions. Cyprian is writing to Cornelius of Rome to warn him against disaffected members of the Church of Carthage who have gone to Rome. Now according to the Vatican decree these men had a right to carry their cause to the Roman tribunal. The Pope has "full and supreme power of jurisdiction".[3]

How did Cyprian regard those who dared to bring complaints from Carthage to Rome? "For it has been decreed by our whole body, and is alike equitable and just, that every cause should be heard where the offence has been committed. A portion of the flock has been assigned to the several shepherds which each is to rule and govern, having hereafter to give account of his administration to the Lord; it therefore behoves those over whom we are set not to run about from place to place, nor, by their crafty and deceitful boldness, break the harmonious concord of the bishops, but there to plead their cause where they will have both accusers and witnesses of their crime; unless perhaps some few desperate and abandoned men count inferior the authority of the bishops established in Africa who have already given judgment concerning them. . . . Already has their cause been heard; already has sentence been given concerning them."[4]

Could there be a more specific and emphatic assertion of the independent authority of a national Church? Could there be by anticipation a clearer disproof of the Vatican decree? Be it remembered that Cyprian is writing in friendliness to the Bishop of Rome. He was utterly unconscious, as was Cornelius, that he was infringing on any rights of the Roman Church; nor that he was repudiating

[1] *Cathedra Petri*, chap. v, p. 150.
[2] Ibid., chap. v, p. 137.
[3] Vatican Decrees, chap. 3
[4] Ep. 54: 14.

the fundamental constitution of the Catholic Church. Is it any wonder that Roman Catholic controversialists so often show themselves distorting historical evidence? Here, the head of their Church, in a carefully prepared encyclical, again and again grotesquely and inexcusably misrepresents not only the words of St. Cyprian but his whole life-long attitude to the Roman episcopate.

3

Two Spanish bishops, Basilides and Martial, were deposed for serious crimes. They (or one of them) went to Rome and were restored to communion and to their sees by Pope Stephen. The Spanish Church appealed against this decision to Cyprian. At a Council in Carthage the Pope's decision was reversed. The appointment of the new bishop in place of one of them "cannot be rescinded by the fact that Basilides, after his sins had been detected and further revealed by the confession of his own conscience, went to Rome and deceived Stephen, our colleague, who was a long way off and ignorant of what had happened and of the truth; and intrigued to be unjustly reinstated in the episcopate from which he had been justly deposed. This means merely that the sins of Basilides have been multiplied rather than absolved, for to his previous wrongdoing he has added the crime of deception and fraud. Nor is one who carelessly allowed himself to be beguiled so blameworthy as the man is to be execrated who through fraud imposed on him".[1]

As always in St. Cyprian's life, the Bishop of Rome is regarded as possessed of no more authority than any other bishop. The idea of obedience to him is undreamt of. In fact in this epistle he is severely censured. The Spanish clergy are told that though some (of whom the Bishop of Rome was foremost) are found among their colleagues who think that discipline is to be neglected this ought not to disturb their faith. The verses of Psalm l. are quoted against the bishops who communicate with the condemned ones: "When thou sawest a thief thou consentest with him: and hast been partaker with the adulterers."[2]

Rome teaches in 1870 that "none may reopen the judgment of the Apostolic See, than whose authority there is none greater, nor can any lawfully review its judgment." Cyprian and a council of

[1] Ep. 67: 5.   [2] Ep. 67: 9.

African bishops in 254 repudiated and denounced the Roman decision and instructed the Spanish church to pay no regard to it.

4

Soon afterwards Cyprian was engaged in bitter conflict that ended in complete rupture with the Bishop of Rome.

It was the custom of the Church of North Africa and of Asia Minor to rebaptise all who came to them from heretical sects. The Church of Rome regarded the baptism of heretics as valid and not to be repeated. Stephen of Rome and Cyprian put forth their contrary views. In 256 a Council of seventy-one bishops met at Carthage and decreed firmly the necessity of rebaptism.

Cyprian wrote to Stephen on terms of complete equality, informing him of what was done and asserting its rightfulness and finality. He hints pretty plainly that if Stephen does not agree it is his fault and that he is free to go his own way. "We have informed you, dearest brother, of these things by reason of our mutual respect and our sincere love, believing that what is religious and true will commend itself to your true faith and religion also. But we know that some will not abandon a position they have once taken up nor easily change their policy. . . . In this matter we coerce no one and lay down the law to no one, since each bishop hath in the administration of the Church freedom of decision according to his own will and is hereafter to give an account of his conduct to the Lord."[1]

Stephen replied in a letter in which Cyprian found "error" and regarded as "arrogant", "irrelevant", "self-contradictory", "rash". He writes : "The harsh obstinacy of our brother Stephen has reached such a pitch." "Does he give honour to God who is a friend of heretics, an enemy to Christians and who deems the priests of God, guarding the truth of Christ and the unity of the Church, should be excommunicated." "For what is that blindness of soul, what is that degradation of faith, to refuse to recognise the unity which comes from God the Father and from the tradition of Jesus Christ." "It happens, however, that a man of presumptuous and stubborn zeal will defend his own wrong and false views rather than yield to another's that are right and true."[2]

Cyprian met the Roman denunciation by holding a larger

[1] Ep. 71: 3.   [2] Ep. 73: 1, 4, 7, 8, 10.

Council of eighty-seven bishops probably towards the end of 256. His opening speech was highly significant. "It remains that we severally declare our opinion on this same subject, judging no one, nor depriving any one of the right of communion if he differs from us. For no one of us setteth himself up as a Bishop of bishops, or by tyrannical terror forceth his colleagues to a necessity of obeying; inasmuch as every bishop, in the free use of his liberty and power, has the right of forming his own judgment, and can no more be judged by another than he can himself judge another. But we must all await the judgment of our Lord Jesus Christ, who alone has the power both of setting us in the government of His Church and of judging of our acts therein."[1]

The Council unanimously pronounced for rebaptism, thus repudiating the Roman bishop's position. Stephen had cut off his Church from the Africans. When the Council sent its delegates to Stephen he would not admit them to an interview and forbade the members of his Church to receive them in their houses. "Shelter and hospitality were denied them."[2] Stephen denounced Cyprian as a "false apostle".

What the Church thought of the Roman bishop's proceedings can be seen in the letter[3] of St. Firmilian which Cyprian translated and issued to the Churches. The African Church and that of Asia Minor continued undisturbed in their policy.

---

[1] Mansi, i, 951.   [2] Ep. S. Firmilian *inter Cypr.*, 74: 25.
                            [3] See *infra.*

CHAPTER XXI

ST. FIRMILIAN

Firmilian was Bishop of Caesarea in Cappodocia from about 232 to 270. He was one of the most eminent bishops of his time and is so celebrated by Dionysius of Alexandria and by Eusebius.[1] He probably presided at the two synods of Antioch occasioned by the heresy of the bishop there, Paul of Samosate.[2]

At the time of the great Council of Carthage, which unanimously disagreed with the views of Stephen, Bishop of Rome, on rebaptism, Cyprian consulted Firmilian. Firmilian's reply is to be found as translated by Cyprian in his Epistle 74. It is an uncompromisingly severe condemnation of Stephen. The vigour of its language reveals how far the Church of the third century was from recognising any overruling, much less infallible, authority in the Bishop of Rome, even by those who regarded him as succeeding to St. Peter's chair.

Firmilian begins by rejoicing at the unity of spirit between the African and Eastern Churches. Stephen may be thanked, because through his unkindness the proof of Cyprian's faith and wisdom has been received, but Stephen has no more merit for this than Judas has for the sacrifice of our Lord. He ascribes "audacity and pride" to Stephen and declares Cyprian has settled the matter according to the rule of truth and the wisdom of Christ. "As regards what Stephen has said as though the apostles forbade those to be baptised who came over from heresy. . . . You have answered most fully that no one can be so foolish as to believe that the apostles delivered this." "That they who are at Rome do not observe those things in all respects which are handed down from the beginning and that they in vain pretend the authority of the apostles, any one may even know from this that in celebrating Easter and in many other divine and sacramental ordinances we may see there are certain diversities among them and that all things are not alike observed by them which are observed at Jerusalem." Diversities

---

[1] *Historia Ecclesiastica*, vii, 28, 30.
[2] Hefele, *Councils*, vol. i, p. 120 (E. T.).

have not broken the peace and unity of the Catholic Church. "This Stephen has now dared to do, breaking the peace with you which his predecessors ever maintained in mutual affection and respect. Moreover, herein defaming the blessed Apostles Peter and Paul as if they had handed this down."

"What is the greatness of his error and the depth of his blindness who says that remission of sins can be granted in the synagogues of heretics, and does not abide on the foundation of the one Church which was once based by Christ upon the rock." Firmilian's strictures show that he, like Cyprian, interpreted the "rock" text as giving no prerogatives to the Bishop of Rome. This is emphasised in what follows: "I am rightly indignant with Stephen for his open and manifest folly since he who boasts so loudly of the place of his episcopate and who insists that he holds the succession from Peter, on whom the foundations of the Church were laid, is introducing many other rocks, and establishing new buildings of many Churches, maintaining baptism in them by his authority. . . . He does not comprehend that one who thus betrays and abandons unity disparages, and in a way effaces, the truth of the Christian rock." "Stephen is not ashamed to announce that remission of sins can be granted by those who are themselves immersed in all kinds of sin."

Firmilian goes on to apostrophise Stephen in terms that no ingenuity can explain away. "Consider with what ignorance you dare to blame those who strive for the truth against falsehood. . . . What strifes and dissensions hast thou stirred up through the Churches of the whole world! and how great sin hast thou heaped up when thou didst cut thyself off from so many flocks! For thou didst cut thyself off, deceive not thyself; for he is truly the schismatic who has made himself an apostate from the community of the unity of the Church. For while thou thinkest that all may be excommunicated by thee, thou hast excommunicated thyself from all. Nor have even the precepts of an apostle been able to help thee to the rule of truth and peace."

"How diligently has Stephen fulfilled these salutary commands and warnings of the apostle, keeping in the first place lowliness and meekness. For what can be more lowly and meek than to have quarrelled with so many bishops throughout the whole world, breaking peace with each one of them in various modes of discord; now with the Eastern Churches, as we feel confident you are aware;

now with yourselves who are in the South! From whom he received episcopal legates with such long-suffering and meekness that he would not admit them even to the common intercourse of speech; so mindful, however, was he of love and charity that he instructed the entire brotherhood that no one should take them into his house; so that on their arrival not only peace and communion but even shelter and hospitality was denied them. This is 'to keep the unity of the spirit in the bond of peace', to cut himself from the unity of love, to alienate himself in everything from the brethren and to rebel in furious bitterness against the sacrament and the faith. Can there be one body and one spirit, and with such an one, in whom perhaps there is not one mind, so slippery is it, so shifting, so uncertain."

Stephen is denounced for siding with the heretics and daring to call Cyprian a "false Christ" and "false apostle" and "deceitful worker". "He is conscious that all these offences are in himself, and has been beforehand with his lies, bringing against another the accusations he himself richly deserves to bear". Stephen is "worse than all the heretics".

In strange defiance of such witness, the Vatican Decree declares that the perpetual practice of the Church confirms that the Roman Pontiff has "the supreme power of teaching"; and that all the venerable fathers have embraced and venerated his apostolic doctrine!

CHAPTER XXII

ST. HIPPOLYTUS

Hippolytus was a bishop in or near Rome at the beginning of the third century. His death took place about 236. "It has seldom happened," writes Dr. Salmon, "in ecclesiastical history that one who enjoyed so much celebrity in his lifetime as Hippolytus has been so obscurely known to the Church of subsequent times."[1] Professor Kirsch states: "Hippolytus was the most important theologian and the most prolific writer of the Roman Church in the pre-Constantinian era."[2] Bishop Lightfoot would extend the period to the time of Jerome.[3] His works were translated into many eastern languages. A seated statue of him was excavated in 1551 and is now in the Lateran Museum. On the back of the chair is a list of several of his writings. The statue was probably set up during or immediately after his lifetime. Several writers in the ensuing centuries refer to him.

The discovery of Hippolytus's book, *The Refutation of All Heresies* and its publication in 1851, aroused the interest of the learned. Still we are unsure about much of his personal history. He was a bishop at Rome. Döllinger considers him the first anti-pope. Lightfoot thinks he was bishop of the floating foreign population of the harbour of Portus.

In the *Refutatio* he makes charges of heresy against Pope Zephyrinus (199–218) and of heresy and other misdemeanours against Pope Callistus (219–223).[4] He accuses them of being deceived by the heretic Noetus and teaching a sort of Sabellianism that identified the Father and the Son. Zephyrinus is represented as an illiterate and avaricious man who was inveigled in that sect. Callistus was his adviser and ally in these evil courses. Hippolytus tells how he

---

[1] *Dict. Chr. Biog.*, vol. iii, pp. 85, 86.
[2] *Catholic Encyclopaedia*, vol. vii, p. 361.
[3] *Apostolic Fathers*, vol. ii, p. 427.
[4] Bk. ix. See Bishop Christopher Wordsworth, *St. Hippolytus and the Church of Rome*, pp. 62 ff.

resisted and confuted this heretical school, though Zephyrinus and Callistus co-operated with them.

Hippolytus gives a terrible account of the life of Callistus. Escaping from the convict mines in Sardinia, he crept into the favour of Zephyrinus, who made him an assistant by hypocrisy and fawning. "He was assuredly a cheat and an imposter." At the death of Zephyrinus, Callistus "thought he had obtained what he sought after". This ambiguous phrase implies he was made Pope. Callistus is also accused of encouraging lax discipline in morals and allowing sinners into the Church on easy terms.

We are not now directly concerned with the justice of Hippolytus's severe strictures on either of these Popes. It is possible that Hippolytus may have been made a rival Bishop of Rome to Callistus. There are two deductions to be drawn. (1) If this famous and learned man was made bishop by an orthodox and rigorist section of the people, and, since no record of such a schism in the Church of Rome is preserved, then it follows that a disputed succession in that Church was a matter of mere local interest and not a cause of consternation to the whole Christian community. (2) The fact that a man of Hippolytus's fame, one honoured always as a saint and martyr in the Roman Church, whose feast is still commemorated, could write as he did about two Popes proves that neither he nor his contemporaries regarded the Popes as the Vicars of Christ and infallible Teachers. "If he owned Zephyrinus as bishop, the most unruly presbyter of our own Church could not show less belief in the infallibility of his bishop than Hippolytus does in that of Zephyrinus."[1] "In his *Refutation of all Heresies* we see a practical refutation of that great heresy . . . a refutation of the heresy of papal supremacy and of papal infallibility."[2]

[1] Salmon, *Dict. Chr. Biog.*, vol. iii, p. 91.
[2] Bishop Christopher Wordsworth, *St. Hippolytus and the Church of Rome*, p. 304.

CHAPTER XXIII

GENERAL COUNCILS

"I confess," wrote Pope Gregory the Great, "that I receive and venerate the four Councils as I receive and venerate the four books of the Gospel."[1] In the early centuries of Christianity the one recognised method of settling disputed doctrines was the assembling of a Council. When the errors of Nestorius disturbed the Church the monks of Constantinople supplicated the emperor to summon a Council to confirm and restore the faith.[2] When the emperor did call the Council he explained it was indispensable on account of the troubles in the Church. When the second Council of Ephesus took the side of the heretics, Pope Leo besought the emperor, "with groans and tears", to summon a Council in Italy to banish offences and remove all doubts concerning the faith.[3]

St. Augustine in all his controversies knew no supreme deciding authority except the consent of the whole Church. Arguing with the Donatists about the position of St. Cyprian, regarding rebaptism, he does not censure Cyprian for refusing to submit to the Bishop of Rome. He explains that no General Council had in his time pronounced on the matter. Cyprian, he maintains, would "undoubtedly have yielded if at any time the truth of the question had been placed beyond all dispute by the investigation and decree of a General Council".[4] Augustine in this treatise makes plain the methods for the confirmation of truth. It can only be set forth by the authority of Councils. Among Councils, local and provincial ones must yield to the authority of universal Councils.[5] Regarding the orthodox view of baptismal validity Augustine declares: "We ourselves would not dare to assert anything such unless we were supported by the most harmonious authority of the universal Church."[6] We can

---

[1] Migne. P. L. 77: 478.
[2] Mansi, iv, 1108.
[3] P. L. 54: 829.
[4] *De Bapt. contra Donatistas*, lib. (Migne) ii. P. L. 43: 129.
[5] Ibid., P. L. 43: 128, 129.
[6] Ibid.

"declare with the confidence of a fearless voice that which under the Government of our Lord God and Saviour Jesus Christ has been ratified by a Council of the universal Church".[1]

Vincentius of Lerins also looked on a General Council as the highest tribunal in fixing doctrine. In accordance with the teaching of the Fathers, "by the decree and authority of a Council the rule of the Church's faith may be settled".[2]

Numerous illustrations might be given of the truth of Newman's statement that when heresy divided the Church "nothing was left to those who desired peace, to say nothing of orthodoxy, but to bring the question under the notice of a General Council".[3]

It is plain, then, that the early Church knew of no method for the authoritative formulating of belief but General Councils. This is obviously in direct conflict with papal theories of one man having the infallible supreme power of teaching; that "if any questions regarding faith shall arise they must be defined" by his judgment; that it is unlawful "to appeal from the judgments of the Roman Pontiffs to an Oecumenical Council as to an authority higher than that of the Roman Pontiff". The early Church showed complete unconsciousness of these powers belonging to any official in the Church.

It is easy to understand the difficulties and disadvantages of taking bishops everywhere from their duties, compelling them to travel in irksome and dangerous conditions over land and sea. Even when assembled in one city, continued residence there often entailed severe sacrifices. "A heathen writer complains that the whole posting system of the empire was deranged through its being constantly occupied by bishops hastening to Councils. Why at so much cost and labour bring a number of fallible men together if one infallible man could have settled the whole question in his closet?"[4]

When the papal power had become strong enough to overthrow the primitive constitution of the Church and make its usurpation supreme then it drastically changed the status of Councils. In the Latin Church they are only a simulacrum of what they were. Pope Pius IX added a new dogma—the Immaculate Conception of the Blessed Virgin Mother—by his own initiative and authority. At

---

[1] *De Bapt, contra Donatistas*, lib. vii. P. L. 43: 242, 243.
[2] *Commonitorium*, chap. 28.
[3] *Arians of the Fourth Century* (new edition), p. 241.
[4] Salmon, *Infallibility of the Church*, p. 288.

the Vatican Council the phrase *Sacro Universali Synodo approbante* superseded the old individual voting—*Ego definiens subscripsi*. Even in the fourteenth century a writer described the part taken by the bishops present at the Council of Vienne as "one hundred and thirty Pastoral Staves".[1] Of course, if the Bishop of Rome is the supreme Judge of the faithful, and if none may reopen his judgment, then it is superfluous and impertinent to apply to other bishops and not to him alone for authoritative decisions on the faith.

If the Roman Pontiffs were "placed over the universal Church", true Vicars of Christ, possessing "the plenitude of power from our Lord Himself", then no one but they could summon a universal Council and no one but they preside over it.

The fact is that not one of the first eight Councils, recognised in the Roman Church as oecumenical, was summoned by a Pope. In the face of an unquestionable truth like this the Romanist may well feel the convenience of the protest of Cardinal Manning that "the appeal to antiquity is both a treason and a heresy"; and appreciate his claim. "How can we know what antiquity was except through the Church."[2]

Nor was it the rule that the Popes must preside at the Councils. They did not preside in person or through their representatives at the first three. The Pope was not even represented at the fifth. At the sixth, while the papal legates had the place of honour, the emperor and his officials acted as presidents. While it might have been expected that, as the holders of the chief see, the Bishops of Rome would preside as a matter of course, we see that actually this was not considered necessary.

The witness of the General Councils as authoritative exponents of Christian doctrine is of conclusive testimony to the novelty of the papal claims.

[1] See Denny, *Papalism*, p. 134.
[2] *Temporal Mission of the Holy Ghost* (4th edition), p. 238.

CHAPTER XXIV

THE COUNCIL OF ARLES

In the beginning of the fourth century a disastrous schism originated in the Church of Africa. The appointment of Caecilian to be Bishop of Carthage was opposed by a powerful party who came to be known as Donatists. They represented the extreme rigorists, who condemned all who compromised during the persecutions. A synod of seventy bishops elected a rival Bishop of Carthage. Their contention was that they were the Catholic Church of Africa. When they found themselves ignored by the officers of the Emperor Constantine they lodged an appeal to him to have the issue judged. They asked that judges be sent from Gaul. The title of their petition begins "*Libellus Ecclesiae Catholicae*".

They were not conscious of any supreme judge divinely authorised to decide such matters. The Bishops of Gaul are asked for, probably as being near to Africa and likely to be impartial outsiders. Constantine in part granted their request. He appointed bishops from Gaul and Italy to hear the case and naturally gave the chairmanship to the bishop of the world's metropolis, Rome. But the terms of his decree exclude any conception of the Bishop of Rome having either peculiar authority or sole power to adjudicate. The imperial letter is addressed to Miltiades, Bishop of the Romans, and to Mark.[1] (It is generally supposed that by Mark is meant Merocles, Bishop of Milan.)[2] It tells of the evils of the commotion in the African Church, where the bishops are at variance among themselves. Constantine orders that Caecilian, with ten bishops of his side and ten of his opponents, proceed to Rome, "that there a hearing may be granted him in the presence of yourselves, and moreover of Reticius and Maternus and Marinus[3] also, your colleagues, whom I have ordered to hasten to Rome for this purpose".

This Council met at Rome, October 313. Fourteen Italian bishops

---

[1] Eusebius, *Historia Ecclesiastica*, x, 5.
[2] *Dict. Chr. Antiq.*, vol. ii, p. 1811.
[3] Bishops from Gaul.

were added. They decided that the charges against Caecilian were baseless. Constantine treats the decision as that of all the bishops The matter was terminated "at the city of Rome by 'qualified and most excellent Bishops'".[1]

The Donatists appealed from the decision. Plainly they knew of no final authority in the Bishop of Rome. Neither did the whole Church. Constantine allowed the protest by calling a larger Council of the West to hear the dispute. This Council met at Arles in August 314. Even the British Church was represented at it. No such representative gathering had heretofore taken place; and it was for a retrial of what the Bishop of Rome and his colleagues had pronounced on.

Nor was there any protest that it was unseemly or profane to ignore thus the verdict of the Bishop of Rome. The then Bishop of Rome, Sylvester, sent his representatives to it. They were not given the chief place. "Marinus of Arles, one of the three judges who had been appointed beforehand by the emperor, appears to have presided over the assembly."[2] Constantine, in a letter summoning a bishop to the Council, explains that the malcontents objected that the Roman trial was the judgment "of a few persons".[3] "Constantine decided to have the case tried over again."[4]

The Council condemned the Donatists and issued a number of important canons on various points of Church discipline. Letters to the Pope survive which show a mode of thought far from consistent with modern Papalism. One letter simply tells the Pope "what we have decreed in common council we signify to your belovedness that all may know what in future they ought to observe".[5] They do not dream of asking for a confirmation of what they have decreed. They request or instruct him to be the means of circulating their decisions. Another letter similarly desires that through Sylvester, who "holds the greater dioceses", the decisions might be chiefly made known.[6] The Council of Arles, by its very existence, proved its authority was higher than that of the Bishop of Rome. The doctrine that "none may reopen the judgment of the Apostolic See" was without meaning to it.

---

[1] Mansi, ii, 465.
[2] Hefele, *Councils*, vol. i, p. 181 (E. T.).
[3] Eusebius, *Historia Ecclesiastica*, x, 5.
[4] Duchesne, *Early History of the Church*, vol. ii, p. 88.
[5] Mansi, ii, 471.
[6] Ibid., ii, 469.

H

CHAPTER XXV

THE COUNCIL OF NICAEA

1

The outbreak of Arianism in the fourth century was one of the most dangerous crises the Church had to endure. In 320 or 321 a Council held under Alexander, Bishop of Alexandria, condemned its leader, Arius. The heresy denying the essential Deity of Christ gained adherents until it provoked widespread divisions, and the feuds excited the ridicule of the heathen. The Emperor Constantine appealed in moving terms to Alexander and Arius to cease their contests.[1] No adequate result being obtained, the emperor called the Council of Nicaea in 325.

In his letters after the Council Constantine makes plain how it was the decision of the assembled bishops that was alone regarded as authoritative in matters of faith. Writing to the Church of Alexandria, he rejoices in the Church being delivered from error. "Let us therefore embrace that doctrine which the Almighty has presented to us." "For that which has commended itself to the judgment of the three hundred bishops cannot be other than the doctrine of God; seeing that the Holy Spirit dwelling in the minds of so many dignified persons has effectually enlightened them respecting the divine will."[2]

Writing to the Churches, Constantine told of his anxiety that one faith should be maintained in the Catholic Church. "But I perceived this could not be firmly and permanently established unless all, or at least the greatest part, of the bishops could be convened in the same place and a decision about our holy religion be arrived at from their assembly."[3]

How was it that at such a crisis no one thought of appealing to the Bishop of Rome as the infallible Teacher and the Vicar of Christ? This was just the crisis when the supreme Pastor, through whom the flock, kept away from poisonous error, "might be

[1] Socrates, *Hist. Eccl.*, i, 7.　　[2] Ibid., i, 9.　　[3] Ibid.

nourished with the pasture of heavenly doctrine", should exert his office. The sorely-pressed Bishop of Alexandria ignored his function.

Bishop Alexander did issue an appeal, but it was "to our beloved and most honoured fellow-ministers of the Catholic Church everywhere. Inasmuch as the Catholic Church is one body and we are commanded in the holy Scriptures to maintain the bond of unity and peace, it consequently becomes us to write and mutually acquaint one another with the conditions of things among us".[1]

Sylvester, Bishop of Rome, did not summon the Council. Neither did he preside at it. He was absent through age and sent two presbyters to supply his place. The evidence is conclusive that Hosius, Bishop of Cordova, presided. Athanasius[2] and Theodoret both ask in similar words, of what Council was he not the president. In the signatures as given by Mansi his name comes first. C. H. Turner has given six forms of the signatures of Hosius and the Roman legates, representing twenty-five codices. Hosius always signs first, and in none of them is any reference to his being a representative of Rome. Two Popes of the sixth century claimed for their predecessors a joint presidency at Ephesus and complete presidency at Chalcedon, but are silent about Nicaea. Puller's conclusion is: "I submit the case is as clear as it is possible for a case to be. It is difficult to understand how, in the face of such a crushing fact, Roman theologians and controversialists can persist in maintaining that the Pope, in the time of the Council of Nicaea, was the divinely appointed monarch of the Church."[3]

2

The canons of the Council of Nicaea furnish further evidence that the supremacy of Rome was unknown. Canon IV legislates about the right order of appointing bishops. After election, the bishops of the province are to appoint or ordain. The right of confirming the appointment belongs to the metropolitan in each province. The jurisdiction of the Bishop of Rome is ignored. Bishops did not then hold their office "by the grace of the Apostolic See".

Canon V deals with excommunications. The sentence passed by the bishops of each province shall have the force of law. "He who

---

[1] Socrates, *Hist. Eccl.*, i, 6.
[2] Athanasius, *Apology for his Flight*, 5.
[3] *Primitive Saints and the See of Rome*, p. 172.

has been excommunicated by some shall not be admitted by others."
Appeals lie from an individual bishop to the bishops of the province.
No other tribunal is recognised. The Vatican Decrees, while professing to adhere to the tradition received from the beginning of
the Christian faith, declare that the Pope "is the supreme judge
of the faithful, and that in all causes, the decision of which belongs
to the Church, recourse may be had to his tribunal". Once again
facts contradict papal assumptions.

Canon VI is, if possible, more destructive of such claims. It
begins: "Let the ancient customs prevail which are in use in Egypt,
Libya and Pentapolis, that the Bishop of Alexandria have authority
over all these, since this also is the custom for the Bishop of Rome.
Similarly the prerogatives of the Churches of Antioch and of the
other Churches in the Eparchies must be preserved."

Here the extended metropolitan rights of the Pope (as he used
to be called) of Alexandria are safeguarded on the analogy that the
Bishop of Rome had similar privileges in his area. One metropolitan's jurisdiction is compared to that of the other. Such language
is clearly impossible if the Fathers were aware that one of these
bishops had by divine right sovereign jurisdiction over the whole
Church. They could not in that case plead ancient customs as
equally justifying the local privileges of both. Here in the first
assemblage of the bishops of the whole Church there is blank
ignorance shown of the sovereignty of an infallible Head. The
Bishop of Rome is only casually cited as by ancient custom possessing authority in his own area.

How impossible it is to reconcile the witness of history with
Papalism is again and again demonstrated by Papalists themselves
in their interpolations in the records. We shall see how a false
version of the Nicene canons was brought forward to impose on
the African Church; and the interpolated form which Pope Leo's
legates produced at the Council of Chalcedon. It was doubtless
on the strength of the same interpolation that he misled the Emperor
Valentinian III.

Through the whole proceedings of the universally venerated
Council of Nicaea there is not a vestige of recognition of any divinely
appointed chief ruler. Its witness is incompatible with papal claims.
They are alien to primitive Christianity.

CHAPTER XXVI

ST. ATHANASIUS

The Arian heresy brought the Church into the most serious doctrinal peril. The Godhead of our Lord was called in question. Then it was not a Bishop of Rome who stood out in the forefront of the defenders of the faith, but a Bishop of Alexandria—St. Athanasius. A Bishop of Rome deserted to the side of the heretics, without the Church feeling any commotion beyond what naturally accompanied the apostasy of a prelate of so great a see.

St. Athanasius, in his voluminous writings against the deadly heresy, never once appeals to the infallible teaching function of the Bishop of Rome. We may search his orations, epistles, apologies, etc., without discovering any recognition that there existed among Christians one divinely constituted authority by whose judgment all questions regarding the faith are to be defined. We find him laboriously appealing to Scriptural testimony, to the ancients, to the Nicene Council, to reason, but never to an inerrant source of truth in Rome. If he believed the Bishop of Rome was divinely appointed to be the infallible Teacher, it is impossible that he would not have urged obedience for his decision.

The attitude of Athanasius towards Rome was clearly seen when Pope Liberius apostasised and renounced him. This pitiable fall into heresy made no difference to Athanasius's position. To him it was only the deplorable defection of a bishop of exalted rank. He censures his Arian enemies for the pressure they put on Liberius. "They respected not his bishopric because it was an apostolical throne; they felt no reverence for Rome because she is the metropolis of Romania."[1] Liberius was but one of "the bishops of illustrious cities and the heads of great Churches",[2] who at one time championed Athanasius. Athanasius was quite unaware that one of these bishops was the Vicar of Christ.

[1] *History of the Arians*, 35.
[2] *Apology Against the Arians*, 89.

Athanasius mentions the fall of the Bishop of Rome as an incident in the unhappy proceedings. Liberius "did not endure to the end the sufferings of banishment, yet he remained in his exile for two years, being aware of the conspiracy against me".[1] "Liberius, after he had been in banishment two years, gave way and from fear of threatened death was induced to subscribe."[2] He writes with pity for the apostate Liberius, who supported him "so long as he was suffered to exercise a free choice". His fall was due to fear and is in contrast with the faithful who have "avoided as they would a serpent the anti-Christian heresy".[3]

As Athanasius was unconscious of the infallible teaching authority of the Bishop of Rome, so was he also of that bishop's supremacy. Neither when he was condemned by the Council of Tyre nor in his repeated banishments did he ever appeal to the Pope's sovereign jurisdiction as "Head of the whole Church". Against the Council of Tyre it was to the emperor he applied. The Council of Egyptian bishops that met in Alexandria (339) pronounced Athanasius innocent without any reference to supreme Roman jurisdiction. It might have been urged that the bishop of the then second see in the Church should not be deposed without the bishop of the first see being at least consulted. No such argument is used in the long encyclical letter of the Egyptian bishops to the "bishops of the Catholic Church everywhere".

It was the enemies of Athanasius who wrote to Rome accusing Athanasius and who asked Julius to call a Council. Athanasius thereupon sailed for Rome to attend the Council. The Eastern bishops refused to attend and wrote a disrespectful letter to Julius. Julius did not try the case himself. A Council of fifty bishops met and received Athanasius into communion (341). Julius sent a remarkable letter to the Arians which makes clear that he was far from attempting to judge personally by right of any divinely given authority.

In this document Julius stresses that he had invited them to be present at a Council. He emphasises repeatedly the authority of Councils. Their own delegates had requested the Council. They had asserted the equality of bishops and deprecated the grasping by bishops at more than their due on account of the greatness and

---

[1] *Apology Against the Arians.*, 89.
[2] *History of the Arians*, 41.
[3] Ibid.

populousness of their Churches. Strange to say, Julius in his dealing with this point does not remind them of the prerogatives of the Petrine see. What Julius had previously written was the opinion, not "of myself alone but of all the bishops throughout Italy and in these parts". He was unwilling to cause all these bishops to write. Athanasius and others had complained "before all the assembled bishops" of the injustice done them. Bishops should not be illegitimately deposed. "Word should have been written of it to us all that so a just sentence should proceed from all . . . and why was nothing said to us concerning the Church of the Alexandrians in particular? Are you not aware that the custom has been for word to be written first to us and so after that for a just decision to be passed?"

This is the translation of the last sentence given by Dr. B. J. Kidd.[1] He cites the authority for it of Dr. Brightman. The words καὶ οὕτως ἔνθεν are often translated "from this place". Even if we take the words in the latter sense they convey the reasonable argument that the Bishop of Alexandria should not be deposed without first acquainting the Bishop of Rome. This is all that the following sentences imply. "If, then, any such suspicion rested on the bishop there, notice thereof ought to be sent to the Church of this place; whereas after neglecting to inform us, and proceeding on their own authority as they pleased, now they desire to obtain our concurrence in their decisions, though we never condemned him. Not so have the constitutions of Paul, not so have the traditions of the Fathers directed; this is another form of procedure, a novel practice." Julius knew nothing of the claim "that by the appointment of our Lord the Roman Church possesses a superiority of ordinary power over all other Churches".[2] Athanasius's comment added to this letter is: "Thus wrote the Council of Rome by Julius, Bishop of Rome."[3]

Mgr. Batiffol finds the attitude of Athanasius to Rome and this letter of Julius hard to explain. He quotes the words of Duchesne: "Athanasius, deposed by the Council of Tyre, does not seem to have had the idea that an appeal to Rome would have been able to establish his position." He writes that the fact was that at that date there was no example known of an Eastern bishop, condemned by an Eastern Council, making recourse to Rome.[4] Then, in the

---

[1] *The Roman Primacy*, p. 49.   [3] *Apology Against the Arians*, 36.
[2] Vatican Decrees, chap. 3.   [4] *Cathedra Petri*, pp. 217, 218.

letter of Julius, "it could be wished that there was a more judicial answer, an affirmation of the right of recourse from every Council to Rome. Pope Julius only sketched this affirmation at the end of his letter".[1]

Batiffol ingeniously tries to expand the "sketch" of Roman authority that he imagines he finds in Julius's letter. But the shadowiness of the sketch troubles him. He adds: "It is remarkable that the Pope Julius does not vindicate openly the privilege of a primacy peculiar to his see. . . . The occasion was favourable to exalt the exceptional authority of the bishop who presided over the Church of Rome, but the Pope Julius did not seize the occasion. He even put a certain insistence on the representation that, though he wrote alone, the response was that of his Council."[2]

Batiffol candidly recalls the letter of St. Ambrose in 381 to the emperor: "As Athanasius of holy memory, and Peter, lately bishops of the Church of Alexandria, and many of the Easterns have done, who are seen to have had recourse to the judgment of the Church of Rome, of Italy and of the whole West."

The decision in Rome did not settle the matter. So the Sardican Council was called by the emperors about 344. It was presided over by Hosius, Bishop of Cordova, although the delegates of the Bishop of Rome were present. "The holy Council of which the great Hosius was president."[3] The fact is so clear that Hefele is forced to make the futile plea that Hosius may had have a special commission for it from the Pope![4] The Council cleared Athanasius and decided that "the decision of our brother and fellow-bishop Julius was a just one".[5] The Council deposed and excommunicated bishops by its own inherent authority. Julius wrote to the Church of Alexandria, congratulating them on the restoration of their bishop, who was "pronounced innocent not by my voice only but by the voice of the whole Council".[6]

It is in accordance with the foregoing that Athanasius, in defending himself to the universal Church, should consistently cite his vindications by assemblies of bishops and not by a supreme Judge at Rome. His cause was tried, he writes, first of all "in my own

[1] *Cathedra Petri.* pp. 223, 224.
[2] Ibid., p. 225.
[3] Athanasius, *History of the Arians*, 16.
[4] *History of the Councils*, vol. ii, p. 97 (E. T.).
[5] Athanasius, *Apology Against the Arians*, 37.
[6] Ibid., 52.

country in an assembly of nearly one hundred of its bishops; a second time at Rome when, in consequence of letters from Eusebius, both they and we were summoned and more than fifty bishops met; and a third time in the great Council assembled at Sardica by order of the most religious emperors, Constantius and Constans". He goes on to tell how the decision in his favour was given by three hundred bishops out of many countries which he enumerates. The Bishops from Italy are mentioned twenty-fourth in the list and those from Britain thirty-sixth and last.[1] Again and again this is his defence—the decision of "so many eminent bishops";[2] "bishops of illustrious cities and the heads of great Churches". "Now if anyone wishes to become acquainted with my case and the falsehood of the Eusebians, let him read what has been written on my behalf, and let him hear the witnesses, not one or two or three, but that great number of bishops."[3]

Assuredly Athanasius knew nothing of one "supreme judge of the faithful". To him the defection of Hosius seems to have been a greater calamity than that of Liberius. He accuses the Arians of having "spared neither the great confessor Hosius nor the Bishop of Rome".[4] They thought they had done nothing so long as Hosius held out. Hosius is "the father of the bishops". "He is the president of Councils and his letters are everywhere attended to."[5]

To St. Gregory Nazienzen, St. Athanasius is he who is entrusted with "the rulership of the whole world".[6] If titles like this had been given to a Bishop of Rome, what misleading assumptions would have been founded on them.

---

[1] Athanasius, *Apology Against the Arians*, 1.
[2] Ibid.
[3] Ibid., 89, 90.
[4] *Apology for Flight*, 9.
[5] *History of the Arians*, 42.
[6] Oratio xxi, 7. P. G. 35: 1088.

CHAPTER XXVII

POPE LIBERIUS

The Vatican Council declared that in the Apostolic See the Catholic religion and doctrine has always been kept undefiled; that the Holy Spirit was promised to the successors of Peter that they might inviolably keep the deposit of faith; that by the divine promise of our Lord the see of holy Peter remains ever free from all blemish of error.[1]

These assertions are confuted by the plain historic facts of Roman bishops becoming heretics. Prominent among those who lapsed from the Catholic faith is Liberius (352–66). It was not on any minor point of the faith that he apostasised, but on the foundation itself. In the most critical time of the struggle against Arianism he deserted Athanasius and the truth that Athanasius defended.

The evidence of this apostasy is overwhelming.

(1) Athanasius himself has twice chronicled it.[2] Liberius for a time stood firm, but was banished by the emperor to Beroea. There his misfortune and the fear of worse penalties overcame him.

(2) Jerome twice records his fall. "Liberius, worn out by the tedium of exile and subscribing heretical pravity (*in haeretican pravitatem subscribens*), entered Rome as a conqueror."[3] Again Jerome writes: "Bishop Fortunatus of Aquileia was to be blamed because when Liberius, Bishop of Rome, was enduring exile for the faith he first solicited him and subdued (*fregit*) him and compelled him to the subscription of heresy."[4]

(3) St. Hilary of Poitiers, also a contemporary, in his work *Contra Constantium Imperatorem* addresses the emperor: "O wretched man, I know not whether there was greater wickedness in your banishing him (Liberius) or in your sending him back."[5]

(4) The fourth witness is Sozomen, who wrote his history less than a century after the time of Liberius. Sozomen records that the

---

[1] See chap. iv.
[2] See supra, p. 122.
[3] *Chron. A. D.*, 354. P. L. 27: 501.
[4] *De Viris Illustribus*, c. 97. P. L. 23: 735.
[5] c. xi. P. L. 10: 589.

emperor when at Sirmium summoned Liberius from Beroea. With the assembled bishops he set to work to induce Liberius to confess the Son was not of one essence (*homoousion*) with the Father. They gathered into one document decisions against certain heretics and the creed put forth at the Antiochene Synod of 341. They succeeded in inducing Liberius to subscribe to this. "But they also received in turn from Liberius a confession which excommunicated those who would not declare that the Son is like the Father in essence and in all things",[1] i.e. the semi-Arian "homoiousion" creed. Puller gives convincing reasons for agreeing with Duchesne that this part of Sozomen's history is based on official and first-hand documents.[2]

(5) Corroborations are not wanting from other sources of Liberius's fall. Faustinus and Marcellinus in 383 presented to the emperors a *Libellus Precum*. In the preface we read that two years after the exile of Liberius the Emperor Constantius came to Rome and the people asked for Liberius. The emperor said: "'You shall have Liberius and he will return better than when he left you.' In this way he indicated Liberius's agreement by which he had joined hands with perfidy (*manus perfidiae dederat*)."[3]

(6) There are the letters of Liberius himself to opponents of the Nicene Creed. "I do not defend Athanasius. . . . Having learned . . . that you condemned him justly, I immediately agreed in your sentence. . . . So then Athanasius, having been removed from the communion of us all . . . I pray you now so work together that I may be released from exile and return to the see entrusted to me by God."[4] In another letter to prominent heretical bishops as Ursacius and Valens, he announces that "Athanasius, who was bishop of the Church of Alexandria, was condemned by me, and that he was separated from the communion of the Roman Church".[5] St. Hilary of Poitiers, when quoting these letters, breaks forth in indignant denunciations: "This is Arian perfidy." "I say anathema to thee, Liberius, and to thy accomplices."[6]

Hefele disputes the authenticity of these letters, but the generality of eminent Roman Catholic historians accept them, scholars like Natalis Alexander, Tillemont, Fleury, Dupin, Mohler, Newman, etc.

---

[1] *Historia Ecclesiastica*, iv, 15. P. G. 67: 1152.
[2] *Primitive Saints and the See of Rome*, p. 276.
[3] P. L. 13: 81.
[4] *St. Hilar. Fragmenta*, vi. P. L. 10 : 689, 690.
[5] Ibid. P. L. 10: 693.
[6] Ibid. P. L. 10: 691.

His arguments have not convinced writers of his own Church, as Duchesne and Renouf ("Hefele's arguments against them are exceedingly weak").[1] Dr. Kidd agrees with Gwatkin that Hefele "does not make out any strong case against them".[2] Hefele admits that Liberius renounced the term Homoousios, and, "yielding to force and sinking under many years of confinement and exile, signed the so-called third Sirmian formula".[3]

Whether the letters are genuine or not, there is incontestable evidence of Liberius's apostasy. As Salmon states, the question of their genuineness affects "not the question of the fall of Liberius but only the amount of humiliations with which that fall was attended".[4] Bishop Gore believes "there is no good reason to doubt their genuineness".[5]

Roman Catholic writers down the ages have not hesitated to expose the sin of Liberius. "Until the sixteenth century the fall of Liberius was accepted as an indisputable historical event. . . . In the martyrology of Ado (14th August) St. Eusebius is said to have 'bewailed that Liberius, the Pope, had expressed his agreement with Arian perfidy', words which occur in other mediaeval martyrologies, and they were formerly in the Roman Breviary, whence they were deleted in the sixteenth century."[6]

Baronius narrates how the people of Rome were alienated from Liberius because he had so "disgracefully [*turpiter*] agreed with Constantius. . . . For it was held that Liberius, on account of his communicating with heretics—manifest from the letters written by himself concerning compromise with the Arians—was entirely exiled from the Catholic communion. . . . For that reason he was completely excluded from the pontifical office". "The execrable contagion of his foul communion with the Arians."[7]

Cardinal Newman, in a book reissued in 1895, writes of the "scandalous" fall of Liberius,[8] "this miserable apostasy",[9] "The Pope a renegade".[10]

[1] *Condemnation of Pope Honorius*, p. 44.
[2] *History of the Church*, vol. ii, p. 157.
[3] *History of the Councils*, vol. ii, p. 245.
[4] *Infallibility of the Church*, p. 427.
[5] *Roman Catholic Claims*, p. xv.
[6] Denny, *Papalism*, p. 390.
[7] *Annal. A. D.*, 357. 56: 57.
[8] *The Arians* (new edition, 1895), p. 319.
[9] Ibid., p. 322.
[10] Ibid., p. 352.

CHAPTER XXVIII

THE COUNCIL OF SARDICA

The pronouncement of Pope Julius and the Roman Council in favour of Athanasius and Marcellus was not accepted by the Eastern Church. A Council was summoned by the emperors to meet at Sardica (the modern Sophia) in 343 or 344. The bishops from the East refused to remain for it when they found that Athanasius and Marcellus were to be received in fellowship. So the Council was almost entirely one of the Western Church. The Pope was represented by his legates, but Hosius of Cordova presided. In reality the very existence of the Council was an evidence that the papal decisions were not regarded as authoritative. Mgr. Batiffol writes that "this Council was a concession on the part of Rome, for Rome had agreed that the cause of Athanasius and of Marcellus of Ancyra be completely referred to it, and without having regard to the judgment of the Council of Rome".[1]

Some of the decrees of the Council mark a new stage in the advancement of the See of Rome, one that was natural for the times. The disputes rendered advisable some sort of Court of Appeal from provincial Synods. Athanasius was a victim of the injustice of the Council of Tyre. No one need dispute the expediency of such appellate legislation or choosing the Bishop of Rome to exercise it. For the scope of the canons of Sardica we may accept Hefele's synopsis with one exception.

"(1) When a bishop has been deposed by his comprovincials at the provincial Synod, but still thinks his cause a good one, he may, according to the fifth canon, either appeal to Rome himself or through the judges of the first court.

"(2) Rome now decides whether the appeal shall be allowed or not. In the latter case it confirms the sentence of the first court; in the former it appoints a second court.

[1] *Cathedra Petri*, p. 226.

"(3) Rome nominates as judges for the second court bishops from the neighbourhood of the province in question.

"(4) To this court the Pope may, however, also send legates of his own who will then take the presidency in his name."[1]

The exception is the last clause. Hefele is not justified in stating the legates were to preside. No such prerogative is decreed in the text. The words of the canon are that if the accused bishop should petition the Bishop of Rome to send presbyters *de latere* then it is in the power of the Bishop of Rome "to determine that they be sent, who, when present, may adjudicate with the bishops, having the authority of him by whom they were sent". This phrase simply gives the Roman presbyters, as delegates of the Bishop of Rome, a right to sit as members of an episcopal tribunal. The delegates of the Roman bishops at the Council of Sardica did not preside —a fact in itself sufficient to show how unwarranted is Hefele's inference.

(1) The Sardican decrees are distinctly a new privilege conferred by the Council on the Roman bishop. They make plain there was no such inherent authority existing in that see. The words of the decree are perfectly clear on this. "Hosius the bishop said . . . If it please you let us honour the memory of the holy apostle Peter. . . . Is it pleasing to all? The Synod answered, It is pleasing." They are the grant of a new and hitherto unknown privilege to Rome. They are irreconcilable with the Vatican dogma that by divine right the Roman Pontiff is the supreme Judge of the faithful. The previous position of the Roman bishop was fixed by the sixth canon of Nicaea which gave him a local authority in Italy similar to that possessed by the Bishop of Alexandria in Egypt, Libya and Pentapolis.

(2) It was a very restricted right, entirely different from the Vatican claim, that, *jure divino*, "in all causes the decision of which belongs to the Church recourse may be had to his tribunal". The Pope (*a*) could not of himself order the case to be retried; (*b*) he could not summon the parties to Rome; (*c*) he had not the power of deciding it at his own tribunal; (*d*) he is limited in his choice of the new judges—they must be bishops of neighbouring provinces with or without representatives from Rome; (*e*) the right of appeal is restrained to bishops.

---

[1] *History of the Councils*, vol. ii, p. 128 (E. T.).

Now all this is in definite conflict with modern papal claims. "On the papalist theory the whole proceeding must appear insufferably impertinent. It did not so appear to St. Athanasius and to the other Fathers of the Synod because they knew nothing of the theory which underlies the Vatican Decrees."[1]

There is a sentence in a letter from the Council to Pope Julius, laid stress on by Allies,[2] which is almost certainly unauthentic. In it the members are made to say that it seems best and most fitting that they refer "to the head, that is, to the see of the Apostle Peter". Although it might not be unlikely for a Western Synod to mention the prelate of the Apostolic See of the West as their head, there are good reasons for rejecting this text. Hefele does not defend it. He admits the Latin is barbarous, and that it interrupts the train of thought and looks like something inserted in parenthesis.[3]

There is something mysterious about the Canons of Sardica. They seem scarcely ever to have been put into practice.[4] The African Church at the time of St. Augustine had never heard of them. A plausible, if not entirely convincing, case can be made out against their authenticity.[5] One of the most extraordinary features of their history is the repeated attempts of Roman bishops—Zosimus, Boniface, Leo—to pass them off as Nicene when striving to claim prerogatives for their Church. If Pope Zosimus be supposed to have been misled by what Chapman calls "an unfortunate accident of transcription",[6] this excuse cannot be urged for Leo the Great. He more than once made improper use of them.

[1] Puller, *Primitive Saints and the See of Rome* (3rd edition), p. 143.
[2] *The See of Peter*, pp. 8, 86.
[3] *History of the Councils*, vol. ii, p. 164.
[4] Cf. Batiffol, *Cathedra Petri*, p. 228.
[5] Cf. Denny, *Papalism*, p. 151 ff.
[6] *Studies in the Early Papacy*, p. 208.

CHAPTER XXIX

ST. BASIL

Basil was Bishop of Caesarea in Cappadocia, 370–9. He accomplished a memorable work in re-establishing the orthodox faith in Asia Minor and other parts of the East. His life affords proofs of how far the Christian leaders of his time were from believing that the Bishop of Rome was the Governor and supreme Teacher of the Church.

Basil's prolonged struggles with the Arians was conducted without any consciousness that there was in Rome an authority whose function it was to declare the true faith, and who was entitled to universal obedience. We never find him striving to ensure unity by appeal to the jurisdiction of the Roman bishop. On the other hand, it is to Athanasius that he looks as the highest authority. He justified his practice of receiving Arians into the Church on their acceptance of the orthodox formulary by appeal to the great name of Athanasius. He tells how he had received and could produce a letter of "the most blessed Father, Athanasius", endorsed by the Bishops of Macedonia and Achaia: "I thought it necessary to follow so great a man because of the trustworthiness of those who made the law."[1] To Athanasius he writes: "It is sufficient to most of the others [bishops] to look each to what concerns himself; this is not enough for you, for to you anxiety for all the Churches is as great as for that especially entrusted to you by our common Master. At no time do you cease discoursing, admonishing, writing, sending men in all directions who advise what is best." He describes himself as consulting Athanasius, "the leader of all".[2] Again: "The greater the maladies of the Churches become, the more we turn to your Perfection, convinced that the sole consolation left to us in our dangers is your presidency."[3] "When we look to your Augustness and consider that our Lord has appointed you to be

[1] Ep. 204. Loeb edition, iii, 170.
[2] Ep. 69. Ibid., ii, 38.
[3] Ep. 80. Ibid., ii, 88.

the physician of the maladies of the Churches."[1] "The most blessed Pope, Athanasius."[2]

In the prolonged troubles in the East, and the dispute about the episcopal succession at Antioch, Basil was brought into contact with Rome, and his letters afford abundant proof of how far he was from recognising the papal position. He was a staunch supporter of Meletius as the one rightful Bishop of Antioch. Rome ignored Meletius and supported his rival, Paulinus.

Basil sought eagerly for the assistance of the Church of the West to heal the sad confusion of the Churches in the East where heresy and persecution had wrought havoc. He naturally turned to the brethren, who enjoyed peace, and were not harassed by persecuting rulers, to aid in reconstructing the orthodox faith. But his appeal was always to the Churches of the West as a whole and only for their brotherly support. He never appealed to the Bishop of Rome as the supreme Governor of the Church. He exhorts to "agreement with the bishops of the West".[3] He addresses his appeals "to the most holy brothers and bishops of the West".[4] He writes as an equal to equals. About 372 a letter was sent, signed by St. Meletius, St. Basil, St. Eusebius of Samosata, St. Gregory the elder of Nazianzus, and twenty-eight other bishops, addressed to "our most God-beloved and holy brethren, fellow ministers, fellow-minded bishops with us in Italy and Gaul".[5]

A couple of years later, after fresh persecutions, another appeal was sent from the East. Basil wrote a personal letter at the same time "to the bishops of Gaul and Italy".[6] The fact that this illustrious saint named the bishops of Gaul before those of Italy and does not even make particular reference to the Bishop of Rome at all is conclusive evidence that he was not aware of a divinely given supremacy of Rome.

In 375 the Bishop of Rome, Damasus, made the blunder of repudiating Meletius by acknowledging Paulinus as sole Bishop of Antioch. This only made far worse the distracted state of the Church there and added to the difficulties of the orthodox Eastern bishops. Basil and the bishops had no hesitation in rejecting the bishop who was admitted to communion with Rome. They did not know that salvation depended on submission to the decision of the Bishop of Rome.

[1] Ep. 82. Loeb edition, ii, 96.
[2] Ep. 258. Ibid., iv, 42.
[3] Ep. 66. Ibid., ii, 26.
[4] Ep. 90. Ibid., ii, 122.
[5] Ep. 92. Ibid., ii, 132 ff.
[6] Ep. 243. Ibid., iii, 434.

Basil, writing to a local governor, Count Terentius, utterly refuses
to give deference to the behests of Rome.[1] He writes: "I hear also
that they are now circulating a letter from the Westerners com-
mitting to them the episcopate of the Church of Antioch, but which
defrauds the most admirable bishop of the true Church of God,
Meletius. I am not surprised at this for they [the Westerners] are
entirely ignorant of things here. . . . But since we accuse no one,
but pray that we may have love to all and especially those of the
household of faith, we congratulate those who have received the
letter from Rome, and if it has some honourable and grand testimony for them we pray that to be true and confirmed by their
actions. Not, however, on that account shall we be able ever to
persuade ourselves either to ignore Meletius or to forget the Church
under him. . . . As for myself, I shall never consent to draw back
because someone has received a letter from men and is puffed up
about it." There could not be a more direct rejection of the Roman
decision and communion. The whole Eastern Church agreed with
Basil in honouring, then and since, Meletius as bishop of the true
Church of God in Antioch.

After this, St. Basil's references to the West were frank and
unfavourable. Writing to Eusebius of Samosata about sending
letters there, he says: "I myself am at a loss to know what one
should write through them or how to agree with those who write.
It occurs to me to speak the words of Diomede, 'Would that thou
hadst never besought', since, saith he, 'Haughty is the man'. For
in truth arrogant characters, treated with deference, tend to become
more than usually disdainful. If the Lord be reconciled to us, what
other support do we need? But if the wrath of God remain upon
us what help is there for us from Western superciliousness? Those
who neither know the truth nor bear to learn it, but, prejudiced
by false suspicions, are now doing just what they did before in
the case of Marcellus,[2] quarrelling with those who announced the
truth to them and giving their own support to heresy. I myself,
apart from the common design, was thinking of writing to their
leader [Coryphaeus]—nothing about ecclesiastical affairs except so
far as to hint that they neither knew the truth of our affairs nor
would accept the way by which they might learn it—but generally

[1] Ep. 214. Loeb edition, iii, 226 ff.
[2] The patronage of the heretic Marcellus of Ancyra by Rome caused hurtful
offence in the East.

about it not being fitting to attack those who are brought low by trials nor to imagine arrogance to be dignity, a sin which of itself is sufficient to make enmity with God."[1]

Such language is absolutely incompatible with the supreme jurisdiction and infallibility claimed for the Roman bishop. Bishop Bossuet remarks on it: "Here it is clear that the confirming of heresy in two pontifical decrees, de fide, was roundly and directly without excuse, without explanation, imputed by Basil."[2]

Writing again about a proposed visit of his brother, St. Gregory of Nyssa, to Rome, he states: "I know he is entirely inexperienced in ecclesiastical affairs, and though with a fair-minded man his intercourse would be respected and very useful but with a high one up in the air, sitting somewhere aloft—and for that reason not able to hear the voice of those who utter the truth from the ground— what advantage would there be to our common purpose from the converse of such a man [as Gregory] who has a character altogether foreign to slavish flattery."[3]

Basil and the other bishops later replied to a communication from Rome. They are mainly desirous of common action between West and East in exposing some unsound ecclesiastics. The heading of the letter is "To the Westerners". The reasons they state for asking the co-operation of the Western bishops furnish a clear refutation of the claim that the papal pretensions are "the ancient and constant faith of the universal Church", which "all the venerable Fathers have embraced and the holy orthodox Doctors have venerated".[4] They explain that their own decisions are suspected as due to personal rivalry. "But you, inasmuch as you happen to live at a distance from them, possess so much the more confidence among the people. . . . Also if a great number of you with one voice declare the same doctrines it is manifest the multitude of those so declaring will render the reception of the doctrine undisputed by all."[5] There is set forth the obvious reasons for so many appeals to the West, and to its headquarters, Rome, in ecclesiastical disputes. An arbiter at a distance was desirable. The verdict of one part of the Church was incomplete without the sanction of the rest. Consent of East and West was essential. Roman controversialists strive unfairly to

[1] Ep. 239. Loeb edition, iii, 418, 420.
[2] Gallia Orthodoxa, c. 65; Oeuvres (Besancon, 1836), p. 42.
[3] Ep. 215. Loeb edition, iii, 236, 238.
[4] Pastor Aeternus and Chapter IV.
[5] Ep. 263. Loeb edition, iv, 92.

represent such resort to the Apostolic See of the West as a recognition of a supreme jurisdiction.

At the end of the letter the bishops remark: "We ourselves are not unaware that the fitting thing is for us to sit in council with your wisdoms and to settle these matters in a common investigation."[1]

It may be added that the Eastern Church always honoured Meletius, the venerated Bishop of Antioch. The fact that he was not in communion with Rome and that Rome insulted him by acknowledging a rival bishop made no difference to their according to him leadership. At the important Council in Antioch, 379 when one hundred and fifty-three bishops met, Meletius was the president. He was also president of the second Oecumenical Council of Constantinople in 381. Being out of communion with Rome did not towards the end of the fourth century militate against a bishop being recognised as practically Primate of the East.

[1] Ep. 263. Loeb edition, iv, 100.

CHAPTER XXX

COUNCIL OF CONSTANTINOPLE

The Arians had gained through many unhappy years predominance in the Church after the Council of Nicaea. When the Emperor Theodosius came to the throne in 379 he gave his support to the orthodox. He summoned a Council, which met in Constantinople in 381. He showed no consciousness that he should have recourse to the Roman bishop as the supreme judge by whose infallible teaching the faith would be made plain.

Damasus, Bishop of Rome, was not even invited to the Council, which was an Eastern one. In the case of this Council there is no possible pretence that the Bishop of Rome was represented, much less presided. The startling fact is that the president until his death was a bishop whom the Church of Rome did not acknowledge—St. Meletius, Bishop of Antioch. Rome accepted as the legitimate Bishop of Antioch his rival, Paulinus.

This is one of the most convincing facts that history affords, that the modern claims of the Bishop of Rome were unknown to the early Church. A Council universally acknowledged as Oecumenical meets without any recognition of the Bishop of Rome, and without his being in any way concerned in it. Its president is a prelate, who was outside the communion of Rome. Not only so, but when Meletius died during the Council the assembled bishops agreed to the appointment of a successor at Antioch in opposition to Paulinus, who was obstinately maintained by Rome to be the lawful bishop.

The second canon of the Council dealt with the territorial jurisdiction of bishops, and safeguarded the rights of provincial synods. It begins: "The bishops of another diocese shall not pass over to foreign Churches and introduce confusion among them." It specifies the spheres of the metropolitans of Alexandria, Antioch, Ephesus, Pontus and Thrace. No mention is made of the supreme "immediate" authority of the Bishop of Rome.

The third canon is a very memorable one. "The Bishop of Constantinople shall hold the first rank[1] after the Bishop of Rome because Constantinople is the new Rome."

Could there be a more sweeping denial of any *jure divino* prerogative in the Roman See? This canon is absolutely subversive of the whole theory that the Bishop of Rome is, as successor of St. Peter, "true Vicar of Christ and Head of the whole Church and Father and Teacher of all Christians". In the opinion of the Fathers composing this Oecumenical Council, the prestige of the Roman Church rested on the civil rank of its city. Among the bishops at this Council were such distinguished ones as St. Gregory Nazianzen, St. Gregory of Nyssa, St. Cyril of Jerusalem, Timothy of Alexandria. Do they fall under the anathema pronounced by the Vatican Council on all who deny the Roman Pontiff to have "full and supreme power of jurisdiction over the universal Church"?

Pope Leo strongly denied the validity of this canon and professed to have no knowledge of it. But as ratified and enlarged by the Council of Chalcedon its conferring of the second place in the Church on the See of Constantinople has prevailed. The Church of Rome at first repudiated the whole authority of this Council. That has not affected its rank among the Oecumenical Councils of the Catholic Church. On this very important point Rome gave way to the East.

Duchesne, writing of the fourth century, admits that there was no central authority recognised to be in Rome. There was no tradition for Rome's interference. That Church "played but a minor part at the Council of Nicaea". There was not "a guiding power an effective expression of Christian unity. The Papacy, such as the West knew it later on, was still to be born".[2]

[1] Lit. "the precedency of honour".
[2] *Early History*, vol. ii, pp. 521, 522 (E. T.).

CHAPTER XXXI

ST. AUGUSTINE

In other chapters it is shown how far St. Augustine was from acknowledging the authority of the Bishop of Rome over the Church of Africa. The voluminous works of this, the greatest Doctor of the Church, constitute an impregnable rampart against the historical assumptions of Papalism.

Augustine's exposition of the Scriptural texts, which are relied on by papal advocates, is irreconcilable with their interpretations. He more than once interprets the Rock to be Christ. "Because I am the Rock (petra), thou art Peter; for the Rock is not from Peter but Peter from the Rock, since Christ is not from the Christian but the Christian from Christ, and upon this Rock I will build My Church; not upon Peter which thou art but upon the Rock which thou hast confessed."[1]

"Thou art therefore, saith He, Peter, and upon this Rock which thou hast confessed, upon this Rock, which thou hast acknowledged, saying, 'Thou art the Christ, the Son of the living God', I will build My Church. Upon Me I will build thee, not Me upon thee."[2]

Sometimes Augustine takes the Rock to be the faith confessed by Peter. "On this Rock I will build—the faith which you confess. On this which you have spoken, 'Thou art the Christ the son of the living God', I will build My Church." He goes on to quote 1 Corinthians x. 4: "that rock was Christ."[3]

When an old man of seventy-four years, St. Augustine wrote his *Retractationes*. He points out that he had as a young man interpreted the Rock as meaning Peter: "But I know that I have afterwards in very many places so expounded the Lord's saying 'Thou art Peter and upon this Rock I will build My Church' as to be understood of Him whom Peter confessed, when he said, 'Thou art the Christ, the Son of the living God'. . . . For it was not said to him, 'Thou art the Rock' (*Petra*), but, 'Thou art Peter' (*Petrus*).

[1] Sermo 270: 2. P. L. 38: 1239.   [2] Sermo 76: 1. P. L. 38: 479.
[3] Sermo 295: 1. P. L. 38: 1349.

But Christ was the Rock, whom Simon confessing, as the whole Church confesses Him, was called Peter. But of these two meanings let the reader choose the more probable."[1] Augustine is entirely unaware that he is dealing with an utterance of the most tremendous doctrinal importance. He does not think it matters very much which of the two interpretations is adopted. He shows that he prefers that which excludes Peter from being the Rock.

The views of St. Augustine on other texts are similarly anti-papal. He taught that St. Peter received the keys only as the representative of the Church. "For these keys not one man but the unity of the Church received."[2] Similarly, in his explanation of "The keys given to the Church" in his *De Doctrina Christiana*, he does not mention Peter.[3] The "Feed My sheep" charge in John xxi Augustine interprets as teaching that the shepherd should lay down his life for the flock. The threefold question and commission was "that he might thrice confess who had thrice denied".[4]

One could fill a book with extracts from Augustine's writings showing how the theories of Papalism were unknown to him. Only a few instances need be given.

While of course honouring the Church of Rome for its Apostolic See and imperial prestige, he does not recognise it as a sovereign authority. His manner of referring to the Apostolic Sees illustrates this. "The Christian Society is diffused by propagation all over the world by the Apostolic Sees and the succession of bishops in them."[5]

How can a man know which are the canonical Scriptures? Augustine's answer shows how far he was from believing a supreme infallible Teacher existed in the Church. The inquirer "must follow the judgment of the greater number of Catholic Churches; and among those, of course, a high place must be given to such as have been thought worthy to be the seat of an apostle and to receive epistles. Therefore he will hold in this way among the canonical Scriptures—to prefer those that are received by all the Catholic Churches to those which some do not receive. Among those again which are not received by all let him prefer those which have the sanction of the greater number and the more important, to those

---

[1] *Retractationes*, 1: 21. P. L. 32: 618.
[2] Sermo 295: 2. P. L. 38: 1349.
[3] bk. i, 18.
[4] Tract 47 *in Joan Evangel*. P. L. 35: 1734.
[5] *Ep. ad Fratres Madaurenses*, Ep. 132: 3. P. L. 33: 1028.

which fewer Churches of small authority receive. If, however, he shall find that some books are held by a majority, others by Churches of higher authority (though this is not likely to be found), I imagine the authority on both sides to be equal".[1] Augustine greatly admired St. Cyprian. Cyprian's opposition to the Bishop of Rome does not seem to him to need excuse. Cyprian was always willing to be convinced by adequate authority. Augustine held a different view from him about rebaptism, but he would not venture to assert it were he not supported "by the unanimous authority of the whole Church to which he himself (Cyprian) would unquestionably have yielded if at that time the truth of the question had been placed beyond all dispute by the investigation and decree of a General Council".[2] Augustine goes on to refer to the full illumination and authoritative decision of a General Council. To Augustine the one supreme authority in the Church was a General Council. The greatest saints could without censure withstand the behests of any particular Bishop of Rome so long as the matter at issue had not been decided by Conciliar authority.

St. Augustine in his prolonged controversies with the Donatists furnishes striking proofs of the non-acceptance of Papalism in his time. Thus, referring to the trial before the bishops at Rome he describes the tribunal as "Melchiades (Miltiades), then Bishop of Rome, judging with his colleagues, the transmarine bishops".[3] He points out how at Arles steps were taken that "the same cause should be more diligently examined and terminated". He has to meet a Donatist accusation that Miltiades had no authority to interfere, as a Council of seventy African bishops had condemned Caecilian. Does he reply that the Bishop of Rome had "full and supreme power of jurisdiction over the universal Church"? That claim was outside the consciousness of Augustine. It was undreamt of in his time. He takes a very different line. He defends the Roman bishop by denying that this bishop was guilty of such usurpation. "For the emperor, being petitioned, sent bishops as judges, who sat with him and decided what seemed right about the whole affair."

We see here, as in the refusal of the African Church in the case of Apiarius, to allow Roman interference,[4] how far Augustine was from perceiving any sovereign authority vested in Rome.

[1] *De Doctrina Christiana*, bk. ii, p. 8.
[2] *De Bapt.*, ii. P. L. 43: 129.
[3] Ep. 43, *Ad Fratres Glorium*. P. L. 33: 166.
[4] See pp. 148 ff.

In another passage in Epistle 43 Augustine explicitly admits the legitimacy of challenging and revising the Roman verdict. "Supposing those bishops who judged at Rome were not good judges, there remained still a plenary Council of the universal Church where the cause could be sifted with the judges themselves, so that if they were convicted of having judged wrongly their sentence could be annulled."[1] Appeal from Rome to a Council could not be more frankly stated. Yet it is from this epistle that Roman controversialists cite a phrase in support of their contentions. We have seen the importance attached by Augustine to the Apostolic Sees. Here he points out to the Donatists that they were not in communion with the Apostolic See of the West. He writes that "the pre-eminence (or priority) (*principatus*) of an apostolic chair has always flourished in the Roman Church"—a natural remark for Augustine to make, but one that by no means corroborates modern papal pretensions.

He more than once deals with Donatist assumptions that they were the real Catholic Church. If he believed the Catholic Church depended by divine command on union with Rome, why did he not remind his opponents of this its fundamental constitution? His method is to argue from the importance of being in communion with apostolic Churches—Rome as well as others. In one document he writes: "What has the chair of the Roman Church done to you, in which Peter sat, and in which today Anastasius sits; or the chair of the Church of Jerusalem in which James sat and in which John sits now?"[2]

He rebukes the Donatists for their abusive language about the Church of Rome. They called an apostolic chair a "pestilential chair" (*cathedra pestilentiae*). But he nowhere reminds them—as he must have done if he believed it—that the Lord had committed His supreme authority to that chair.

Augustine wrote a treatise on the Unity of the Church. This was to confute the error of the Donatists who claimed that they alone constituted the Catholic Church. The title is given by Leo XIII in his *Satis Cognitum* as *Contra Donatistas Epistola, sive De Unitate Ecclesiae*. The epistle is commonly cited as *De Unitate Ecclesiae*.

Augustine brings in it many arguments against the Donatists' claim, but he never recalls them to the fact that the Catholic Church is inseparable from the Pope. He never asserts that the Church has a supreme Ruler, a centre of unity. In contesting the exclusive

[1] Ep. 43. P. L. 33: 169.   [2] *Contra Literas Petil.*, 51. P. L. 43: 300.

claims to Catholicity of the African Donatists he did not dream of confronting them with the assertion that it is "the teaching of Catholic truth from which no one can deviate without loss of faith and salvation"[1] that the Bishop of Rome is the supreme Pastor of the flock. He makes no reference whatever to communion with the Roman Pontiff being in any special way involved in settling the question of what is the Catholic Church.

Augustine lucidly propounds the issue at stake. "The question assuredly to be debated between us is—where is the Church; whether with us or with them?"[2] This crucial point is hammered home. The question is "Where is the Body [of Christ], that is, where is the Church?" The editors of the Migne collection summarise the scope of the epistle as an enquiry: "Is the Church of Christ among the Catholics or the Donatists?"

The fact that Augustine argues the matter without the least suggestion that there was any one bishop in the Church having sovereign powers or unique divinely given prerogatives is conclusive that Papalism was unknown in his day. To him the Bishop of Rome was just one "of the transmarine bishops where the greatest part of the Catholic Church is spread"[3] who ought to judge about the dissensions. Augustine insists on the evidence from Scripture. "Let us not hear, 'This is what you say', 'This is what I say', but let us hear, 'Thus saith the Lord'."[4] Yet he does not adduce the verses on which the Roman claims are based.

Augustine's attitude to the Papacy was naturally one of deference to the holder of the Apostolic and Metropolitan See. He recognised no jurisdiction or superiority of teaching in him. He withstood him when he considered his theology was erroneous or his interference unwarranted. His position was well expressed in his own words to Pope Boniface. "The pastoral watchtower is common to all of us who have the office of the episcopate although that on which you stand is a loftier height."[5]

A much-relied-on testimony from St. Augustine is the epigram: "*Roma locuta est: causa finita est.*" This is another instance of how Roman controversialists manufacture evidence. The phrase is not Augustine's. It misrepresents the passage from which it is supposed to be taken. His argument is that since two African Councils have

[1] *Vatican Council*, chap. 3.   [3] P. L. 43: 394.
[2] P. L. 43: 391.   [4] Ibid.
        [5] *Ad. Bonifacium contra duas Epp.*, i, c. 2. P. L. 44: 551.

decided against the Pelagians and have sent to the apostolic seat about the matter and "from thence rescripts have come: the cause is finished".[1] His contention is that both the African Church and the Roman have condemned Pelagianism, so there is no more to be said. When the Roman Church later under Zosimus favoured Pelagius, Augustine opposed him as strongly as ever.

If any unfairness in Roman methods could astonish us we might well marvel to find Cardinal Hergenrother in his "Anti-Janus", a belauded attempt to discredit "Janus", falling back on the old falsification (p. 67): "*Roma locuta est: causa finita est.*"

[1] Sermo 131: 10. P. L. 38: 734.

CHAPTER XXXII

POPE ZOSIMUS AND PELAGIANISM

The history of the relations of Pope Zosimus (417-18) with the Pelagian heresy is incompatible with the theory that the Bishop of Rome is endowed with the "gift of truth and never failing faith", that the flock of Christ might be by him kept away from the poisonous food of error.

Celestius, the disciple of Pelagius, was condemned for heretical teaching at a Council in Carthage (411). Pelagius and Celestius obtained credence in the East. Pelagius was accused there by two western bishops, Heros of Arles and Lazarus of Aix, at a Council held in Dioscopolis, but was acquitted (415). Letters from the two bishops aroused the anxiety of Augustine and the African Church. Councils were held at Carthage and Milevum. The decision against Celestius was confirmed and a letter sent to Pope Innocent I, requesting his support.

It was the natural course for the African bishops to seek to obtain the high authority of the bishop of the Apostolic See of Rome when they were at variance with some bishops of the East on a grave doctrinal issue. But they showed no consciousness that he was the supreme and infallible Teacher. They did not leave the question to his judgment. They announce to him their firm decision and urge that the *auctoritas* of his see be added to it.

Innocent in his replies makes high-flying claims for his see. He agreed with the African view. The bishops there were gratified, and Augustine wrote his much-misquoted sentence about the matter being finished. It is the joint condemnation of the African and the Roman episcopate he stresses. Similarly, later, he wrote to a Pelagian: "Your cause has indeed been finished (*causa finita est*) by a competent judgment of the bishops in common."[1]

But the matter was far from finished. Zosimus succeeded to Innocent. He befriended Pelagius and Celestius and declared them of unimpeachable doctrine (*absolutae fidei*). He was shocked that it

[1] *Contra duas Epp. Pelagianorum*, 3: 5. P. L. 44: 704.

was possible for such orthodox men to be defamed. He declared they were condemned by false judges. He denounced their accusers, Bishops Heros and Lazarus, in unmeasured language and even vulgar abusiveness. They are whirlwinds and tempests of the Church. It is their custom to slander the innocent. They are calumniators and diabolical accusers—men whose names should blush for shame— they are "two pests". The African bishops are severely lectured for paying heed to such ridiculous slanders and "trifling whisperings". They are reminded that false witnesses rose up against Christ. They are warned not to credit every empty report or to become unjust witnesses. Let the African bishops know that those wrongly condemned men "have never been separated from our body and from Catholic truth".[1]

Zosimus issues his judgment as the representative of St. Peter, vested with all the authority of his see. He invokes "the authority of the Apostolic See to which the decrees of the Fathers sanctioned a peculiar reverence in honour of the blessed Peter". He has not come to his decisions "hastily or untimely" in this matter. He delivers his injunctions *apostolicae sedis auctoritate*. It cannot, then, be pleaded that his approval of the Pelagians was a mere private opinion or *obiter dictum* or not formally put forth as a papal judgment on the faith.

The African Church, when the Pope's letters came, hastily held a Council, probably at the end of 417. The members maintained their former position about Pelagianism and let the Pope know he was in error.

In 418 (probably) a great Synod assembled at Carthage. Bishops were present even from Spain to the number of two hundred and fourteen. They issued several canons anathematising the errors of Pelagianism. They were so unconscious of any supreme teaching authority in Rome that they wrote: "We have determined [*constituimus*] that the sentence put forth by the venerable Bishop Innocent about Pelagius and Celestius shall stand until by an open confession they acknowledge, etc."[2] When the Bishop of Rome agreed with them, the African bishops welcomed his support and rejoiced that his powerful influence would contribute to unity of doctrine and discipline in the Church. When he disagreed with them they reaffirmed their position and rejected his decisions. Of the canons of this Council of Carthage Fleury writes: "It is thought that these

[1] Ep. 3 and 4. Mansi, iv, 350 f., 353 f.   [2] Mansi, iv, 376.

canons were drawn up by Augustine who was the soul of this Council."[1]

The Africans proceeded to bring the scandal of the Pope's countenancing of heresy before the emperor. The emperor, Honorius, issued a rescript on 30th April condemning the "noxious contagion", banishing Celestius and Pelagius, "the original heads of this execrable doctrine", from the city and prohibiting their meetings.[2] The edict was to be published through the whole empire. Duchesne considers: "It was too harsh a step. The African episcopate might well have acted with less precipitation, have permitted religious arguments to act on Pope Zosimus instead of hurling *gendarmie* across the deliberations of the Roman Church."[3]

Zosimus ignominiously retreated. He condemned Pelagius and Celestius and their doctrines in a document called his *Tractoria* to which he required all bishops to subscribe. Julian, a distinguished bishop, and eighteen other Italian bishops refused and appealed to a General Council. Even in Italy the theory of papal infallibility was unrecognised in the fifth century. Augustine, having secured the triumph of his views, was politic in his treatment of the discredited Pope. He, "when once success had been attained and the Pope brought over more or less willingly to his views, devoted himself in his discourses and in his books to toning down any disturbing features that there might have been at certain moments in the attitude of Rome".[4]

Once again it was not the Pope who defended orthodox doctrine. "The supreme power of teaching" was in abeyance. Zosimus is linked with Liberius and Honorius in admitting what orthodox Church doctrine rejects. It was the Bishop of Hippo and not the Bishop of Rome who guided the course of Catholic belief.

[1] *Ecclesiastical History*, vol. xxiii, p. 48 (E. T.).
[2] P. L. 44: 1726 f.
[3] *Early History*, vol. iii, p. 167 (E. T.).
[4] Duchesne, loc. cit.

CHAPTER XXXIII

THE AFRICAN CHURCH AND APPEALS TO ROME

Pope Zosimus and the Church of Africa were involved in another dispute. A priest of Sicca, named Apiarius, having been deposed by his bishop, went to Rome and applied to Zosimus for reinstatement. The Bishops of Rome were accustomed to welcome such irregular appeals as assisting their encroachments on national Church authority. It was this appeal probably that made the African Church assert its independent jurisdiction by the canon passed at the Synod of Carthage (1st May 418). "If priests, deacons and inferior clerics complain of a sentence of their own bishop, they shall, with the consent of their bishop, have recourse to the neighbouring bishops, who shall settle the dispute. If they desire to make a further appeal, it must only be to their primates or to African Councils. But whoever appeals to a court on the other side of the sea may not again be received into communion by any one in Africa."[1]

The Vatican Decrees states that "by the appointment of our Lord the Roman Church possesses a superiority of ordinary power over all other Churches"; to which all are bound "to submit, not only in matters which belong to faith and morals but also in those that appertain to the discipline and government of the Church throughout the world". We have seen that the African Church did not believe this as regards matters of faith. They showed also that they repudiated the papal claim in matters of discipline.

Zosimus took extraordinary steps to impose his will on the Africans. He sent three legates, a bishop, Faustinus, and two priests with his commands. They were received by Archbishop Aurelius of Carthage at a small Synod in 418. The Pope, in support of his demand for the right of appeal to Rome, declared that the Nicene Council had so legislated. The canons he cited were not Nicene but those of the Council of Sardica. The African bishops were puzzled. They cautiously replied that, pending further investigations, they would observe the canons adduced.

[1] Mansi, iii, 726.

Pope Zosimus died in December 418. He was succeeded by Boniface. A large African Synod met in May 419. The papal legates attended. The copy of the Nicene canons was read and the unauthentic papal ones. Bishop Alypius remarked of the papal canons: "When we inspected the Greek copies of the Nicene Synod, somehow or other, I know not why, we utterly failed to find them there."[1] It was resolved to send to Constantinople, Alexandria and Antioch for valid copies of the Nicene Council. On the proposal of Augustine it was agreed that for the present the disputed canons be accepted. A letter was sent to Pope Boniface telling him what was decided and that Apiarius, on asking pardon for his faults, had been allowed to exercise his priesthood elsewhere than at Sicca. The letter, of which Augustine was one of the composers, reflected on the conduct of Faustinus. The African bishops make plain that they did not recognise any sovereign power in Rome but only such privileges as may have been enacted by Nicaea. Nor did the Pope in his message venture to rely on any higher prerogatives than those decreed by the Councils. All this is inconsistent with modern Papalism. The letter reminds the Pope that even supposing the canons are genuine they do not cover the papal action in this case. "We request of your holiness to cause us to keep whatever was really ordained by the Fathers at Nicaea, and also to take care that those rules which are written in the instructions brought by the legates be really carried out by you in Italy." They go on to say that if the canons are genuine and are so observed at Rome "we could by no means be compelled to endure such treatment as we are unwilling to mention or could suffer what is unbearable. But we trust by the mercy of God that while your holiness presides over the Roman Church we shall not have to endure such arrogance and that a course of proceeding will be maintained towards us such as ought to be observed even without our having to speak of it."[2]

So matters remained for some years. Then the question was revived. Apiarius, being again guilty of evil conduct, was excommunicated. Again he went to Rome. Very strangely, the then Pope, Celestine, took up his case, restored him to communion, and sent him back to Africa accompanied by Faustinus. He pronounced Apiarius innocent and required him to be admitted to communion.

A plenary Council was held at Carthage in 424. Faustinus was as arrogant as before. After three days Apiarius broke down and made a full confession of his crimes, convicting himself of "every kind of

---

[1] Mansi, iv. 404.   [2] Mansi, iii, 830 f.

K

incredible infamy". The African bishops then sent to Pope Celestine the famous Synodical letter known as *Optaremus*. Thus is a comprehensive and powerful rebuttal of papal claims. It shows that nearly two centuries after Cyprian the spirit of independence in the national Church and of resolute resistance to Roman aggression was maintained.

The African fathers do not fail in plain speaking to their papal disturber. They give their opinion of his legate. After recording his partiality, they say: "He vehemently opposed the whole assembly, inflicting on us many affronts under pretence of asserting the privileges of the Church of Rome." After telling of Apiarius's confession, they proceed in outspoken fashion:

"With all due regards to you, we earnestly beg of you that for the future you do not too easily admit to a hearing persons to Rome from Africa, nor consent any more to receive to your communion those who have been excommunicated by us, because your reverence will readily perceive that this has been prohibited by the Nicene canons. For while this seems to be there forbidden in respect of the inferior clergy or the laity, how much more did the Council will this to be observed in the case of bishops lest those who have been suspended from communion in their own provinces might seem to be restored to communion hastily or precipitately in some sort by your holiness. Let your holiness reject as is worthy of you that unprincipled taking shelter with you of priests and of the clergy of lower degree, both because by no ordinance of the Fathers has this right been withdrawn from the African Church, and also because the Nicene decrees have most plainly committed the inferior clergy and the bishops themselves to their own metropolitans. For they have ordained with great prudence and justice that all matters shall be terminated in the places where they arise; and they did not think that the grace of the Holy Spirit would be wanting to any province by which grace the bishops of Christ would discern with prudence and maintain with constancy whatever was equitable; especially since any party who thinks himself wronged by a judgment, may appeal to the synod of his province, or even to a general Council; unless it be imagined by any one that our God can inspire a single individual with justice, and refuse it to an innumerable multitude of bishops assembled in council. How shall we be able to trust a sentence passed beyond the sea since it will not be possible to send the necessary witnesses, whether on account of the weakness of sex, or of advanced age or through any other impediment? That your holiness should send any on your part we can find ordained by no council of the Fathers."

Could there be a more absolute and precise contradiction to the dogmas of Papalism than this conciliar pronouncement of the African Church? Yet the Church of Rome claims that the Pope is "the supreme judge of all the faithful, and that in all causes, the decision of which belongs to the Church, recourse may be had to his tribunal and that none may reopen the judgment of the Apostolic See." This Council shows how novel and intolerable is the dominion over the Church of Christ usurped by the Bishop of Rome.

The Council's stand is also remarkable as witnessing to the tradition of independence that was maintained by Cyprian.

The Council's letter to Pope Celestine goes on to expose the imposition of palming off on them the pretended canons of Nicaea. They quietly write that nothing of the kind is to be found in the authentic letters of that Council which they have received from the Bishops Cyril of Jerusalem and Atticus of Constantinople.

Then they conclude in forcible style: "For the rest, whosoever desires you to delegate any of your clergy to execute your orders do not comply lest it seem that we are introducing the smoky arrogance of the world into the Church of Christ, which sets before those who desire to see God the light of simplicity and the splendour of humility. For now that the miserable Apiarius has been removed out of the Church of Christ for his horrible crimes, we feel confident respecting our brother Faustinus that through the uprightness and moderation of your holiness, our brotherly charity not being violated, Africa will by no means any longer be forced to endure him. Sir and brother, may our Lord long preserve your holiness to pray for us."[1]

[1] Mansi, iv, 515 f.

CHAPTER XXXIV

ST. JEROME

There is a passage of St. Jerome which is laid much stress on by papal controversialists. At first sight it does seem to favour their cause more than any other testimony that can be produced from patristic writings. Even if Jerome held the view of modern Romanists about the authority of the Roman bishop this would only show that he was in conflict with the belief and practice of the universal Church before, during and after his time. The impetuosity of Jerome's character and the customary unbridled extravagance of his language would not lend weight to his judgment. A proper understanding of the circumstances in which he wrote shows, however, that his words cannot be taken as supporting the inferences drawn from them.

The letter in question to Pope Damasus (Ep. 15) was written when Jerome was a young layman not many years baptised. The probable date for it was March to September 375[1]. At that time he was living in the Syrian desert and was harassed by the surrounding monks who wanted to compel him to profess a theological formula which he objected to. The Easterns held the formula of three hypostases in the Trinity—the form which has become universal. Rome then maintained one hypostasis. A further bewildering dissension was between the three bishops struggling for the episcopate in the neighbouring Church of Antioch—St. Meletius who was honoured and revered by the orthodox Church leaders of the East, and is now regarded as a canonised saint by Rome itself; Paulinus, who afterwards was blunderingly acknowledged as legitimate bishop by Rome; and Vitalis, a heretic. In these disturbing contentions Jerome turned to the head of the great Church of his baptism, the Church where unity of discipline and doctrine prevailed, for direction on the course he should pursue. What was more natural for a young layman—a "man of Rome" as he calls himself—to do? He emphasises that he is still entitled, though distant, to the oversight of the bishop of his

[1] See Puller, *Primitive Saints and the See of Rome*, pp. 311–13.

own Church. His appeal to Rome was then the obvious course. It is the extravagance of his mode of doing so that has given cause for misunderstanding.

He tells Damasus how since the East is so shattered by long-standing furious divisions that it is difficult among the broken cisterns to find the true fountain. "Therefore by me is the chair of Peter to be consulted, and that faith which is praised by the apostle's mouth. I appeal for spiritual food to the Church whence I received the garb of Christ. Neither the vast expanse of ocean nor all the breadth of land which separate us could preclude me from seeking the precious pearl. . . . Whilst the bad children have wasted their goods, the inheritance of the fathers is preserved uncorrupt among you alone. . . . At present the Sun of righteousness rises in the West; but in the East the fallen Lucifer has placed his throne above the Stars. You are the light of the world; you are the salt of the earth. . . . Though your greatness terrifies me, your goodness attracts me. From the priest I demand the safe-keeping of the victim; from the shepherd the protection due to the sheep. . . . My words are spoken to the successor of the fisherman, to the disciple of the cross. I who follow none as my chief but Christ so I communicate with none but your blessedness, that is, with the Chair of Peter. For this is the Rock on which the Church is built. This is the house where alone the paschal lamb can be rightly eaten. This is the ark of Noah and he who is not found in it shall perish when the flood prevails. But since, by reason of my sins, I have betaken myself to this desert which lies between Syria and the uncivilised waste, and I cannot, owing to the great distance between us, ask of your sanctity for the holy thing of the Lord. Consequently I here follow the Egyptian confessors who share your faith, and I anchor my frail craft under the shadow of their great ships. I know nothing of Vitalis; I reject Meletius; I have nothing to do with Paulinus. He that gathers not with you scatters; he that is not of Christ is of Antichrist.

"Just now, I am sorry to say, those Arians, the Campenses, are trying to extort from me, a man of Rome, the unheard-of formula of three hypostases. . . . Because I do not learn their words I am counted a heretic. . . . If you think fit, enact a decree, and then I shall not hesitate to speak of three hypostases. Order a new creed to supersede the Nicene and then, whether we are Arians or orthodox, one confession will do for us all."[1]

[1] Ep. 15. P. L. 22: 355 et seq.

A few months later, having received no reply, Jerome wrote again. He tells how he is surrounded on the one side by raging Arians and on the other by a Church torn in three parts. "Meantime I keep crying, 'If any one is united to the See of Peter, he is mine'" . . . He beseeches to be told by letter with whom he ought to communicate in Syria. "Despise not a soul for whom Christ died."[1]

This is the outpouring of a distracted Roman, irritated by the confusing feuds around him, calling for advice to the bishop whose flock he belonged to. In a foreign land he sets himself to glorify the Church of his baptism. "What he recognised in Rome is recognised rather in the way of personal predilection than of ecclesiastical dogma."[2]

Jerome was a great scholar of unbalanced temperament. He was prone to unrestrained language. His manner of describing his theological opponents was, "mad dogs", "two-legged asses", "wild beasts", "hissings of the old serpent". His laudations of asceticism and virginity are grotesque and hysterical. He was wont to revile marriage in an insensate way. (*sordes nuptiarum*; *tumor uteri*). His letters to girls are of incredible coarseness. Writing to Eustochium, he rages against the married life. He only excuses it as the means whereby virgins are produced, as roses from thorns, gold from the soil, pearls from shells.[3]

Roman Catholic writers admit his excesses. Father Bottalla writes of his "tendency to give too ready credence to unauthorised rumours".[4] Dom. Chapman refers to "the holy man's violent tongue"[5] "St. Jerome does not measure words when his temper is up."[6]

In any case, Jerome does not look upon Damasus as the divinely appointed Ruler and infallible Teacher of the Church. His appeal is as "a man of Rome" in a foreign land to the Roman bishop. At that particular time it was an understandable working rule for a Roman to adhere to ecclesiastics in communion with Rome. Rome then preserved the faith. It was not so previously in the time of Liberius, nor was it so later in the time of Honorius. Nor did it give Jerome right guidance in practice when it sided against Meletius.

[1] Ep. 16. P. L. 22: 359.
[2] Gore, *Roman Catholic Claims*, p. 115.
[3] *Ad. Eustoch.* P. L. 22: 406.
[4] Quoted by Puller, *Primitive Saints and the See of Rome*, p. 161.
[5] *Studies on the Early Papacy*, p. 118.
[6] Gore, *The Church and the Ministry* (5th edition), p. 347.

Besides, it is clear from his other and later writings that Jerome did not hold the theories of the modern Roman Church. More than once he contradicts the fundamental dogma of Peter being the rock. "Christ is the Rock who granted to His apostles that they should be called rocks: Thou art Peter and upon this rock I will build My Church."[1] "Upon this rock the Lord founded His Church (Matt. xvi. 18), from this rock the Apostle Peter derived his name. The foundation which the apostle, as architect, laid (1 Cor. iii. 10) is our Lord Jesus Christ alone. On this foundation, secure and firm . . . the Church of Christ is built."[2] "That which the teaching of Peter had founded on Christ the Rock."[3]

Exalting the virginity of St. John, he maintains that this is why he was the most loved of the disciples. When our Lord appeared on the lake shore after the resurrection it was John who recognised Him. "A Virgin alone recognised a Virgin. If John was not a virgin why was he more loved than the other disciples? But you say the Church was founded on Peter though this is done in another place on all the apostles and all receive the keys of the kingdom of heaven, and the solidity of the Church is established equally upon all. Nevertheless among the twelve one is therefore chosen that by the appointment of a head an occasion of dissension may be taken away. But why was not John chosen who was a virgin? Deference was paid to age, because Peter was the elder, lest one who was a young man, almost a boy, should be thus far preferred to a man of mature age; and lest the good Master who ought to remove an occasion of quarrel from the disciple would seem to present a cause for envy against the young man whom He loved. . . . Peter was an apostle and John an apostle, one married, the other a virgin, but Peter was only an apostle while John was an apostle and an evangelist and a prophet."[4]

This is far removed from the Roman doctrine about the sovereignty of Peter. Jerome represents him as first among equals—his is a leadership of order to prevent confusion.

Jerome, like Cyprian, regards the bishop as the supreme authority in his diocese. He knows nothing of any supreme Pastor over the universal flock. The bishop is the *summus sacerdos*. "The safety of a Church depends upon the dignity of the chief priest to whom if some exceptional and eminent power be not given by all there will

---

[1] *In Amos*, vi, 12. P. L. 25: 1118.
[2] *In Matt.* vii, 26, 27. P. L. 26: 51.
[3] *Adv. Jovin*, lib. ii. P. L. 23: 350.
[4] *Adv. Jovin.*, lib. i. P. L. 23: 258, 259.

be as many schisms in the Church as there are priests."[1] The chief authority he knows of for the Church is the local bishop. He had no conception that there was by divine institution a Head of the whole Church, a "supreme Pontiff" with universal power of jurisdiction "over each and all the pastors and the faithful".

The Vatican Council pronounces anathema on all who say that "Blessed Peter the apostle was not appointed the prince of all the apostles". Jerome is in peril of falling under that anathema when he styles Peter and Andrew "Apostolorum principes".[2] How far Jerome was from holding the dogma of papal inerrancy is shown by his repeated statement of the apostasy of Pope Liberius.[3]

[1] *Contra Luciferanos.* P. L. 23: 173.
[2] Brev. *in Ps.* 67. P. L. 26: 1080.
[3] p. 126.

CHAPTER XXXV

COUNCIL OF EPHESUS

I

The Third General Council was held at Ephesus in 431. Cyril, Bishop of Alexandria presided over it and managed its proceedings. Nestorius, Bishop of Constantinople, was condemned and deposed.

It was a period in the life of the Church on which we must look back with grief. Unchristian and violent elements had sway, which culminated in another regularly constituted Council eight years afterwards in the same Church at Ephesus under the presidency of Cyril's successor. At it the then Bishop of Constantinople was beaten to death. Cyril was a man of repellent character, whose attitude to the Bishop of Constantinople was truculent. His uncle and predecessor, Theophilus, had disgracefully persecuted the saintly Bishop of Constantinople, Chrysostom. The teaching of Nestorius was open to objection, but was capable of an orthodox interpretation.

Cyril began his operations against Nestorius at the begnning of the year 429. He had an acrimonious correspondence with him. In such a conflict, fraught with the gravest issues for one of the patri-archs, it was natural that both should seek the support of the Church of the West, represented by its head, Celestine, the Bishop of Rome. Celestine took the side of Cyril in no uncertain manner. He held a Council in Rome (August 430), and wrote to Nestorius that if within ten days after receiving the letter he would not renounce his impious novelty and profess the same faith as that held by the Church of Rome and of Alexandria and the orthodox everywhere then Cyril is authorised to excommunicate him.[1] To Cyril he wrote: "The authority of our see, having been joined with yourself and freely occupying our place, execute this sentence with strictness and vigour; so that unless in ten days from this monition he condemns

[1] Mansi, iv, 1035.

157

in writing his unholy doctrine, and declares that he holds that faith concerning the birth of Christ our God which is held by the Roman Church and your Holiness's Church, and by all who belong to our religion, your Holiness may provide for his Church and let him know that he must needs be cut off from our body."[1]

The vagueness of the Pope's account of how Nestorius had erred and what precise definition he was to profess is astonishing. Here is no attempt of the infallible Teacher "faithfully to expound the revelation or deposit of faith".[2] Once again, as in the Arian conflict, it is the Bishop of Alexandria and not the Bishop of Rome who promulgates orthodox doctrine. Romanist scholars have to admit this. Battifol writes that it is the defect of the letter that Celestine did not enumerate the errors for which he reproached Nestorius. "It deplores that 'many of the things which you impiously preach the universal Church condemns', without mentioning what were the impious propositions."[3]

Duchesne notes the failure of Celestine to lay down "what was exactly the doctrine that he rebuked in Nestorius, or in what consisted this teaching common to Rome, to Alexandria and to the universal Church to which the patriarch of Constantinople was so severely recalled. Between what was taught at Alexandria, what was believed at Rome, and what was set forth at Antioch there were notable differences."[4] The statement in the encyclical *Lux Veritatis*, that "Cyril was in wonderful agreement with the teaching of the Roman Church", is therefore amusing. As Archbishop Chrysostom of Athens notes: "It is the contrary which is accurate, namely, that the Church of Rome adopted the teaching of Cyril."[5]

2

Cyril, having received the support of the Western Church, proceeded to make full use of his advantage. At every stage he showed he had no consciousness that the supreme Judge had spoken. His actions showed he believed he had received the co-operation of an important ally. He proceeded to utilise this accession to his side in seeking for other support in the campaign against Nestorius. He

[1] Mansi, iv, 1019, 1020.
[2] Vatican Decrees, chap. 4.
[3] *Le Siège Apostolique*, p. 354.
[4] *Early History of the Christian Church*, vol. iii, p. 235 (E. T.).
[5] *The Third Oecumenical Council and the Primacy of the Bishop of Rome*, p. 27.

sent out letters to John, Bishop of Antioch, to Juvenal of Jerusalem, and others. His arguments to John are most significant and entirely out of keeping with the idea that the universal Pastor had pronounced a final judgment which all must obey. He never refers to it as such.

Though he is very anxious to use all possible arguments to dissociate John from his friend Nestorius, he relies only on the inducements of expediency. It is the judgment of the bishops who assembled in Rome he puts forward, and the dangerous position any one will be in who isolates himself from them. It is these bishops (plural) whom it is necessary to hearken to. It is the "union with all the West" he exalts, and the fact that the bishops of Thessalonica and Macedonia always concur with them.[1] "We will follow their decision lest we shall fall away from the communion of such a great number", and he gives John the ominous advice that he would do well to "consider the advisability" of standing in with them. John saw clearly the seriousness of the campaign against Nestorius. He wrote imploring him to come to terms and to cease opposing the word "Theotokos". But though he uses many eager arguments he never thinks of telling him the obvious one—on papal theories—that it is his duty to obey the sovereign Head of the Church. He presses, instead, the expediency argument of not falling out with the Western Church. He begs him not to disturb the lately secured union between East and West.[2]

Cyril did not consider the Pope's judgment of sufficient authority in itself, nor did he by any means regard himself as merely the Pope's agent to announce it. He held in November 430 a council of his own in Alexandria. Then he felt in a position to overcome Nestorius. He wrote to Nestorius his famous third letter in which, so far from merely transmitting the decision of the supreme authority, he writes in the name of his own synod as well. He looks on the decree as a reinforcement by Rome of his own work "Therefore," harshly wrote Cyril, "together with the holy Synod which met in Great Rome under the presidency of our most holy and venerable brother and fellow minister, Bishop Celestine, we notify you by this third letter advising you to renounce these crude and perverse doctrines which you hold and teach and to accept the right faith instead." He goes on to state that Nestorius must within the time set, in express words, "declare that you anathematise these your infamous and

[1] Mansi, iv, 1052. [2] Ibid., iv, 1063.

profane opinions and will hold and teach as we all do, the bishops and doctors and heads of the people in the West and the East; and both the holy Council at Rome hath agreed, and we all, that the letters written by the Church of Alexandria are right and blameless."[1]

Here is no call to submit to a sovereign Judge. More than once Cyril brings forward his own Church as joined with Rome in issuing the order. Writing to the monks of Constantinople, he says: "We have thought it right to admonish him with a third letter, that sent from us and from our most holy and religious brother and fellow-minister, Celestine, the Bishop of the Great Rome."[2] Moreover, he composed twelve forms of dogma to which he demanded subscription entirely without the knowledge or sanction of Rome.

The ultimatum was delivered to Nestorius on 6th December, 430. He replied with twelve anathemas against Cyril.

3

The messengers of Cyril must have met on the way the imperial messengers summoning representatives of the bishops to meet for a general council in Ephesus, at Pentecost the following year—7th June. This decree was a definite ignoring—a repudiation—of the Pope's authority. It plainly showed that he was not supposed to have any power to issue final decisions on doctrine. The condemnation of Nestorius by the Pope was complete. There was no idea in the Church of the fifth century that it was "irreformable". The emperor orders the whole matter to be decided by the bishops as if no decision had been given. He states that the Council is indispensable and orders that no new step must be taken by any one until the Council meets. The final judgment is to be "the common sentence which will be given by all".[3]

Bishop Maret, in his book *Du Concile Général*, submitted to the Vatican Council, wrote: "The Pope had pronounced in the affair of Nestorius a canonical judgment, clothed with all the authority of his see. He had prescribed its execution. Yet, however, three months after this sentence, and before its execution, all the episcopate is invited to examine afresh and to decide freely the question in dispute; and it accepts the invitation. The execution of the pontifical sentence is suspended with the acquiescence even of the Pope."

[1] Mansi, iv, 1069, 1072.   [2] Ibid., iv, 1097.   [3] Ibid., iv, 1113.

"Here are facts worthy of very serious attention; facts which clearly prove that in these memorable circumstances the chief and final authority was, for Catholics as for heretics, for emperors as for bishops, for the Pope himself—not the Pope alone or with a limited number of bishops—but the Pope with the episcopate, the Pope forming with all the bishops one grand unity."[1]

Bossuet, the great seventeenth-century champion of Romanism, agrees entirely with this view. "It was fixed that all was in suspense once the authority of the universal Synod was invoked even though the sentence of the Roman Pontiff about doctrine and about persons accused of heresy had been uttered and promulgated."[2]

The Pope himself saw nothing improper in this nullification of his sentence. He was summoned (like any other bishop) to attend the Council to investigate a matter on which he had already pronounced his decision. In his reply to the emperor he makes no objection whatever. He says he is unable to be present but is sending representatives. Four hundred years after the founding of Christianity, the theory that the Pope is the supreme Judge of the faithful, that is, unlawful to appeal from the judgments of the Roman Pontiffs to an Oecumenical Council, had not been heard of even in Rome.

Further, he wrote a letter which was presented to the Council by his delegates. In it he declared that their Master's commission to the apostles to teach has descended to all the bishops in common (in commune). Quoting the command "Go, teach all nations", he enjoins: "You ought to observe, my brethren, that we have received a general commission. He who committed the common duty to them all wills that you all carry it out. . . . We ought to take on ourselves their labours to whom we succeed in office."[3] In this remarkable document Celestine, as the Roman Catholic historian Fleury says, "places himself in their (i.e. the bishops') rank."[4]

4

On 7th June many bishops had not arrived at Ephesus. The Pope's delegates were not yet there, nor John of Antioch and the Eastern bishops. Cyril had a majority and refused to wait, though the emperor's representative and sixty-eight bishops protested.

[1] vol. i, p. 183.
[2] *Defensio Declarationis Cleri Gallicani*, lib. vii, c. x.
[3] Mansi, iv, 1284 f.
[4] *Ecclesiastical History*, vol. xxv, chap. 47 (E. T.).

The Council met on Monday 22nd June. Nestorius refused to attend. It is remarkable that the Council did not feel it advisable to wait for the representatives of Rome to arrive.

Cyril presided as bishop of the see of highest rank present. It is alleged he presided in virtue of a commission from the Pope. This is quite unfounded. The commission he had received from the Pope was for the definite purpose of announcing the terms of the papal condemnation of Nestorius which was carried out in the preceding December. The Council was not thought of when the Pope gave him this commission in August. In none of the Pope's letters after the Council was summoned does he appoint Cyril his representative. On the contrary, he appointed as his delegates Bishops Arcadius and Projectus and the priest Philip.

Even when the papal delegates were present at later sessions of the Council Cyril still presided.

When Cyril was not present it was Juvenal, Bishop of Jerusalem, who presided, though the papal delegates were there and signed after him.

The legates expressly stated at the Council that they were commissioned to supply the presence of Celestine.[1] In the letter of the emperor they are described as those who "supply the presence of the most holy Bishop Celestine".[2] In the Council's letter to Celestine they are similarly designated as having by "their presence exhibited Celestine to them and filled the place of the Apostolic See".[3]

In the Acts of the Council (which are open to suspicion) Cyril is represented as Bishop "of Alexandria who also had the place" of the Bishop of Rome. That is, his own rank comes first, then he claims to represent *also* Celestine. Other bishops took the place also of absent ones. Cyril was faced with powerful opposition. His unscrupulousness was too well known.[4] Generally he signs himself simply as Bishop of Alexandria. The legates signed after him.[5]

Duchesne considers that Cyril's original commission to represent Celestine "seems clearly to have expired. Besides the best proof that

---

[1] Mansi, iv, 1295.
[2] Ibid., iv, 1303.
[3] Ibid., iv, 1337.
[4] "True Christianity would avert its sight in shame and anguish that such a champion should be accepted as the representative of the Gospel of peace and love" (Milman, *Latin Christianity*, vol. i, p. 186).
[5] Mansi, iv, 1304, 1363.

the Pope had no idea of causing himself to be represented by him is the fact that he was sending legates".[1]

Dom. Chapman writes that Cyril, "as the first bishop in the world after the Bishop of Rome, assumed the presidency of the Council. . . . It does not appear that Celestine had commissioned Cyril to be his representative at Ephesus".[2]

If the papal claims were true all that the Council had to do was to ascertain if Nestorius had fulfilled the Pope's conditions, and, if not, straightway condemn him. The matter had been investigated and pronounced on by the Vicar of Christ. Nestorius, by papal decision, was already a heretic, outside the Church, and the see of Constantinople was vacant.

Completely different was the procedure of the Council. The charge against Nestorius was investigated as if no papal decision had been given. The Pope's letters were heard on a level with those of Cyril as evidence against him. But he was regarded as Bishop of Constantinople and so cited to attend. Three times "the most religious Bishop Nestorius" is summoned to appear.

The method of trial adopted by the Council was that first the Creed of Nicaea was read, then Cyril's second letter to Nestorius. This letter had already received the enthusiastic approval of the Pope, yet Cyril formally asked the Council to pronounce whether he had "written correctly, blamelessly and in harmony with" the Nicene creed. The bishops voted approval. Then Nestorius's answer was put to the vote and condemned with anathemas. As Bossuet comments: "By the same form and rule Cyril is approved, Nestorius reprobated. Twice by the same procedure of the Ephesian Synod the judgment pronounced and promulgated of the Roman Pontiff on a question of the Catholic faith is reviewed. What he had approved and what he had reprobated are equally brought into court. Only after investigation is the judgment confirmed."[3]

It is exceedingly significant that this, the crucial turning point of the Council, was reached without any mention of the Bishop of Rome's decision. Could there be clearer evidence that the bishops knew themselves to be exercising a completely independent judgment?

---

[1] *Early History*, vol. iii, p. 243.
[2] *Bishop Gore and the Catholic Claims*, p. 89.
[3] *Defensio Declarationis Cleri Gallicani*, lib. vii, c. ii.

Once Cyril's theology was endorsed and Nestorius anathematised,[1] the whole issue was virtually settled.

It was only after this that the Pope's letter was read. Then followed Cyril's third letter. Even then, after hearing the Pope's letter, extracts from the Fathers were read to make clear what was orthodox doctrine. Passages from the writings of Nestorius were heard. Then the final decision was taken, condemning Nestorius. It records that, Nestorius not having appeared, the bishops were necessarily bound to examine his ungodly doctrine. "Necessarily urged by the canons and in accordance with the letter of our most holy Father and fellow minister, Celestine, Bishop of Rome, we have come, abundantly weeping, to this sorrowful sentence against him, namely, that our Lord Jesus Christ, whom he has blasphemed, decrees by the holy Synod that Nestorius be excluded from the episcopal dignity and from all priestly communion."[2] The sentence was signed by all the bishops, the first signature being: "I, Cyril, Bishop of Alexandria, subscribe to the judgment of the Council."

That the condemnation of Nestorius was the action of the Council hearing the case *de novo* and formulating its own decision is apparent also in the sentence served on Nestorius. "The holy Synod . . . to Nestorius the new Judas: Know that for thy impious doctrines thou wast deposed by the holy Synod agreeably to the laws of the Church, and declared to be excluded from all ecclesiastical dignities on the 22nd day of the present month of June." Until this sentence Nestorius was "the most religious Bishop of Constantinople". After it he was the "new Judas". "Nestorius was always regarded and treated as Bishop of Constantinople until he was deposed at Ephesus; and he was deposed there, not in virtue of the Pope's judgment which was read there but of proof adduced of his false doctrine."[3]

5

The fact of the Council being held, and its independently trying and condemning Nestorius, is crushing refutation of the Vatican Council's theology. Much is made of the compliments given to the Pope and the prominence attached to his name. It is easy to understand why such use should be made of his consent.

---

[1] The Bishops cried out : "Whosoever does not anathematise Nestorius let him be anathema."

[2] Mansi, iv, 1212.

[3] Tillemont, *Memoires*, vol. xiv, p. 364.

When John of Antioch arrived in Ephesus and found what Cyril's manœuvres had effected he held a rival Council of forty-three bishops and deposed Cyril and his chief ally, Memnon, Bishop of Ephesus. The imperial commissioner denounced to the court the improper proceedings of Cyril. Cyril's Council excommunicated the Bishop of Antioch. So the unseemly row went on between the prelates of Alexandria and Ephesus on the one side and those of Constantinople and Antioch on the other (though John did not share Nestorius's doctrine). The decisive question was: which side will the emperor take? Cyril knew that the support of the Western Church gave him a tremendous advantage over his opponents. He needed to use every weapon, for in August the new imperial commissioner arrived with the decision that Cyril and Memnon as well as Nestorius were deposed and they were all three also put under arrest.

So it is not at all surprising to find eager and constant references all through to Celestine, and his Western colleagues. In the Council's letter sent to the emperor at the third session the Council of "the bishops of the West" at Rome is put in the forefront, as agreeing with their decision. Celestine has, it is urged, confirmed this through the delegates who represented him at the Council. No mention is made of any personal supreme authority belonging to Celestine. The important point stressed is the union with the Western Empire and Church. "For as the men who came made known to our Synod, and have witnessed in writing, that the opinion of the whole Council of the West is in agreement with that of this Synod, and that they were of one mind with us . . . we, having necessarily taken a decision based on our common agreement, have presented it to your authority that your piety may know that our recent judgment was pronounced by a common vote of the whole universe."[1]

Cyril, in writing afterwards to the emperor, said: "Both the Church of the Romans and the whole Council which has assembled, so to speak, from all over the world bore witness to the rightness of my faith."[2]

In the synodical letter to Celestine himself his condemnation of Nestorius is not regarded as being final or authoritative. The Council look on the sentence as proceeding from their own authority. "We have condemned, as we have declared above, this heresy as impious and most wicked." There is no word of executing what Celestine had before ordained.

[1] Mansi, iv, 1301.   [2] Migne. P. G. 76: 481.

L

A decision of the Eastern Church only, or of the Western, could not bind the whole Church. It is easy to understand, therefore, the weight placed by Eastern Synods on the corroboration of Rome, the Head of the West. This desire did not imply, as is so often wrongly argued, any recognition of supremacy in Rome but marked the all-importance of united action.

CHAPTER XXXVI

VINCENTIUS OF LERINS

The *Commonitorium* of St. Vincent was written about the year 434. He resided in the island monastery of Lerins—the retreat founded by Honoratus, famous for its illustrious inmates such as Patrick, Hilary of Arles, Benedict Biscop, etc. Vincent's short tractate is one of the most valuable documents of the fifth century. It is written in bright, concise style. Its object is to furnish a method for guarding against heresies. He writes: "I have often enquired most earnestly and attentively from very many experts in sanctity and learning how, and by what definite, and, as it were, universal rule I might distinguish the truth of the Catholic faith from the falsity of heretical perversion."[1]

It is obvious that if the Romanist dogma was known in the early Church the simple rule would be to conform to the teaching of the divinely authorised infallible Guide, the Bishop of Rome. Such instructions as Vincent and the many other patristic writers against heresies laid down would be superfluous. The fact is that Vincent never once suggests this sovereign method. Nowhere in his *Commonitorium* does he show the least consciousness that the Church had such a medium for discovering truth. The rules he gives and his elaborations of them are not only absolutely inconsistent with the Vatican theories but are also an inexorable condemnation of their novelty.

1

His direction to any one who wishes to detect the frauds of heresies and to remain sound in the faith is to resort to, first, the authority of the divine Law, secondly, to the tradition of the Catholic Church. Since men interpret Scripture differently, he enunciates his famous maxim—we are to hold to "that which has been believed everywhere, always and by all"—*Quod semper, quod ubique, quod*

[1] bk. i, chap. ii.

ab omnibus. In other words, true doctrine has "universality, antiquity, consent". This Vincentian rule can be criticised if it be
pressed unduly, but it is, in general terms, an admirable test for
the Catholic orthodoxy.

Vincent goes on to explain the application of the rule in terms
that at every stage rule out the papal claims. What is the Catholic
Christian to do if part of the Church goes wrong? He is to prefer
the soundness of the whole body to a corrupt member. What if
some novel contagion affects the whole Church? He is to cling to
antiquity. What if some of the ancients erred? Then he is to honour
the decrees of a General Council. But if some new error springs
up which has not been so rejected? He must take pains to find
out and compare the opinions of those ancients who remained in
the communion and faith of the one Catholic Church, "and whatever he shall find to have been held, written and taught, not by
one or two only, but by all equally and with one consent, openly,
frequently and persistently, that he must understand is to be believed
by himself also without the slightest hesitation".[1]

This is exactly the Anglican method of investigating the belief
and practice of the primitive Church which is derided by the advocates of the easier method of simply consulting the "living voice"
of Rome. Vincent shows that in the fifth century this papal novelty
had not been invented.

Again and again Vincent emphasises the indispensable method.
"It is the characteristic of Catholics to keep the deposits committed
to them by the holy Fathers, to condemn profane novelties, and,
as the apostle said more than once, to anathematise anyone who
preaches anything but what has been received."[2] How are the
Catholics to distinguish truth from falsehood in interpretation of
Scripture? he asks in another place. And his answer again is by
the decrees of a General Council, "and, what is next best, the consentient opinions of many and great teachers".[3] The "collection
and comparison of the unanimous opinions of the Teachers of old"
is the standard of orthodoxy. As soon as error of interpretation
shows itself, "the opinions of the Fathers in interpretation of the
canon ought to be collected".[4]

When referring to St. Paul's words (1 Cor. xii. 28) he makes
abundantly clear that he knew of no infallible Teacher whose

[1] chap. iii.   [2] chap. xxiv.   [3] chap. xxvii.
                    [4] bk. i, chap. xxviii.

function it was to have the full power of feeding, ruling and governing the whole Church. He quotes the enumeration of those whom God hath placed in the Church, apostles, prophets, teachers, and adds: "Whosoever therefore despiseth those who have been placed by God in His Church in their several times and places, when they agree in Christ in the interpretation of some one point of Catholic doctrine, despiseth not man but God."[1] Again, citing 1 Timothy vi. 20: "O Timothy, keep the deposit, avoiding profane novelties of speech," he writes, "who today is Timothy but either the universal Church in general, or the whole body of the prelacy in particular whose duty it is themselves to hold the knowledge of religion complete and to communicate it to others."[2] It is the glory of the confessors that, "following the decrees and definitions of all the bishops of the holy Church, the heirs of apostolic and Catholic truth, they preferred to surrender themselves rather than the faith of antiquity and universality".

2

Vincent, in certain references to the Bishopric of Rome, conveys the same evidence of being unaware of its divine prerogatives. Giving instances of the "many examples" of teachers who withstood novelties, he includes Pope Stephen, who is praised for that "acting indeed with his colleagues, but giving them the lead . . . deeming it right, I imagine, so far to surpass all the rest in his devotion to the faith, as he was above them by the authority of his position".[3] Here there is only such recognition of the preeminence of the metropolitan of the West which we can all endorse. The unyielding and excommunicated opponent of a Bishop of Rome, Cyprian, is celebrated as "that light of all saints and martyrs and bishops who, with the rest of his colleagues, will reign with Christ for ever".[4] When Vincent deals with the Council of Ephesus (431), held in his own time, his witness is clear and detailed against the papal pretensions. It is claimed by Romanists that this Council duly obeyed and observed the condemnation of Nestorius by Pope Celestine.

Vincent's account of the procedure of the assembled bishops is very different.[5] They, he writes, "agreed to this as the most Catholic, the most loyal, and the best thing to do, namely, to bring forth

---

[1] bk. i, chap. xxviii.   [2] bk. i, chap. xxii.   [3] bk. i, chap. vi.
[4] bk. i, chap. vi.   [5] bk. ii, chaps. xxix and xxx.

openly the opinions of the holy Fathers . . . in order that duly
and solemnly by their consent and decree the religious tie of ancient
doctrine might be strengthened and the blasphemy of profane
novelty might be condemned. Which, having been done, the impious,
Nestorius was rightly and deservedly adjudged to be at variance
with Catholic antiquity, and blessed Cyril, on the other hand, to
be in agreement with it".

But Nestorius was by the Pope's decree condemned and excommunicated before the Council met! The ignoring of the Pope's
supreme authority is demonstrated. It is Cyril who is singled out
as the leader of the Church in exposing Nestorius.

Vincent goes on to enumerate ten of the Fathers whose opinions
were cited before the Council as those through whom "the words
of the sacred Law were expounded and the rule of divine doctrine
established". Pope Celestine's name is not once mentioned among
them. The testimonies of two Bishops of Rome, Felix and Julius,
were included—not as of supreme infallible authority but entirely
on a level with the others. It is expressly stated by Vincent that they
were brought forward "in order that it might be proved that not
only Greece and the East but also the Western and Latin world
always so thought". Cyprian and Ambrose were cited that "not
only the capital of the world but its flanks also might yield their
judgment". All this shows the importance placed on the West
agreeing with the East. It explodes the idea of one sovereign infallible
authority to settle doctrine. It was by following the advice and
obeying the judgment of all the Fathers appealed to that the blessed
Council "gave pronouncement concerning the rule of faith without
shirking or presumption or favour".

It may be noted that Vincent, referring to St. Paul's words
(Gal. i. 8), "though we or an angel from heaven preach any other
gospel", asks what he means by "we". He answers that "he means
even if Peter or Andrew or John or in fact the whole company of
the apostles preach any other gospel to you than we have preached
let him be accursed".[1] Peter was not exempted from liability to
err. St. Paul is to Vincent "that chosen vessel, that teacher of the
gentiles, that trumpet of the apostles, that herald of the world, that
intimate of heaven".[2]

[1] bk. i, chap. viii.   [2] bk. i, chap. ix.

CHAPTER XXXVII

HILARY OF ARLES

S t. Hilary was an inmate of Lerins when St. Vincent and probably St. Patrick were resident there. His struggle with the Papacy shows how far the Church of Gaul in the fifth century was from acknowledging the supremacy of Rome. Hilary became Bishop of Arles in succession to St. Honoratus about 429. The very fact of his election is a proof of how little the Church was disposed to heed papal protests. Pope Celestine in a letter to the Bishops of Vienne and Narbonne had condemned the choosing of a monk from Lerins, Honoratus, to be bishop. He objects to choosing outsiders (*peregrini et extranei*) and monks as bishops, and enjoins that each man ought to have the fruit of his service in the Church where he had spent his life.[1] The response of the diocese of Arles was to choose another monk of Lerins, Hilary, to succeed Honoratus.

Hilary was revered for the sanctity of his life and the devotedness of his episcopal labours. "The fifth century does not present a nobler and more beautiful character."[2]

In the year 444 (accompanied by Germanus of Auxerre, St. Patrick's friend) he held a Synod, probably at Besançon, and excommunicated a bishop named Celidonius. This bishop betook himself to Rome. Leo admitted him to communion and seems to have illegally instituted an enquiry. Hilary, on hearing of such an outrage on Church principles, went to Rome himself. Hilary was careful to declare that he did not recognise the papal jurisdiction but only intended to protest against the irregularity.[3] Fleury thus represents his attitude to Leo: "I am come only to show my respect for you, not to plead my cause and I inform you of what has passed

[1] Migne. P. L. 50: 434. Cf. Prof. Oulton, *History of the Church of Ireland*, vol. i, p. 39 f.
[2] Gore, *Leo the Great*, p. 107.
[3] *Ecclesiastical History*, vol. xxvii, chap. 4.

not by way of accusation but as a simple recital; if you are of a different way of thinking I will not importune you further."[1]

At the Roman Council Celidonius was acquitted. Hilary refused to enter into communion with him and boldly challenged the authority of Rome to interfere thus in the affairs of the Gallic Church. His biographer, Honoratus, tells how he did not yield to the powerful; that though he was in danger he would not admit to his communion him whom he and Germanus and other Gallican bishops had condemned. Duchesne[2] writes: "The explanations which he gave to the Pope, in language rude enough, amounted to nothing less than a refusal to admit the competence of the holy See in such a matter." Hilary's style was "*propre à effaroucher les orcilles romaines*".

St. Leo himself has told that Hilary "would not suffer himself to be subject to the blessed Apostle Peter"; that he "depreciated in arrogant terms the reverence due to the blessed Peter";[3] that his utterances were "such as no layman would dare to speak; no bishop to listen to." It is evident that in the fifth century papal encroachments were not tamely submitted to.

The result was that Hilary's liberty was in danger. He found it advisable to leave Rome without ceremony and return as quickly as he could to Gaul. Leo was enraged. According to Fleury he deprived Hilary of his authority, prohibited him from being present at ordinations, declared him cut off from the communion of the holy See and represented it as an act of grace that he was left in the Church and not deposed.[4] The letter Leo wrote to the bishops of Vienne is a discreditable tirade, revealing his spite and fury. He denounces Hilary for presumption and self-seeking. He tells the bishops that Hilary wanted to subject them to his own supremacy. "Whoever, puffed up with the spirit of pride, denies the dignity of Peter, only sinks himself to hell." Hilary is accused of repeated insolence. His activity in journeying through his diocese is sneered at. His diligence is more like "the speeding of a buffoon [*scurrili velocitate*] than episcopal moderation. . . . This is not to return but to flee, it is not showing the wholesomeness of pastoral visitation but resorting to the violence of a thief and a robber".[5] John x. 1

---

[1] "*Se ad officia non ad causam venisse, protestandi ordine non accusandi.*" Honoratus, *Vita Hilaü*. P. L. 50: 1237.
[2] *Fastes Episcopaux de l'ancienne Gaule*, vol. i, chap. 3, p. 115.
[3] Leo, *Verbis arrogantibus minuendo*, Ep. 10. P. L. 54: 630.
[4] Fleury, *Ecclesiastical History*, vol. xxvii, chap. 5.
[5] P. L. 54: 633.

is applied to the venerated bishop. Leo's rage even carried him further. There was a charge of Hilary having consecrated a bishop before the existing one was dead. Leo's abusiveness extended to writing that "Hilary was not so desirous to consecrate a bishop as rather to kill off the one who was ill". Hilary is an habitual liar (*pro suo more mentiri*).[1] He has withdrawn himself from the apostolic communion by a "disgraceful flight".

This letter casts a sinister light on Leo's unscrupulous and domineering character. He far surpassed his predecessors in exalting the power of the Papacy and persistently magnifying its claim.

Subsequently negotiations took place, but Hilary would not yield the main point and was never reconciled to Rome. His death was the occasion of a wonderful outbreak of grief and love from his flock and even from outsiders. He is today honoured as a saint in the Roman Church.

His story reveals how increasingly dangerous it became to resist the audacious encroachments of Rome. Leo fell back on the secular arm. He obtained from the Emperor Valentinian III an edict that was of tremendous importance in riveting the supremacy of the Popes on hitherto independent national Churches. "The terms of the rescript of Valentinian III in 449 are unhappily discreditable to Leo the Great, who also himself reproduced what he must have known to be the detected misquotation of Sardican canons as Nicene."[2]

[1] P. L. 54: 636.
[2] Dr. Wm. Bright, *Waymarks in Church History*, p. 213.

CHAPTER XXXVIII

IMPERIAL RESCRIPTS

1

The reasons for the growth of the power of the Bishops of Rome were manifold: the unique imperial rank of the city; the early richness and wide benefactions of the Church; its apostolic prestige; its, in general, orthodox faith and leadership of the United Western world when the East was torn with heresy and dissensions; the destruction of the once great, independent African Church; the acceptance in the dark ages of a series of forged documents. The Roman bishops were often men of uncommon ability, ambitious to extend the authority of their see.

The removal of the imperial residence from Rome resulted in a great accession of power and influence to the bishops of Rome. They succeeded to a share in the glory that attached to the imperial traditions of the city.

In the place where the princes of the State had long wielded their sovereign sway there were now instead princes of the Church, who gradually came to regard themselves and to be regarded as heirs of the Caesars. We find the Western emperors ready to maintain and extend the powers of the bishop of the still venerated city. A vital factor in imposing the jurisdiction of the Roman bishop on the Western Church was the interference of the State. Papal supremacy may be said to be largely due to secular tyranny. Two edicts of the emperors had incalculable results in forcibly subjecting the Church to the sway of Rome.

When Pope Liberius died in 366, less than a year after the death of the anti-pope, Felix, there was a disputed election. Ursinus was ordained by one party. Damasus was ordained a week later by a larger section. Sanguinary riots ensued. The adherents of Damasus attacked those of Ursinus in their church. When the fight was over one hundred and thirty-seven dead bodies were taken out of the church. The Emperor Gratian sided with Damasus and banished his rival. "As for Damasus, his victory had cost him too dear; his promotion had been accompanied by too much police action, too many imperial rescripts, too many corpses."[1]

About the year 380 a Council under Damasus at Rome petitioned the Emperor Gratian for powers to deal with recalcitrant bishops. Gratian replied by a rescript to his "Vicar" at Rome, Aquilinus. In it he orders that a contumacious bishop condemned "by the judgment of Damasus with a Council of five or seven bishops" or by a Council of Catholic bishops, or one who had refused to appear before an episcopal tribunal, should be compelled by State officials to answer before the episcopal tribunal or come to the city of Rome. If the case arose in more distant regions it was to be submitted to the metropolitan of the province; or if the metropolitan himself was accused he must answer at Rome or before judges chosen by the Roman bishop. If the condemned bishop suspect partiality on the part of the metropolitan or any of his judges he can appeal to the Bishop of Rome or to a Council of fifteen neighbouring bishops.

By this secular ukase the Bishop of Rome obtained powers he did not possess previously. (1) All metropolitans of the West were made so far subject to him that he could either try them at Rome or appoint judges to try them. (2) Bishops tried anywhere in Western Europe might by this law either appeal to the judgment of the Bishop of Rome at Rome or to a Synod of local bishops. The extension of papal power in the fourth century was thus based on civil force, not on ecclesiastical consent or tradition.

2

In the middle of the fifth century another emperor by his secular power immensely extended the jurisdiction of the Popes. This is the sequel to Hilary of Arles's resistance to Leo the Great. Leo, to rivet his aggressive ambition on the Church, "called in the police". The emperor then was the contemptible and vicious Valentinian III. There is no room for doubt that his edict of 445 was at the dictation of Leo. In it he refers to Leo's complaint to him against Hilary. Hilary's independence is censured as offending against "the majesty of the empire and the respect due to the Apostolic See". "Inasmuch, then, as the primacy of the Apostolic

---

[1] Duchesne, *Early History of the Church*, vol. ii, p. 366.

See is assured by the merit of St. Peter, prince of the episcopal crown, by the dignity of the city of Rome and the authority of a sacred Synod, let not unlawful presumption endeavour to attempt anything contrary to the authority of that see. For then at last will the peace of the Churches be everywhere maintained if the whole body [*universitas*] acknowledges its ruler." After references to the contumacy of Hilary and the disorders in the Churches beyond the Alps, the edict goes on: "Not only, then, do we put away so great a crime but in order that not even the least disturbance may arise amongst the Churches, or the discipline of religion appear in anything to be weakened, we decree by this perpetual edict that it shall not be lawful for the bishops of Gaul, or of other provinces, contrary to ancient custom, to attempt aught without the authority of the venerable Pope of the eternal city; but whatever the authority of the Apostolic See has sanctioned or shall sanction let that be held by them and by all for a law; so that if any of the bishops shall neglect, when summoned, to come to the tribunal of the Roman bishop let him be compelled to attend by the governor of the province, in all respects regard being had to what our divine parents conferred on the Roman Church."[1]

This brutally tyrannical law destroyed the free constitution of the Western Church. It made "the irresponsible absolutism of the Roman Pontiff part of the law of the empire".[2] By it "the Romish bishop became the supreme Head of the whole Western Church".[3] Puller does not exaggerate when he writes: "There is nothing more absolutely certain in the history of the Church than that the papal *jurisdiction* outside the suburbicarian provinces mainly arose out of the legislation of the State. One may truly say that Erastianism begat it, and forgery developed it. . . . Thus did the decrepit autocracy of the dying empire plant in the home of freedom, the Church of God, the hateful likeness of itself."[4] The great Roman Catholic historian, Tillemont, acknowledges:[5] "This law is very appropriate, as Baronius says, to make it evident that the emperors much assisted to establish the grandeur and authority of the Popes. . . . We are not able to refrain from stating that in the mind of those who have any love for the liberty of the Church, or any knowledge of her

---

[1] *Apud.* Leo, Ep. 11. P. L. 54: 636 et seq.
[2] Gore, *Leo the Great*, p. 109.
[3] Gieseler, *Eccl. Hist.* i, 452.
[4] Puller, *Primitive Saints and the See of Rome*, pp. 196, 201.
[5] *Memoires*, vol. xv, p. 83.

discipline, it will bring always as little honour to him whom it praises [Leo] as hurt to him whom it condemns [Hilary]."

The rescript was addressed to the patrician Aetius, the Victor of Attila and main support of the empire, whom Valentinian afterwards basely murdered. Valentinian's own miserable life was put an end to the next year by the husband of a woman he had outraged.

In this rescript the dignity of the city of Rome is joined with the merit of St. Peter as instituting its authority. A third ground is alleged, the authority of a sacred synod. This is the familiar device of Roman bishops at that period. Leo apparently was able to deceive Valentinian. Dr. Gore writes: "Leo in urging, as he constantly did, Nicene authority for receiving appeals from the universal Church was distinctly and consciously guilty of a *suppressio veri* at any rate, which is not distinguishable from fraud. Of this crime we cannot acquit him; and how large a part this and similar 'lies' —which they are none the less, though they be believed to be 'for God'—have contributed to the advancement of the Roman See, it is quite impossible to estimate."[1]

It is noteworthy that Theodoret, writing to Leo, bases the precedency of the Roman Church on the city being the largest, the most splendid, the most illustrious in the world; on the faith of the Roman Church and on her having the tombs of Peter and Paul. These reasons must have irritated Leo.[2]

[1] *Leo the Great*, p. 114. [2] Ep. 113. P. G. 83: 1313.

CHAPTER XXXIX

THE COUNCIL OF CHALCEDON

The fourth General Council met at Chalcedon on 8th October 451. Leo the Great had been Bishop of Rome then for eleven years. His impressive personality, ability and soaring ambition had much advanced the power and prestige of the See of Rome. His episcopate marks an era in its rise. The civil convulsions due to the breaking up of the Roman Empire contributed to the need for some centre of authority being recognised, and the Bishop of Rome succeeded to much of the prestige due to the former emperors. The bishops of the great Eastern sees continued their unholy contests. In 449 another Bishop of Alexandria had at a properly summoned General Council deposed and maltreated another Bishop of Constantinople. Appeals naturally came to Rome from the distracted Churches and the victims of ecclesiastical violence.

Leo had just the qualities to exalt the position of his great see in such a time of chaos. He formulated in new and daring language claims that through Peter he had supremacy in the Church. He developed the arguments to justify the powers that circumstances thrust upon the see. "The rule which governed Leo's conduct as Pope was a very simple one: it was to take every opportunity which offered itself for asserting and enforcing the authority of his see; he was not troubled with historical or Scriptural doubts or scruples which might cast a shadow of indecision . . . on his resolutions and actions."[1]

After the disgraceful doings at the second Ephesian Council, Leo besought the Emperor Theodosius to call a General Council in Italy. The Church of Rome still regarded a Council as the means to settle disputed articles of the faith. Theodosius declined. The new emperor, Marcian, brought about such a favourable change that Leo became strongly opposed to the project of a Council. When it was

[1] Gore, *Leo the Great*, p. 101.

called he acquiesced, but more than once expressed his dissatisfaction to the emperor.

The scope of the Council's deliberations, as well as its being held at all then, reveal the absence in the Church of any knowledge of the sovereign authority of Rome either in jurisdiction or doctrine. In more than one letter to the emperor Leo protested against doctrinal issues being treated at it. There must not be discussions as to what kind of faith is to be held.[1] He adjured the emperor in the name of Jesus Christ and besought him that he would not allow the faith to be brought into question.[2] He wrote similar deprecations of doctrinal discussions to the Council and told it that apostolic doctrine was most fully and luminously set forth in his letter to Flavian, i.e. the Tome.[3] The Council of Chalcedon paid no heed and enacted momentous doctrinal definitions.

We need not be surprised to find the Roman legates having the chief place at the Council of Chalcedon. Leo was the bishop of the first see. The Bishop of Constantinople had an unsatisfactory record. The Bishop of Alexandria was on trial and was deposed by the Council. Still it was, as the Acts of the Council show, a limited honour, for the imperial representatives were the real business presidents and frequently acted as such and exerted the final authority. The letter of the Council to Leo states: "The believing emperors presided for the sake of order."[4]

1

At the beginning of the proceedings the Roman legates demanded that Dioscurus, Bishop of Alexandria (who had excommunicated Leo), leave the Council. "Either he must retire or we depart." The imperial commissioners gave them the reproof. "If you hold the character of a judge you ought not to plead as an accuser." Eventually Dioscurus was placed in the middle of the assembly with his accuser. He had not the right to vote, but he took a very active part in the discussion.

Theodoret, Bishop of Cyrus, had been deposed at Dioscurus's Ephesian Council. He appealed to be judged by the bishops of the West. Leo declared his deposition invalid. When he appeared at the Council his right to sit was vehemently objected to. The bishops

[1] Mansi, vi, 113.
[2] Ibid., vi, 128.
[3] Ibid., vi, 134.
[4] Ibid., vi, 148.

at Chalcedon did not know that Leo "had full and supreme power of jurisdiction over the universal Church". Theodoret was only allowed for the time being to sit in the middle without the right of speech.

In the eighth session his case came forward again. Leo's restoration of him to his episcopal rights was directly ignored. The bishops eventually compelled him to clear himself of Nestorianism by pronouncing explicitly an anathema on Nestorius. It was only when he did so that he was accepted.

The condemnation of Dioscurus was decreed at the third session. The Roman legates who presided proposed his deprivation and gave their votes for it. They went on: "Now, therefore, the Synod will vote in accordance with the canons"—that is, the final judgment rested with the Council.

The bishops did not understand that a final infallible judgment had already been given, for they proceeded to give their votes individually. "I agree"; "I am of the same mind"; "I decree". Some associated their votes with the condemnation by "Leo and Anatolius, archbishops of the most holy Churches with whom I agree".[1] The sentence passed on Dioscurus ran in the name of "the holy and great Oecumenical Synod". He is "deposed by the holy Oecumenical Synod from the episcopal office". The whole authority to depose is expressly vested in the Council. "Dioscurus has been stripped of his episcopate by the Oecumenical Council."[2]

2

Before the 449 Council Leo wrote his celebrated doctrinal treatise called his Tome. It is the one outstanding document explanatory of the faith that the See of Rome has given to the ancient Church. Roman controversialists are accustomed to appeal to it as an exercise of the infallible teaching office. If any papal declaration is *ex cathedra* this is.

At the second session Leo's Tome was read, among other standard doctrinal utterances, as also were those of Cyril. Was it received by the Council as the voice of the infallible Father and Teacher of all Christians? Far from it. Some of the bishops were doubtful about parts of its teaching and declined to agree to it. A few days were asked for to consider its orthodoxy. The imperial

---

[1] Mansi, vi, 1047.   [2] Ibid., vi, 1099.

commissioners granted a delay of five days for examination and consultation.

When the matter came up again at the fourth session the critical bishops were found to be satisfied. Then the commissioners called on the Council to decide if the decisions of the Councils of Nicaea and Constantinople and the letter of Leo were in agreement.

Beginning with the Bishop of Constantinople, the bishops one by one gave their opinion that Leo's statement was orthodox. Some of them sanctioned it as agreeing with Cyril's theology. The former objecting bishops of Illyricum, in their subscription, said: "We are persuaded that the most holy Archbishop Leo is most orthodox; we have been instructed concerning his letter by his legates, Paschasinus and Lucentius, and they have cleared up the seeming difference which arose from modes of expression. . . . Being persuaded that the letter is perfectly agreeable to the faith of the Fathers, we gave our consent to it and subscribed it." The bishops of Palestine, who had also previously demurred, said they were satisfied with the legates' explanations and now assented to Leo's letter. One hundred and sixty-one bishops gave their consent, using phrases like: "It agrees and I therefore subscribe"; "I subscribe as it is correct"; "As I find it agrees"; "As far as I have been able to perceive". The remaining bishops sanctioned it by acclamation.

By its prolonged examination of Leo's theology and its careful expression of individual approval of his orthodoxy—and of his agreement with Cyril—the Council demonstrated in the most emphatic way that it knew nothing of the doctrine of infallibility attaching to *ex cathedra* papal definitions.

Bossuet's account is: "It was resolved to refer Leo's epistle to a legitimate examination of the Council." He concludes: "Thus the greatest unshakable strength is added to the apostolical decree after that it is confirmed by the investigation, examination, discussion and consequent agreement and testimony of the whole body."[1]

There is even higher corroboration than Bossuet's for this. Pope Vigilius himself has argued from the manner in which Leo's letter was received after being found "to agree with the doctrines set forth of the Nicene and Constantinopolitan Synods and also with the doctrines of the blessed Cyril in the first Ephesian Synod."[2]

The Council in its formal definition of faith puts its attitude to Leo's Tome beyond question and shows how it regarded that

[1] *Defensio*, vol. vii, chap. 17.   [2] *Constitutum*, Mansi, ix, 473.

utterance as on a level with Cyril's. "The holy Synod receives the Synodal epistles of the blessed Cyril both to Nestorius and to the Easterns. . . . With these the Synod has reasonably combined the letter sent by the most blessed and holy Leo, archbishop of the great and older city Rome . . . inasmuch as it is in accordance with the confession of St. Peter and fitted to oppose error and strengthen orthodox doctrines."[1]

In fact at this Council Cyril is regarded as the orthodox standard. Leo and others are hailed as being in harmony with him. "Leo says the same as Cyril; Celestine affirms what Cyril says; Xystus affirms what Cyril says."[2]

Very remarkable also is the allocution sent to the emperor by the Council. It is a defence of Leo's Tome! Leo is praised as a champion given by God to the Synod. No one, therefore, must accuse his letter as being contrary to the canons. "Leo has in fact altered nothing in the faith proclaimed by the Fathers." In proof of Leo's orthodoxy citations are added from several of the Fathers, including Cyril.[3]

Providing tests for the new Bishop of Constantinople's orthodoxy Leo wrote: "Let him not scorn to examine my letter which he will find entirely agreeing with the piety of the Fathers."[4] Writing to the Empress Pulcheria, he requires Anatolius to acquiesce in Cyril's letter or (vel) assent to his.[5] After Chalcedon he claimed the authority of the Council for his Tome.[6]

3

At its fifteenth session the Council decreed its famous twenty-eighth canon. "We following in all things the ordinances of the holy Fathers, and recognising the recently read canon of the one hundred and fifty religious bishops [i.e. of the Council of Constantinople], do ourselves adopt the same determination and resolution in regard to the privileges of the most holy Church of Constantinople, New Rome. For the Fathers properly rendered privileges to the see of elder Rome on account of it being the imperial city; moved by the same opinion the one hundred and fifty religious bishops awarded the same privileges to the most holy See of New

---

[1] Mansi, vii, 113.
[2] Ibid., vii, 104.
[3] Ibid., vii, 456 f.

[4] Migne. P. L. 54: 891.
[5] Ibid. P. L. 54: 894.
[6] Ibid. P. L. 54: 1052.

Rome judging with good reason that the city which is honoured with the sovereignty and the Synod and which enjoys the same privileges as the elder imperial city of Rome should also in ecclesiastical concerns be magnified as she, holding the second place after her."

It is obvious how this canon strikes away the foundations from the papal theory for the primacy of Rome. It attributes the privileges to the action of the Church and explains the reason as the civil greatness of Rome. It assigns in the same way and for the same reason equal privileges to Constantinople, Rome having the precedence. Such a regulation would be unthinkable if the Fathers knew that "by the appointment of our Lord the Roman Church possesses a superiority of ordinary power over all other Churches".[1] On papal theories the General Council of Chalcedon is guilty of little less than blasphemy.

The Roman legates had absented themselves from the session at which this canon was passed. Notice about it was given at the preceding session. Probably they knew they would be outvoted.

At the following session they requested from the presidents permission to speak.[2]

They complained of what was passed in their absence. It was explained that everything was done regularly, and the canon was read with one hundred and ninety-two signatures, including those of the Bishops of Antioch, Jerusalem and Heraclea. A Roman legate then alleged that the bishops were coerced or surprised into signing it. This was indignantly denied. Then the legate fell back on the plea that the ordinances of Nicaea had been set aside and those of Constantinople followed. He denied the validity of the latter canons. The remarkable thing is that he never brought forward the plea of the God-given authority of Rome. The presidents asked for the canons to be produced. The Roman legate then read a corrupted form of the sixth canon of Nicaea with the words interpolated: "The Roman See has always held the primacy."

By this or a similar fraud Leo induced the Emperor Valentinian in the famous rescript to assert "the authority of the holy Synod" for the primacy of Rome. He tried to influence Theodosius by the same reprehensible device. He claimed that the decrees of the Nicene canons, drawn up by the bishops of the whole world, gave

[1] Vatican Decrees, chap. 3.   [2] Mansi, vii, 425.

him the right to hear appeals.[1] He even said he was sending a copy of them to Theodosius. Under his tutelage Valentinian[2] wrote similarly, and Valentinian's mother, Galla Placidia, was induced to write, basing the claim as being "in accordance with the provisions of the Nicene Synod".[3] The exposure of the fraud in the time of Zosimus leaves Leo without excuse. He "reproduced what he must have known to be the detected misquotation of Sardican canons as 'Nicene' ".[4] That at such an early date there should be a falsification of even the Nicene canons in Rome is ominous of the forgeries to come.

When the legate had finished, the authentic text was read. The polite Greek bishops abstained from comment just as they were wont to do when Roman legates at General Councils indulged in grandiloquent pretensions for their see. Then the relevant canon of Constantinople was read.

Nor was the position of the legates improved when the commissioners asked the bishops if they had voluntarily agreed. They solemnly declared they had. The commissioners gave their decisions that the first rank of all and the chief honour be preserved for the archbishop of old Rome but that the archbishop of New Rome was to have the same prerogatives of honour and have the rights specified in the canon. They asked the Synod to express its mind, and the canon was passed with acclamations. Lucentius, a Roman legate, hotly protested. "The Apostolic See cannot be humiliated in our presence." He demanded that the resolution be rescinded. The commissioners curtly replied: "Our proposition has been ratified by the Council." As Duchesne writes, the legates "could do nothing more than protest".[5]

Pope Leo, when he heard the news, protested vehemently. He wrote to the emperor, the empress, and the Archbishop of Constantinople. The archbishop was severely scolded. It is interesting to find Leo rebuking the prelate of Constantinople for ambition and recommending him to practise modesty and humility.

The Easterns wrote in their most conciliatory and flattering strain to Leo. These fulsome Oriental compliments are much stressed by Roman writers, forgetful of similar language used to others. They dreaded that Leo might not assent to the dogmatic decrees of the

[1] Mansi, vi, 18.   [3] Ibid., vi, 51.
[2] Ibid., vi, 50.
[4] Bright, *Waymarks in Church History*, p. 213.
[5] *Early History*, vol. iii, p. 321.

Council. Opposition to them in Egypt and the East was rife and was growing into disastrous calamities for the Church. They did not want their work discredited by the Western Church disavowing it and so more disunion caused. Leo sanctioned the dogmatic decrees, but refused to acknowledge the offending canon. The Archbishop of Constantinople went on quietly exercising the rights the canon gave, and Leo's opposition was disregarded in practice. In spite of him the See of Constantinople has ranked since as the second in the Church, and the Council of Constantinople stands universally revered as the Second General Council. In 690 the Council in Trullo confirmed the exact words of the canon. At the Fourth Lateran Council (1215) it was decreed that the Latin Patriarch of Constantinople should rank immediately after Rome.

Bishop Gore, reviewing the bearing of the Council of Chalcedon on the phenomenon of papal authority, writes: "When Pope Pius IX proclaimed, 'with the consent of the hóly Vatican Council, that the personal infallibility of the Pope was a 'dogma divinely revealed' and his 'definitions are irreformable of themselves and not by the consent of the Church', and proclaimed also that in announcing the dogma he was but 'faithfully adhering to the tradition received from the first beginnings of the Christian faith', he is using language which in the light of history we can simply call unintelligible."[1] He adds that the Papacy "represents also the conscious effort of personal ambition and fraudulent dealing".

[1] *Leo the Great*, pp. 125, 126.

CHAPTER XL

POPE VIGILIUS

The Council of Chalcedon did not bring peace to the Church. The Tome of Leo was rejected over much of the East and in nearly all Egypt. The Emperor Justinian endeavoured to heal the injurious divisions and placate the Monophysites by condemning (1) Theodore of Mopsuestia and his writing, (2) certain writings of Theodoret, (3) and of Ibas. So arose the controversy of the "Three Chapters".

Vigilius, Bishop of Rome (537–55), had obtained his position by pledging himself to support the Monophysite schemes of the empress. Hefele states that the empress promised Vigilius "the papal dignity on condition that he would again reinstate Anthimus of Constantinople, and declare against the Synod of Chalcedon".[1]

Having obtained the Popedom by such nefarious means, involving the deposition and death of his predecessor, he declined to carry out his pledges. His subsequent conduct displays him as a man of deceit and dishonour.

The Western Church was strongly opposed to the imperial policy. The emperor compelled Vigilius to come to Constantinople. Arriving there, Vigilius refused to condemn the Three Chapters and rejected communion with Mennas, Patriarch of Constantinople, and with those who had signed the edict. The Patriarch of Constantinople in turn excommunicated the Pope. Before long Vigilius turned right round and wrote to the emperor anathematising the Three Chapters. In 548 he issued his celebrated *Judicatum* in which he formally anathematised the Three Chapters.

Violent opposition to the Pope's decree ensued. He excommunicated two of his Roman deacons and several other clergy. The bishops of Illyria met and pronounced for the Three Chapters. The Church of Africa excommunicated the Pope for his *Judicatum* until he would do penance.[2]

[1] Hefele, *History of the Councils*, vol. iii, p. 457.
[2] Ibid., vol. iv, p. 264 (E. T.).

Vigilius again turned round and withdrew the *Judicatum*. The emperor promised a Council. Without waiting for the Synod Justinian renewed his edict. Vigilius fled to the basilica of St. Peter in Constantinople and again excommunicated Mennas and others "in the person and authority of the blessed Peter the Apostle". The presence of several Western bishops gave him temporary courage. The emperor ordered him to be forcibly removed from the basilica and he was mishandled by the soldiers while clinging to the altar. Under an oath of protection he left the church next day. Finding fresh grounds for fear of molestation he fled to the famous church of St. Euphemia in Chalcedon.

Futile negotiations ensued about the calling of a Council. It met without the Pope's consent in 553 in Constantinople. The Pope refused to attend. Eutychius, the new Bishop of Constantinople, presided. Yet this Council is held by the Roman Church to be the Fifth General Council.

During its sitting Vigilius drew up his *Constitutum*, which he sent to the emperor. By this time Justinian held him in well-deserved contempt and refused personally to receive it, sending back the answer: "If you have in this condemned the Three Chapters I have no need of this new document, for I have from you many others of the same content. If, however, you have in this new document departed from your earlier declarations you have condemned yourself."[1]

Justinian forwarded to the Council documents proving the shameless vacillations of the Pope. In the *Constitutum* the Pope defended the person of Theodore and the writings of Theodoret and Ibas and appealed to the Council of Chalcedon and to the judgment of Popes Leo and Simplicius. The decree ends with the solemn warning: "We ordain and decree that it be permitted to no one belonging to any ecclesiastical order or office to write or bring forward or compose or teach anything contrary to the contents of this *Constitutum* in regard to the Three Chapters, or after this present definition to move any further question. And if anything has been done, said or written by anyone anywhere about the Three Chapters contrary to what we here assert and decree . . . this in all ways we refute by the authority of the Apostolic See in which by the grace of God we preside."[2]

If this is not a formal *ex cathedra* utterance concerning the faith

[1] Mansi, ix, 349.   [2] P. L. 69: 112.

for the guidance of the whole Church, what can be? It uses the technical term "define" and was meant to be final.

Bishop Maret writes: "It is not possible to doubt that this decree was a solemn judgment of the Holy See, a judgment invested with all its authority. . . . The decree bears on matters of faith or on dogmatic facts. . . . It contains the most formal orders and is addressed to a Council which regards itself as General."[1] He shows that it abounds in anathemas.

The Council, in utter disregard and repudiation of the Pope's authority, proceeded to give their decision as those "to whom is committed the charge of ruling the Church of the Lord".[2] They condemned and anathematised Theodore and "his impious writings, likewise all that which Theodoret wrote impiously against the true faith. . . . Besides this we anathematise the impious letter which Ibas is said to have written to Maris . . . we also anathematise the Three Chapters named . . . together with their defenders who declare the Three Chapters to be right and who sought or shall seek to protect their impiety by the names of holy Fathers or of the Council of Chalcedon". Fourteen formal anathemas follow in which in detail the defenders of Theodore and of the writings of Theodoret and Ibas are condemned.

The Pope fell under more than one of these anathemas. The significant decree was added: "If any one ventures to deliver or to teach or to write anything in opposition to our pious ordinances, if he be bishop or cleric he shall lose his bishopric or office." The Pope's name was struck off the diptychs of the Church of Constantinople and he was probably banished.

In about six months Vigilius again turned round—for the fourth time. He made an ignominious submission and fully agreed with the findings of the Council in direct contradiction of his official decree in the *Constitutum*. In fact he ascribed his (*ex cathedra*) teaching to the Devil. "No one is ignorant of the scandals which the enemy of the human race excites in all the world. How he is active to carry through in every way all his designs for the overthrowing the Church of God that is spread through the whole world. He incites to putting forth divergent things, sometimes in speaking, sometimes in writing, not only in his own name but even in ours and in that of others. Thus he has attempted by tricks, craftiness and wicked deceit to separate us ourselves who are at

---

[1] *Du Concile-Général*, vol. i, p. 268.   [2] Mansi, **ix**, 368.

one with our brethren and fellow bishops dwelling in the royal
city. . . . In order that we who were and are united with them in
brotherly love and in the constituted faith might wander into
discord."

He goes on to tell that now all confusion is removed from his
mind and that Christ is recalling His Church to peace. He argues
that it is not discredit'.ble to retract one's judgment when something may have been omitted that afterwards by further study is
found. He cites the example of the blessed Augustine for altering
his views. He, incited by such examples, continued investigating
what was more exactly to be found in the Fathers about the Three
Chapters. So now he anathematises Theodore and the writings of
Theodoret and Ibas and finds they are blasphemous.

"Also we subject to the same anathema anyone who believes that
the Three Chapters could be supported or defended or who try to
overthrow the present condemnation. But all those who, holding
the right faith declared by the Synods, have condemned or do condemn the Three Chapters we define to be brothers and fellow priests.
What things were done by myself or by others in defence of the
aforesaid Three Chapters, by this our present definition we declare
void."[1]

A man could scarcely put forth a more grovelling and abject
repudiation of his own decisions. The Pope adopted the very words
in which the Council had condemned his views. Yet the Vatican
Decrees require us to believe that the Pope is the infallible Father
and Teacher of all Christians—that his definitions are irreformable
of themselves. The Vatican Decrees adduce a Statement of Pope
Nicholas: "It is allowed to none to revise its judgment and to sit
in judgment upon what it has judged."[2] The fifth General Council
not only judged and anathematised a Pope's solemn judgments but
the Pope prostrated himself before the judgment of the Council.
As Bishop Maret states it, the Council "regarded as void this Act
of Vigilius, and its sentence on a principal matter differed essentially
from that of Vigilius. The Council declared *impious* and *heretical*
this letter of Ibas which the Pope declared orthodox; and the sentence of the Council triumphed over the sentence of the Pope, since
the Pope retreated and annulled his own to confirm that of the
Council. Here arises a very delicate but inevitable question. What
was the authority of a Council which, in presence of a Pontifical

[1] P. L. 69: 122 ff.   [2] chap. 4 note.

decision, took a contrary decision, excommunicated its opponents and finished by recalling the Pope to its doctrine?"[1]

By his recantation the Pope purchased the restoration of his see. But as at the Council the Eastern bishops repudiated the pronouncement of the Pope, so now did Western ones. The Church of Northern Italy headed by the Archbishops of Aquileia and Milan formally broke off communion with Rome and rejected at a Synod the condemnation of the Three Chapters. They regarded Vigilius's successor Pelagius as a heretic for his agreement with the Council.[2] The schism lasted for over a century. The African Church also maintained its opposition.

The history of Pope Vigilius is an insurmountable barrier to the acceptance of Roman claims. It reduces them to absurdity. Apologists like Dom Chapman, while angrily abandoning the character of Vigilius ("His shameful pontificate";[3] "No one respected Vigilius nor did he deserve respect"; "His changes of policy rendered obedience impossible"; "His shilly-shallying brought the Papacy to humiliation"; "The weakness of the wretched Vigilius"), yet had the temerity to assume that "no objections to papal infallibility can possibly be based on the case of Pope Vigilius".[4] He does not face the fact that the infallible Pope, with the full force of all his official authority, repeatedly contradicted himself and that finally he submitted to and adopted the decrees of the Council which anathematised his decisions.

The *Catholic Encyclopedia*, with less candour, passes very lightly over this part of Vigilius's history. It omits all mention of the *Judicatum* and of the details of his submission to the Council. It is content to let its readers know that Vigilius "wavered frequently in his measures".[5]

---

[1] *Du Concile-Général*, vol. i, p. 269.
[2] Hefele, *History of the Councils*, vol. iv, p. 355 (E. T.).
[3] *Studies on the Early Papacy*, p. 227.
[4] *The First Eight General Councils*, pp. 53–9.
[5] vol. xv, p. 428.

CHAPTER XLI

ST. COLUMBANUS

The ancient Celtic Church did not know of obedience being due to Rome. Until the eighth century it maintained its own customs (as the time of Easter and form of tonsure) in defiance of Roman authority. The influence of the invading Danes, who became Christians, prepared the way for the growth of Roman prestige.[1] Not until the twelfth century did the Celtic Church of Ireland enter into formal relation with Rome by the acceptance of the Palls from Pope Eugenius III. John Paparo, who attended the Synod of Kells in 1152, was the first *legatus a latere* to come from Rome to Ireland. The Norman Conquest later in the century completed the overthrow of the Celtic Church as an independent organism.[2] Kenney writes that the plot which lies at the centre of Bede's History is "the struggle between the Irish and Roman forms of Church discipline for control of the British Isles".[3]

Columbanus of Bangor, Co. Down, was born in the first half of the sixth century. He was the most distinguished missionary of his era. There are two letters of his extant to Bishops of Rome which demonstrate how far he was from regarding them as Vicars of Christ and infallible Teachers.

Whilst in France he came into conflict with the bishops there, who objected to his Celtic observance of Easter. He wrote a letter to Pope Gregory the Great, calling on him in arbitrary fashion to sanction or at least tolerate the Irish custom. The letter is naturally written in respectful terms to the great Prelate of the Western Apostolic See, but it does not conceal his conviction that the Pope will err grievously, and be repudiated by the Irish if he decides otherwise. "He summonses so to speak the Pope to pronounce" for his cause.[4]

---

[1] Cf. Gougaud, *Les Chrétientés Celtiques* (2nd edition), p. 356.
[2] See my *Independence of the Celtic Church in Ireland*, chap. xiv.
[3] *The Sources for the Early History of Ireland*, vol. i, p. 230.
[4] Gougaud, *Les Chrétientés Celtiques*, p. 182.

He believed (mistakenly) that Jerome had approved of the Irish computation and warns the Pope to be careful "that there be no disagreement between yourself and Jerome. . . . For plainly I confess to you that the man who contradicts the authority of St. Jerome will be looked upon as a heretic and rejected with scorn by the Churches in the West."[1] This is not the utterance of a man who was taught to believe in either the supreme jurisdiction or the infallibility of the Pope.

Later, in his great Monastery of Bobbio in Northern Italy, Columbanus became involved in the "Three Chapters" controversy. He wrote to the then Pope, Boniface IV, at the request of the King of the Lombards, calling on him in the most peremptory and threatening way to dissociate himself from the position adopted by the Roman See. The letter, at the same time, abounds in extravagant terms of adulation. Columbanus shared the tendency to rhetoric of his race.

He declares that it is grief rather than presumption that compels him to tell the Pope that the name of God is blasphemed through him among the Gentiles. "For I am pained, I confess, at the infamy to the chair of holy Peter."[2] The Irish, though dwelling at the end of the earth, are all disciples of St. Peter and St. Paul. The Pope is told to preserve the apostolic faith in order that he may not lack apostolic honour.[3] He is exhorted to let "the occasion of schism be cut off immediately with the knife, as we may say, of St. Peter, that is, by a true confession of the faith in a Synod, and by the abominating and anathematising of all heretics; that so you may cleanse the chair of St. Peter from all error, if there have been any, as they say, introduced—if not, that its purity may be acknowledged by all. For it is a painful and lamentable thing if the Catholic faith be not held in the Apostolic See".[4]

At the time this letter was written the Church of North Italy had formally renounced communion with the Bishops of Rome and regarded them as fallen into heresy by their agreeing to the condemnation of the Three Chapters. Columbanus has no conception of the Pope being himself the infallible Teacher by whom alone all questions of faith must be decided. "Therefore I beseech you, for Christ's sake, clear your reputation which is mangled among the nations, lest it be accounted to you for perfidy by the envious if

---

[1] P. L. 80: 261, 262.
[2] P. L. 80: 275.
[3] P. L. 80: 276.
[4] P. L. 80: 278.

you continue to be silent. Cease then further to dissimulate. Cease
to be silent. . . . Dispel confusion from the face of your children
and disciples who are confounded on your account. And, what is
more serious, that the fog of suspicion may be lifted from the chair
of Peter. Convoke, therefore, an assembly in order to clear yourself
of the things which are alleged against you, for it is no child's play
that is alleged." The action of Vigilius at the fifth General Council
is severely reflected on and his successor is told: "If you know
Vigilius himself to have died so infected why do you against conscience attest him? . . . Now to you belongs the blame if you
have gone astray from the true faith and made void your first faith.
It is on just grounds that your juniors resist you and on just grounds
that they refuse to communicate with you until the memory of the
wicked be effaced and consigned to oblivion. For if there be in all
this more of certainty than fable, your sons are in their turn changed
to be the head and you to the tail, which indeed is painful to be
said. Therefore also shall they be your judges who have always
maintained the orthodox faith, whoever they may be, even should
they appear to be your juniors."[1] The Pope is enjoined to cease to
support heretics, and his opponents to cease to support men of
suspicious character. Both should mutually ask pardon for the
prolonged discord; "And as both have been blameworthy you may
the sooner come to an agreement."

Columbanus apologises for his plainness of speech as being the
custom of his country. "For with us it is not persons but reason
which prevails." He refers to the ancient national glory of Rome
and how the city has become more illustrious on account of the
twin (geminos) Apostles of Christ, Peter and Paul. "You are almost
celestial, and Rome is the head of the Churches of the world, saving
the singular prerogative of the place of the Lord's resurrection.
And as great is your honour through the dignity of your chair
so great care is required by you that you lose not your dignity
through some perversity. For the power will be with you just so
long as right reason continues. For he is the real keeper of the
keys of the kingdom of heaven who through true knowledge opens
to the worthy and shuts to the unworthy. Otherwise, if he acts in
a contrary way he will have power neither to open nor to shut.
These principles then being true and admitted beyond all contradiction by everyone who rightly knows the truth, although it be

[1] P. L. 80: 279.

understood by all, and no man is ignorant how our Saviour bestowed on St. Peter the keys of the kingdom. If you perchance on account of this assume some arrogance (*superciliosum*) as if you had greater authority than others or more power in divine matters, be assured that your power shall be less in the sight of God if you even harbour such a thought in your mind."[1]

"To return to the point from which I have digressed, let me beg of you, seeing that many are doubtful of the purity of your faith, to remove speedily this tarnish from the lustre of the Holy See. For this existing rumour of fickleness is not fitting to the dignity of the Church of Rome, as if she may be moved by any influence from the solid ground of the true faith."[2] He tells how at his first arrival in Italy he received a letter from a certain person warning "that I must be on my guard against you as having lapsed into the sect of Nestorius".

The Vatican Council's assertion that its claims are in accordance with "the ancient and constant faith of the universal Church" is contradicted by the illustrious representative of the Celtic Church, St. Columbanus. In his bold, independent attitude towards the authority of Rome he is in harmony with the Celtic Church through centuries of its renown, before and after his time.

[1] P. L. 80: 280.   [2] P. L. 80: 282.

CHAPTER XLII

POPE HONORIUS

The condemnation for heresy of Honorius, who became Bishop of Rome in 625, is one of the most signal and irrefutable evidences that a Pope in his official teaching is not exempt from error. In the face of it the Vatican Decrees' claim that "the see of Holy Peter remains forever unstained by any error" is untenable.

The Monophysite schism continued to divide the Church and the Empire with tragic results. Bishops and emperors were constantly seeking to bring back the lost unity.

Cyrus, Patriarch of Alexandria, succeeded in obtaining a considerable measure of union by a formula which was a compromise. Sergius, Patriarch of Constantinople, gladly approved, but Sophronius, a learned monk who became Patriarch of Jerusalem, opposed it. Sergius wrote a "dogmatic letter" to Honorius of Rome, giving his reasons at length for favouring the proposed formula. He formally asked Honorius to signify his view through his "holy letters" on the theological issue involved.

The reply of the Bishop of Rome was definitely heretical in a two-fold way. He pronounced for the compromise and declared his full agreement with the views of Sergius. He wrote, definitely, "we confess one will of our Lord Jesus Christ"[1] and rejected the use of either of the expressions one or two "energies" or "operations" in Christ. Honorius concludes his letter: "These things your fraternity will preach with us as we ourselves preach them like-minded with you."[2]

The Monothelite ("one will") heresy resulted, which was to inflict grievous ills on an already distracted and confused Christendom. It minimised or abrogated the human nature of Christ.

It is the responsibility of Honorius that he not only sanctioned this heresy but was one of its chief fomenters.[3] The

[1] Mansi, xi, 539.
[2] Ibid., xi, 545.
[3] Dom Chapman fully admits that, in his *The Condemnation of Pope Honorius*, "the result of his letter was the so-called heresy of Monothelitism" (p. 17).

authorities who spread it appealed to the sanction of Sergius and him.

This was just the occasion when the vicegerent of God should have used his "charisma of truth and never failing faith". The Patriarch of the second see in the Church consulted him in a matter vital to the faith. The Patriarch of the fifth see was in doctrinal conflict with the Patriarchs of the second and third sees.

Honorius was not appealed to in his private capacity. He gave his decision officially as Bishop of Rome. After his letter to Sergius, the orthodox Patriarch of Jerusalem sent him and other bishops a defence of the faith, but Honorius wrote again to Sergius, maintaining his error in dogmatic terms. "These things we have decided to make manifest by the present letters to your most holy fraternity for the instruction of those in perplexity. Moreover, as regards the ecclesiastical dogma (*quantum ad dogma ecclesiasticum*) and what we ought to hold and teach, on account of the simplicity of man and to avoid controversies, we must, as I have already said, define neither one nor two operations in the mediator between God and man.[1] . . . We must not define or preach one or two operations . . . and these things we have decided to make manifest to your most blessed fraternity in order that by putting forward of one confession we may show ourselves to be of the same mind as your Holiness, clearly agreeing in one spirit with a like teaching of the faith. . . . And we have written to our common brethren, Cyrus and Sophronius, that they may not persist in the new expression of one or two energies."[2] Honorius left nothing undone to proclaim authoritatively what the Church was to believe.

His dogmatic teaching has been condemned as completely and ignominiously as any heretic's could be.

(1) Pope St. Martin I held the first Lateran Synod in Rome in 649. This Synod is described by Chapman as "a Council in importance the rival, in authority the equal of Oecumenical Synods, and in interest the superior of many of them".[3] The Council condemned, under anathema, anyone who following the wicked heretics should

---

"The emperor's 'Echthesis', which imposed the heresy on the Church, enforces the decision of Honorius" (p. 24). "It was simply modelled on the first letter of Honorius" (p. 25).

[1] Mansi, xi, 579.   [2] Ibid., xi, 582.
[3] *The Condemnation of Pope Honorius*, p. 48.

confess one will and one operation in Christ. It declared there were two wills and two operations in Him—the contrary to Honorius's teaching.[1] In repudiating the teachers of the heresy by name it omitted by a "conspiracy of silence" the name of Honorius. "The Pope betrays his consciousness that he was implicitly condemning one of his predecessors."[2]

(2) The sixth General Council (Constantinople III) was called by Emperor Constantine Pogonatus and presided over by him, in 680. It judged that as the teachings of Sergius and Honorius were entirely alien from apostolic dogmas and followed the false doctrines of heretics, "we altogether reject them and execrate them as soul-destroying and we have judged that the very names of those whose impious doctrines we execrate should be cast out of the Holy Church of God. . . . With them also we have judged that Honorious, who was Pope of elder Rome, should be together with them cast out of the Holy Church of God, and be anathematised together with them because we have found from the letter written by him to Sergius that in all things he followed his mind and confirmed his impious dogmas".[3] It is to be noted that the Greek word used here (κυρώσαντα) has the sense of authoritative confirmation.

The Council exclaimed: "Anathema to the heretic Sergius! Anathema to the heretic Honorius!"[4] It included "Honorius, who was Pope of ancient Rome" among the instruments the Devil found apt for his purpose in teaching one will and operation.[5] The conciliar decree was signed by the papal legates and all the bishops. The Council ordered the writings of the heretics, including Honorius's second letter, to be burned as impious and hurtful to the soul.

(3) The Council in its letter to Pope Agatho stated: "Those who erred concerning the faith we have slain by our anthemas . . . according to the previous condemnation pronounced on them in your holy letters."[6] Among the heretics named is Honorius.

(4) The emperor, in his decree giving effect to its decisions, wrote: "We anathematise and reject those also who are the heretical promoters and patrons of the superfluous and new dogmas." He names among these "Honorius, who was Pope of elder Rome, who in

[1] Mansi, x, 1155.
[2] Chapman, *The Condemnation of Pope Honorius*, p. 51.
[3] Mansi, xi, 553, 556.
[4] Ibid., xi, 621.
[5] Ibid., xi, 636.
[6] Ibid., xi, 684.

N

all things promoted and co-operated with and confirmed their heresy".[1]

(5) Pope Leo II, in a letter to the emperor confirming the decrees of the Council, admits the heretical pollution of the Roman See. He anathematises, among others, "Honorius, who did not attempt to sanctify this apostolic Church with the teaching of apostolical tradition but by profane treachery tried to subvert its spotless faith"[2] (*profana proditione*).

(6) Pope Leo, writing to the Spanish bishops, states that "those who had been traitors against the purity of apostolical traditions, those who are gone, have been punished with eternal condemnation, that is Theodore . . . with Honorius, who did not extinguish the flame of heretical dogma but fanned it by his negligence".[3]

(7) The same Pope, Leo II, writing to the Spanish king, is even more definite. Mentioning the heretics who have been cast out of the unity of the Catholic Church, he goes on: "Together with them Honorius, Bishop of Rome, who consented that the immaculate rule of apostolical tradition which he had received from his predecessors, should be polluted."[4] He classes Honorius with Arius, Apollinarius, Nestorius, Eutyches, etc., as endeavouring shamelessly to defend heretical doctrine.

(8) The seventh and eighth General Councils renewed the condemnation of Honorius.

(9) The *Liber Diurnus* contains the oaths that had to be taken by every new Bishop of Rome from the eighth century to the eleventh. All the Popes in this period—at least over fifty—solemnly pronounced an eternal anathema on certain heretics, "together with Honorius, who added fuel to their wicked assertions".

The condemnation of Honorius was included in the Roman Breviary for 28th June. Every priest of the Church of Rome thus for centuries had the heresy of a Pope in his sacred manual. Why was the condemnation omitted in the sixteenth century? Bossuet, referring to this erasing of the name "in our own age", the efforts to suppress the *Liber Diurnus*, and other devices, observes: "A cause is clearly lamentable which needs to be defended by such figments."[5]

---

[1] Mansi, xi, 710.   [3] Ibid., xi, 1052.
[2] Ibid., xi, 731.   [4] Ibid., xi, 1057.
[5] *Defensio Declarationis Cleri Gallicani*, pars iii, lib. vii, chap. 26.

The case of Honorius is fatal to the infallibility dogma. The attempts of Romanists to explain it away are many and self-contradictory.

(1) Some like Baronius and Bellarmine put forward (*more Romano*) a charge of falsifications of documents. This is not now taken seriously. Hefele has scarcely troubled to show its absurdity.

(2) Another excuse was to throw the blame on Honorius's secretary as misunderstanding or wilfully misrepresenting him.

(3) Others tried to shift the condemnation from the sixth General Council to the Quinisext.

(4) Others pleaded Honorius was condemned only for leniency to heresy. This was resorted to by important writers. The Council may have, it is urged, condemned him by mistake.

(5) Cardinal Manning boldly states that the two epistles of Honorius "are entirely orthodox", that he was only "censured" (sic.) for "omission of apostolic authority".[1]

(6) The favourite plea in modern days—as by Dom. Chapman—seems to be that he was speaking in his private capacity and not *ex cathedra*. This is as hopeless a defence as the others. "The question was put to him as Pope, and he answered as Pope, in the same tone and style in which his predecessors Celestine and Leo had answered on dogmatic questions."[2] It was not, however, as a private Roman theologian that the Patriarch of Constantinople asked for "holy letters" from him on the doctrinal issue at stake. Hefele, the supreme authority in the Roman Church on the Councils, rejects this plea. "Honorius intended to give to the Church of Constantinople and *implicite* to the whole Church an instruction on doctrine and faith."[3] He points out that, expressly dealing with "ecclesiastical dogma", Honorius uses the word "define". This is the word on which Roman theological experts attempt to attach exaggerated technical significance. We have seen from the authoritative language that Honorius used how he conceived himself prescribing the doctrine that should be held. Dom. Chapman, however, is so pleased with his expedient that he gaily writes: "On the whole I conclude that no Council has by acts and words more fully recognised the authority and infallibility of Rome than the

[1] *Petri Privelegium*, p. 223.
[2] Cardinal Luzerne, quoted by Dollinger, *Fables About the Popes of the Middle Ages*, p. 249.
[3] *History of the Councils*, vol. v, p. 61 (E. T.).

sixth Council which condemned—rightly condemned—Pope Honorius."[1] It was not as merely expressing private opinions that Pope Leo II branded Honorius for having by profane treachery allowed the immaculate Church of his predecessors to be polluted.

The theory of an infallible Guide to protect the Church from error is rendered meaningless by those Romanists who insist on laying down all sorts of rules to contract—and in practice, virtually—to guard against admitting "infallible" utterances. The experts are not even agreed among themselves as to these rules. Dom. Chapman adds another to those often enumerated—Honorius cannot have been speaking *ex cathedra*; he "utters no anathema".[2] These refinements are obvious subterfuges for getting rid of indefensible papal decisions. They illustrate Salmon's remark: "The pope is always infallible except when he makes a mistake."[3] It is as if the admirers of a physician maintained he had an infallible remedy for a certain disease; and when the patients who used it died made the excuse that in such cases the physician had not supplied the unfailing remedy.

The sixth General Council expressly noted that the original letter of Sergius was a "dogmatic" one. The reply would obviously be of the same sort. "The Pope speaks *ex cathedra* and as universal Teacher when, speaking with supreme authority as Pope in an official document, he proposes and appoints something to be observed, avoided or believed, and instructs the universal Church about some dogma." "*Ex cathedra* means nothing more than *ex cathedra*."[4]

Membership of the Roman Church involves believing the dogma of Papal infallibility with the same faith as belief in the Incarnation;[5] and also of believing that this dogma is "the ancient and constant faith of the universal Church"; and that the Fathers and orthodox Doctors venerated and followed the Apostolic doctrine of the Popes, "knowing most fully that this see of holy Peter remains ever free from all blemish of error".[6]

A recent Anglican writer, zealous for the prestige of the Papacy, wavers between the old discredited attempts to explain away the

---

[1] *The First Eight General Councils and Papal Infallibility*, p. 67.
[2] *The Condemnation of Pope Honorius*, 17ᴰ.
[3] *Infallibility of the Church* (3rd edition), p. 444.
[4] Renouf, *The Case of Pope Honorius*, pp. 73, 74, 77.
[5] Encyclical of Pius XI, *On Fostering True Religious Union*, p. 12.
[6] Vatican Decrees, Pastor Aeternus and chap. 4.

condemnation of Honorius.[1] He distinguishes between Honorius
and his secretary—surely the most puerile of all the excuses. He says
it was on the ground of negligence that Pope Leo II justified the condemnation.[2] One has only to read the evidence already cited to see
how inaccurate this is. He doubts the justice of the Council's Condemnation.[3] The unchallenged facts are that three General Councils
branded Honorius as a heretic, that the Roman Council of 649
condemned the teaching he promulgated, that the Popes for centuries pronounced an eternal anathema on him for his positive
heresy. These facts show how the Church repudiated him as a heretic.
Dr. Jalland and others may by the exercise of private judgment re-
pudiate the Councils as wrong. The all-important point is that an
oecumenical Council included Honorius in a list of anathematised
heretics. That demonstrates that the Church in the latter part of the
seventh century had no conception of papal infallibility.

It is noteworthy how Dr. Jalland refrains from quoting the terms
of the Councils' denunciations of Honorius; and also from quoting
the most offending parts of Honorius's writings (for example, *unam
voluntatem fatemur Domini nostri Jesu Christi*). The only extract Dr.
Jalland cites from the proceedings of the sixth General Council are
a fulsome laudation of the Roman See and Pope Agatho. The
Orientals could cynically hear and participate in praise of the Roman
See while in practice solemnly execrating the "impious" "soul-
destroying" doctrines of a bishop of that see and anathematising
him and ordering his pernicious writings to be burned.

Dr. Jalland has, however, felt it necessary to invent a strange, new
plea for Honorius. "The Pope was actually discussing a psychological
problem."[4] The Easterns were "concerned with metaphysics".
He cannot bring himself to admit Honorius taught heresy. "It was
believed by the Easterns and others" that he supported the doctrine
of a "single will". "If Honorius was to blame"; "his supposed
Monothelitism."

The dropping of the condemnation of Honorius from the formula
sworn to by the Popes for three centuries gives pleasure to Dr.
Jalland. "None of them before Gregory VII had the wit or perhaps

[1] Jalland, *The Church and the Papacy*, p. 363.
[2] "If Leo meant this he would have been mistaken. Honorius did positively
approve the letter of Sergius as the Council pointed out" (Chapman, *The Condemnation of Pope Honorius*, p. 114).
[3] Jalland, *The Church and the Papacy*, p. 366.
[4] Ibid., p. 363.

the courage" to do so. The suppression of awkward facts is generally otherwise regarded. Lord Acton's account of the transaction is: "When it was discovered in the manuscript of the *Liber Diurnus* that the Popes had for centuries condemned Honorius in their profession of faith, Cardinal Bona, the most eminent man in Rome, advised that the book should be suppressed if the difficulty could not be got over and it was suppressed accordingly."[1] Dr. Jalland does not tell us that the condemnation of Honorius had a place in the Breviary until a much later period.

"The condemnation is recorded in the Roman Breviaries until the sixteenth century, at which period the name of Honorius disappears. The theory of papal infallibility was at that time being rapidly developed. A fact opposed it. The evidence for the fact is suppressed."[2] The documents brought before the sixth General Council are considered by Dr. Jalland to illustrate "the strange, even mystical continuity persisting throughout papal history".[3] This apologist's dislike to the decisions of the Council should not have carried him so far as to refer to it as "the Easterns and others", "the Easterns". This is in line with the futile, now abandoned, Roman plea that Honorius was condemned by Eastern bishops only. The legates of Agatho, Bishop of Rome, joined in the condemnation. The Roman Council of 649 (as we have seen) condemned under anathema the doctrine laid down by Honorius. Pope Leo II was outspoken in denouncing him. (Dr. Jalland, in consequence, makes uncomplimentary remarks about Leo.)[4] Such methods serve to make plain how vain are the oft-repeated efforts to clear Pope Honorius of heresy.

---

[1] *History of Freedom*, p. 516.
[2] Willis's *Pope Honorius*, quoted by Bishop Gore, *Roman Catholic Claims*, p. 111.
[3] Op. cit., p. 366.
[4] Op. cit., p. 367.

CHAPTER XLIII

POPE GREGORY THE GREAT

The Vatican Council declared that "the Roman Church, by divine dispensation, possesses a superiority of ordinary power over all other Churches and that this power of jurisdiction of the Roman Pontiff over all other Churches is truly episcopal and immediate, that all of whatever rank are bound to submit to it by their duty of hierarchical subordination and obedience".[1] The Pope is styled "the supreme and universal Pastor".

In this connection there is inserted a peculiar paragraph maintaining that this power of the supreme Pontiff is not prejudicial to the power of the ordinary diocesan bishops. Some words of St. Gregory the Great (590–604) are appealed to: "My honour is the honour of the universal Church. My honour is the firm strength of my brethren. I am truly honoured when the honour due to each and all is not withheld."

The use here of these words of Gregory is extraordinarily misleading. They are made to imply that Gregory taught honour done to him resulted in honour and strength to other bishops; that is, that other bishops benefited by the Pope being exalted. The real meaning is the very opposite of this. The words are part of a vigorous protest against the bishops' honour being diminished or destroyed through too much honour being ascribed to himself or to any single bishop. "Gregory said this when repudiating a title which would have exalted him above his fellow bishops. Pius IX repeated it precisely when asserting a prerogative which exalts him to a height of unapproachable isolation."[2] In reality Gregory presents a trenchant and insurmountable rebuttal of papal claims to a supreme bishopric over the Church.

The bishops of Constantinople had adopted the title of Universal or Oecumenical Bishop. Gregory repeatedly denounced such a title in the most emphatic way. Here is how he deals with it in the letter to

---

[1] chap. 3.
[2] Sparrow-Simpson, *Roman Catholic Opposition to Papal Infallibility*, p. 353.

Eulogius, Bishop of Alexandria, from which letter the Vatican Council unscrupulously takes its quotation. He objects to Eulogius having addressed him "with that haughty appellation, calling me Universal Pope. This I beg your Holiness, who art most agreeable to me, to do so no more, because whatever is given to another more than reason requires is so much taken away from yourself. It is not in titles but in character that I wish to advance. Nor do I consider that an honour by which I recognise that my brethren lose their own. For my honour is the honour of the universal Church. My honour is the firm strength of my brethren. Then am I truly honoured when due honour is not denied to each one in his own degree. For if your Holiness calls me Universal Pope you deny that you yourself are what you admit me to be—Universal. But away with this! Let words disappear which inflate vanity and wound charity".[1]

Gregory wrote a series of letters protesting vigorously against the title of Universal Bishop. Some extracts will show his abhorrence for the conception implied in the phrase. He tried to persuade the Emperor Maurice to prohibit the Bishop of Constantinople from adopting it. "Since it is not my cause but God's, and since not I only but the whole Church is thrown into confusion; since sacred laws, venerable Synods, since the very commands even of our Lord Jesus Christ are disturbed by the invention of this haughty and pompous language, let the most pious emperor lance the wound." "But far from Christian hearts be that blasphemous name in which the honour of all priests is taken away whilst it is insanely appropriated by one to himself." Gregory states, in error, that the title was offered to the Roman Pontiff during the Council of Chalcedon. "But not one of them ever consented to use this singular name that all priests might not be deprived of their due honour by something peculiar being given to one. . . . He ought to be coerced who injures the universal Church."[2]

The emperor disregarded the vehement entreaties of the Pope who wrote again: "I confidently affirm that whoever calls himself, or desires to be called, Universal Priest, in his pride goes before antichrist because through pride he prefers himself to the rest. . . . Since the Truth says 'everyone who exalteth himself shall be abased', I know the more any pride inflates itself, the sooner it bursts."[3]

---

[1] *Ep. ad Eulogium*, lib. viii, ep. 30. P. L. 77: 933.
[2] *Ep. ad Mauritium*, lib. v, ep. 20. P. L. 77: 745 et seq.
[3] Ibid., lib. vii, ep. 33. P. L. 77: 891, 892.

To the Bishop of Constantinople, John the Faster, Gregory wrote pointing out that by such presumption the peace of the Church is disturbed, and urging him to refrain "from usurping a proud and foolish name, and you profit in the degree that you do not study to arrogate to yourself by derogating from your brethren". "Who, I say, in this perverse title is set forth for imitation but he who despised the legion of angels joined as companion to himself and endeavoured to shoot up to a height unapproached by all, that he might seem to be subject to none and be alone superior to all." John is shown his likeness to the Spirit of the Devil while he seeks to set himself over the other bishops "by a lofty title and to tread under foot their names in comparison with your own". "Let then your Holiness acknowledge how great is your pride who seek to be called by that name by which no one has presumed to be called who is really holy."

Gregory declares that none of his predecessors in Rome ever was guilty of this. "No one ever wished to be called by such a title. No one seized for himself this audacious name lest if he seized for himself the glory of singularity in the rank of the pontificate he might seem to deny it to all his brethren. . . . By this abominable title of pride the Church is torn asunder, the hearts of all the brethren are provoked to scandal."[1]

Gregory tried to induce the patriarchs of Alexandria and Antioch to join in his protest. He told them : "If a single patriarch is called universal the name patriarch is taken from the rest. But far be this from the mind of a Christian that any one should wish to seize for himself that by which the honour of his brethren may seem to be in the smallest degree diminished . . . wherefore let your holiness in your letters never call any one universal lest in offering undue honour to another you should deprive yourself of that which is your due." The Bishop of Constantinople is declared to be aiming "by the pride of this pompous language to subjugate to himself all the members of Christ who are joined together to the one sole Head, that is, Christ". Gregory is compelled, with profound sorrow, to say this "brother and fellow bishop" (*frater et coepiscopus*), John, is "despising the Lord's commands, the apostles' precepts, and the rules of the Fathers when through pride he tries to surpass in name. . . . If this be allowed to be said freely the honour of all patriarchs is denied. And when perchance he who is termed universal perishes in error, presently no bishop is found to have remained in the state of truth". It

<hr>

[1] *Ep. Ad Joan.*, lib. v, ep. 18. P. L. 77: 739 et seq.

is a "diabolical usurpation". "Stand firm, stand secure, never venture to give or receive writings with the untruth of the name universal."[1]

After the death of John, Gregory wrote to the Patriarch of Antioch explaining he did not think it wise on account of a profane appellation to cause delay or friction by not receiving the Synodal letter of the new Bishop of Constantinople, "our brother and fellow-priest, Cyriacus". "Nevertheless I was careful to admonish him about that same superstitious and haughty title, saying that he should not have peace with me unless he corrected the pride of the aforesaid expression, which the apostate first invented. You should not call this a cause of no importance, because if we bear this calmly we corrupt the faith of the whole Church. . . . And not to speak of the injury done to your honour, if one be called universal, the whole Church tumbles down if that one, being universal, falls. But far be such folly [*stultitia*], far be such trifling from my ears. I trust in the Almighty Lord that what He hath promised He will quickly perform; every one that exalteth himself shall be abased."[2]

Writing to the bishops of Thessalonica, Gregory again pointed out the satanic origin of the title, Universal Bishop. It is a "new and audacious name of superstition".

He implored that none of them "ever admit this name, ever agree to it, ever write it, ever receive a writing wherein it is contained, or add his subscription; but, as behoves the ministers of Almighty God, keep himself clear from such poisonous infection, and give no place within him to the crafty stratagem; since this is done to the injury and disruption of the whole Church, and, as we have said, in contempt of you all. For if one, as assumed, be universal, it follows that you are not bishops".[3]

These extracts from Pope Gregory the Great—many more might be produced—expose graphically the falsity of the papal claims. Gregory insists that the title destroys the position of other bishops. Yet in the Vatican Decrees the title of "supreme and universal Pastor" is not only assumed but is enforced to an extent far surpassing anything that was involved in its original use by the bishops of Constantinople. The Vatican Decrees pronounce anathema on any who say the Roman Pontiff has "not full and supreme power of jurisdiction over the universal Church". This is an extension of the

---

[1] *Ep. ad Eulogium et Anastasium*, lib. v, ep. 43. P. L. 77: 771 et seq.
[2] *Ep. ad Anastasium*, lib. vii, ep. 27. P. L. 77: 883.
[3] lib. ix, ep. 68. P. L. 77: 1004.

concept of Universal Bishop that would have shocked Gregory out of measure . The present Pope, Pius XII, in his first encyclical, *Darkness over the Earth*, repeatedly refers to himself as "supreme Bishop".

Yet it is Gregory who is cited in the Vatican Decrees as a witness to this prerogative of the Roman Pontiff! A more audacious perversion could scarcely be perpetrated. Such methods are an offence against ordinary morality. Gregory is quoted as approving not only what he protested against but for far more extravagant excesses than what he abhorred. Principal F. J. Paul declares: "If Gregory had had the Vatican claims for the Papacy lying before him in writing, his criticism could not have been more pertinent to the situation in 1870."[1] After the passing of five centuries a successor of Gregory, Gregory VII, is found laying it down in his *Dictatus* that "the Roman Pontiff is alone to be called universal".[2]

Bishop Gore wrote: "Even conscious fraud is a familiar element in official acts of the Roman See."[3] The Vatican Decrees resort to repeated fraudulent representation of texts. How can men accept a dogma depending on such preposterous fabrications and misrepresentations? "Has God then need of your falsehoods that ye speak deceitfully for Him?"

Dom Chapman has a brief reference to the title Oecumenical Patriarch, "which St. Gregory the Great was later to misunderstand in so unfortunate a manner".[4]

[1] *Romanism and Evangelical Christianity*, p. 327.
[2] Mirbt, no. 278, p. 146.
[3] *Roman Catholic Claims* (5th edition), p. 111.
[4] *Studies on the Early Papacy*, p. 24.

CHAPTER XLIV

FORGERIES

1

Reference has been made to the attempts of Pope Zosimus and Leo I to utilise counterfeit copies of the Nicene canons. It is noteworthy that just at the period when papal encroachments on the liberty of the Church began, the forging of authorities also began. The process rapidly and portentously developed.

In the fifth or sixth century various documents were manufactured such as stories of Roman martyrs, and an account of the conversion and baptism of Constantine, glorifying Pope Sylvester. With the object of preventing a Roman bishop being tried by the courts, the Acts of a Council of Sinuessa were devised with a legend of Pope Marcellinus. Several other fabricated records glorifying the Papacy were circulated. A work that had a wider influence was the *Liber Pontificalis*, which, composed (as regards its first part) about 530, gave numerous spurious particulars about early Bishops of Rome. Subsequent editions spread the idea of the Pope being the lawgiver of the Church.

2

The foundation of the territorial kingship of the Pope is connected with some famous forgeries. When the Lombards, by that time Catholic and civilised, were pressing towards Rome, Pope Stephen II appealed to Pepin, king of the Franks, for aid. Pepin not showing much readiness to respond, a letter was composed from St. Peter to him. In the dismal ignorance and superstition of the time it was accepted as an authentic apostolic message. Pepin hurried to give battle to the Lombards. The letter was incorporated in the *Codex Carolinus*.

This ludicrous concoction purports to be a direct message from the apostle. "I, Peter the Apostle, of whom you are adopted sons, admonish you to defend the city of Rome, the people committed to

208

my charge, and the Church in which my body lies, from the hands of enemies." "Our Lady, the mother of God, the virgin Mary, joins with me in laying this obligation upon you." If Pepin does not act at once as the apostle admonishes him he is told that he will be "lacerated and tortured, body and soul, in the eternal and inextinguishable fires of hell with the Devil and his pestilent angels".[1]

The success of this document probably impelled to further efforts. About the same time another daring forgery was fabricated and was useful to Leo III to make Pepin's great son, Charlemagne, confirm his father's grants. This was the Donation of Constantine. Duchesne writes: "By most of the critics this document is dated back to the beginning of the year 744; it was manufactured at Rome, probably at the Lateran, the very palace where Leo was at that time beginning his career in the administration of the Sacristy."[2] The *Cambridge Medieval History* ascribes the origin of this "cornerstone of papal power" also to the papal chancellery and states that startling coincidences of phrases connect it with the documents of Stephen II and Paul.[3] Bryce describes it as "the most stupendous of all the medieval forgeries which . . . commanded for seven centuries the unquestioning belief of mankind. . . . A portentous falsehood".[4]

This document sets forth that Constantine, having been cured of leprosy by the prayers of Pope Sylvester, resolved to depart from Rome to the Bosphorus "because it is not right an earthly monarch should have his seat in the place where the spiritual *lordship* and the head of the Christian religion is fixed by the heavenly King". Constantine is made to bestow on the Pope the city of Rome, his palace, all the provinces of Italy and of the Western regions. It is designed to make the Roman Pontiff succeed to the glory and position of the old Roman emperors. It helps to explain the resolution whereby the Bishop of the Imperial City inherited the renown of the Caesars. It orders that the Pope shall rule over the sees of Antioch, Alexandria, Constantinople, and over all Churches in the world.

The Donation expressly awards to the Pope and his clergy the dignities and privileges belonging to the emperor and his senate. The authority of the Pope is set forth as superior to the imperial power. "We have decreed that the most holy Roman Church is to be

[1] Migne. P. L. 89: 1004 f.
[2] *The Beginnings of the Temporal Sovereignty of the Popes*, p. 120.
[3] vol. ii, p. 586.
[4] *Holy Roman Empire*, p. 100.

reverently honoured and the see of the Blessed Peter to be more gloriously exalted than our imperial and earthly throne, attributing to it power and glorious dignity, and strength, and imperial magnificence". The Pope is higher than all the bishops of the whole world, and by his judgment whatsoever pertains to the worship of God and to the procuring of stability of the Christian faith is to be decided. Constantine gives to Sylvester and all his successors in the see of the Blessed Peter "our imperial palace the Lateran", his diadem, crown, purple chlamys and scarlet tunic, all imperial vestments, sceptre, insignia and ornaments.

This forgery became a chief title-deed of the Church. It was used as occasion arose; for example, the claiming of Corsica and Sardinia, the bestowal of Ireland on Henry II. It was incorporated in the Isidorian Decretals and the Decretum of Gratian. It remained down the centuries as part of the Canon law. The Popes in claiming Italian territory did not ask them as gifts but as the restitution of rights.

3

The securing of territorial dominions was only part of papal ambition. For the achieving of spiritual sovereignty over the Church a hideous mass of forged documents was made use of.

About the middle of the ninth century the Isidorian Decretals appeared. It is agreed that they were composed outside Rome. The composer was interested in protecting diocesan bishops and other clergy from the discipline of their metropolitans, and in securing for them the right of appeal to Rome. The scope of his work far exceeds this particular object.

The fiction begins with a series of sixty letters ascribed to various Bishops of Rome up to the year 314. All are spurious and all the work of the supposed Isidore except two, which are earlier forgeries. Then follow the Donation of Constantine and various papal decrees down to the eighth century. Thirty-nine of these are spurious. Finally acts of Councils are given of which many are also fictitious.

These letters exhibit the early Bishops of Rome exercising a sovereign supremacy over the Church. They are shown carrying out the jurisdiction that is now claimed for them. The fact that such spurious writings had to be concocted and attributed to the Popes is damning evidence that such powers were then non-existent. It is the complete absence of any genuine epistles of the sort that necessitated the fabrications.

These forgeries serve to explain how in a grossly ignorant age the antiquity of the authority of Rome came to be credited. To Anacletus, who is received as Bishop of Rome in the first century, there are attributed three lengthy documents in the full papal style. The third has as part of its title words that have since become familiar in the glorification of Rome: "The Church is the hinge and head of all Churches."[1] It asserts that "by the order of the Lord all Churches are ruled by the authority of this holy See".[2] In another letter Anacletus is made to state that the apostles ordained this, by the order of the Saviour, that "the greater and difficult questions be referred always to the Apostolic See".[3]

Calistus is made to use the phrase—much relied on since—that the Church of Rome is "the mother of all Churches".[4] In this almost incredible mass of childish forgeries the Church of Rome is endowed with authority that Scripture and the Fathers knew nothing of. It would be tiresome to multiply citations. Suffice it to give one further specimen. Athanasius is represented as writing to Pope Felix: "The canons certainly enjoin that apart from the Roman Pontiff we must not decide anything about the greater causes." God has appointed Felix and his predecessors as the summit of the citadel of all the Churches, to whom the judgment of all bishops is committed. "For we know that in the great Nicene Synod of three hundred and eighteen bishops it was unanimously enjoined that without the assent of the Roman pontiff a Council could not be held nor a bishop be condemned."[5]

Though the papal court did not fabricate the False Decretals it made instant and abundant use of them and incorporated them into its canon law.[6] Gratian's Decretum—the great system of canon law from the twelfth century—made them part of the standard Church legislation, studied in universities and seminaries. Gratian buttressed their errors with plentiful other fabrications, but the extent to which he relied on them is seen when from the three hundred and twenty-four quotations he gives from the Popes of the first four

---

[1] See Paulus Hinschius, *Decretales Pseudo—Isidorianae*, p. 81.
[2] Ibid., pp. 83, 84.
[3] Ibid., p. 73.
[4] Ibid., p. 136.
[5] Ibid., p. 479.
[6] "Nicholas and those who came after him cited the spurious decretals no less freely than the genuine" (Dr. Barry, *Papal Monarchy*, p. 137).

centuries three hundred and fifteen are from the pseudo-Isidorian work. For hundreds of years this Decretum was the supreme accredited repository of patristic authorities bearing on the constitution of the Church.

The False Decretals made the Pope supreme. In the centuries following, his pretensions were believed to be unchallengeable. His sovereignty was regarded as a constituent part of Christianity. The Christian world was the victim of a monstrous and ludicrous hoax. The conceptions embodied in the Vatican Council are explainable from it.

Nicholas I was a great personality who was daring in pushing forward papal claims. The False Decretals were probably brought to Rome in his time. Writing to the Gallic bishops in 865 he severely rebukes them for challenging the validity of the decrees. They had objected that the decrees attributed to early Pontiffs were not to be found in the codex of canons. He ridicules this argument by saying that on that ground we would not receive the Old or New Testament since neither of them is inserted in the codex of ecclesiastical canons. The decretal letters of the Roman Pontiffs are to be accepted even if they are not incorporated in the codex. He stresses the importance of so many and great decretal statutes and actually assures the dubious bishops that the decretals have been carefully treasured from antiquity in the archives of the Church of Rome and duly venerated among its ancient annals.[1] His letter is a fervid assertion of the authority of these hitherto unknown "*decretalia priscorum pontificum*".

The efforts to clear Nicholas of downright mis-statements here are unavailing. The plea that he is not referring to the False Decretals is vain. Professor Saltet, in the *Catholic Encyclopedia*, shows he has not much confidence in it and admits the *parfum Isidorean* of the letter and that if the decretals are not explicitly quoted they are at least alluded to.[2] The Pope knew that no such documents were in the Roman archives. He knew that their statements, for example about the Council of Nicaea, were false. Funk fully admits that Nicholas I made use of the decretals and that "he unmistakably refers to them".[3] Denny is not a scholar to make grave charges lightly. He writes that "Nicholas's conduct in employing the fabrication is worse than that of the forger".[4]

[1] Mansi, xv, 694–6.   [3] *Manual of Church History*, vol. i, p. 313 (E. T.).
[2] v, 779.   [4] *Papalism*, p. 113.

The next Pope, Hadrian II, cites them beyond the possibility of quibble. Writing to the bishops of the Synod of Duziacensis, he explicitly quotes a spurious decree imputed to Pope Anterus who was Pope for only forty days at the end of 235.[1] Salmon's simile is apposite: "When you catch a man presenting a forged cheque, it is all very well to say he could not possibly have known it to be forged, he is such a very respectable clergyman. But if you find that this very respectable clergyman makes a constant trade of presenting forged cheques and living on the proceeds, our judgment can hardly be quite so charitable."[2]

The fraud was not exposed until the sixteenth century. But the fabric of papal monarchy erected on it was by that time so dominant that it has survived the removal of its props. Nicholas I, in his letter to the Emperor Michael, asserts the privileges of the Roman Church "were published by the holy universal Synods".[3] He quotes as divinely inspired a Synodical decree of Pope Sylvester. The Synod is due to the forger of the False Decretals.

4

Another species of the forgeries that served to impose the papal sovereignty on an uncritical age was the corruptions of the Fathers. The most remarkable of these was the *catena* of passages produced in the thirteenth century from the Greek Fathers, plentifully mingled with concocted extracts from the Eastern Councils. The chief Fathers thus "doctored" were Chrysostom, Cyril of Alexandria and Cyril of Jerusalem. Urban IV (1261–4) hailed the collection as genuine and actually forwarded it to the Greek emperor. It must have caused wonder and amusement to the Eastern ecclesiastics.

Productive of more influence was the copy he sent to St. Thomas Aquinas. That renowned theologian was completely taken in by it. Aquinas is celebrated as one of the greatest intellects of all time. Yet in his book, *Contra errores Grecorum*, he seized eagerly on these ridiculous deceits. Henceforth they had the authentication of this Doctor of the Church, whose teaching cannot be questioned. Deceived himself, he deceived all who accepted his authority. Even though Aquinas was ignorant of Greek and lived at a time when the mental atmosphere was corrupted by the False Decretals, still it is

---

[1] Mansi, xv, 852.   [2] *Infallibility of the Church*, pp. 454, 455.
[3] Migne. P. L. 119: 791.

O

marvellous that he could have been so easily bamboozled into thinking that the great Eastern theologians accepted thus the monarchy of the Pope.

The fraud once again exposes the bankruptcy of the claims for papal supremacy and infallibility. Had there been valid testimonies to it from Eastern Christian antiquity there would have been no need to fabricate these bogus ones.

At least five times Aquinas in his books falls back for proof on one particular tit-bit from Cyril of Alexandria.[1] It may be presented as a specimen of the forger's audacity. "That we may remain members of our head, the Apostolic See of the Roman Pontiffs, it is our duty to seek what we ought to believe and hold, venerating him and asking him for all things, since it is his duty alone to blame, to correct, to determine, to dispose, to loosen, and bind in place of Him who created him and gave His own fulness to no other than to him alone; to whom by the divine law all bow the head, even the leaders of the world, as if they obey the Lord Jesus Christ Himself."

Sparrow-Simpson tells how the eminent theologian, Melchior Cano, said that the quotations given by St. Thomas from St. Cyril of Alexandria afford a much clearer evidence for the papal doctrine than that in any other patristic writer. When he sought for the original passages they were not to be found. "'This is the work of the heretics,' he exclaims indignantly. 'They have mutilated the writings and erased everything that concerned pontifical authority.'"[2]

The earlier Clementine fictions from which the Roman episcopate of Peter is derived have already been referred to. Papal doctrinal structure developed in what Gratry calls a "*école d'erreur et de mensonge*". Salmon writes: "It is not more than the truth to say that the Roman claims have principally taken their growth out of two forgeries"[3]—the pseudo-Clementines and the pseudo-Isidorian Decretals. The testimonies of two most learned Roman Catholics are: "It is so far true to say that without the pseudo-Isidore there would have been no Gregory VII, that the Isidorian forgeries were the broad foundation the Gregorians built on."[4]   Lord Acton, writing of the Renaissance, states: "Religious knowledge in those days suffered not only from ignorance and the defect of testimony, but from an excess of fiction and falsification. Whenever a school

---

[1] See Denny's quotation from Launoy's exposure, *Papalism*, pp. 633 ff.
[2] *Papal Infallibility*, p. 30.
[3] *Infallibility of the Church*, pp. 447, 448.
[4] Janus, p. 105 (E. T.).

was lacking in proofs for its opinions it straightway forged them, and was sure not to be found out. A vast mass of literature arose, which no man, with medieval implements, could detect, and effectually baffled and deceived the student of tradition."[1]

Papal ambition, by such means, brought about the disruption of the ancient order of the Church and destroyed the primitive authority of the episcopal order. Bishops became the helpless dependants of the Pope who could at his will depose them. The frantic demand for sovereignty, spiritual and secular, of the Bishops of Rome over the whole world is the most monstrous imposition in the history of Christianity.

As Acton wrote: "The passage from the Catholicism of the Fathers to that of the modern Popes was accomplished by wilful falsehood; and the whole structure of traditions, laws, and doctrines that support the theory of infallibility and the practical despotism of the Popes stands on a basis of fraud."[2]

[1] *Lectures on Modern History*, p. 78.
[2] *North British Review*, October 1869, p. 130.

CHAPTER XLV

TEMPORAL POWER

The record of the Bishops of Rome as territorial sovereigns is in itself destructive of their claims to be representatives on earth of the meek and lowly Christ.

The temporal power dates from 756, when, deceived by fraudulent devices, Pepin made the Pope lord of a great part of Italy. He bestowed on him, or, rather, on St. Peter, large remaining possessions there of the Eastern Emperor. Soon afterwards, when rivals were disputing for the Lombard throne, Pope Stephen II secured other important areas. Obedient to the Donation of Constantine, the Countess Matilda of Tuscany bequeathed her dominions, nearly a quarter of Italy, to the Pope. The temporal power continued until 1870. During many centuries the Popes were occupied in sanguinary wars either against their own subjects or against neighbouring princes. Their political manœuvres and ruthless campaigns rendered blasphemous their spiritual pretensions. "The theocratic principle had been exchanged for a tyranny. The prince who then sat on the marble throne of the Vatican only differed from the other dynastic princes of Italy in his title and his dress."[1] Lorenzo de Medici had justification for his statement: "The States of the Church have always been the ruin of Italy."[2]

The Vicars of Christ again and again showed themselves ambitious monarchs, extending their dominions by callous treachery and bloodshed. No other bishopric in the world is so defiled with a history of sanguinary warfare. Some Popes personally conducted campaigns. Leo IX, having taken possession of Benevento and Capua, went on to attack the Normans and was taken prisoner by them. Lucius II was slain in the streets of Rome fighting against the revolting citizens.

Julius II was "a soldier in a cassock". His pontificate was spent in a series of ferocious campaigns. He invaded and helped to ruin the

---

[1] Gregorovius, *History of the City of Rome*, vol. vii, p. 429.
[2] Creighton, *History of the Papacy*, vol. iii, p. 128.

republic of Venice. Sometimes he fought with the French; sometimes against them. He was cruel and unscrupulous. As head of the Holy League he succeeded in spreading his conquests. Guicciardini, a contemporary authority, lauds him for his courage and resolution, but writes that his eulogists are those who "judge that it is the office of the Popes to bring empire to the apostolic seat by arms and by the shedding of Christian blood more than to trouble themselves by setting an example of holy life and correcting the decay of morals for the salvation of those souls for whose sake they boast that Christ set them as His Vicars upon earth".[1] At the battle of Ravenna on Easter Sunday, 1512, ten thousand corpses are said to have been left on the field.[2] Julius, a seasoned warrior, was wont to fulminate anathemas and excommunications against cities before attacking them with material weapons.

The Popes in their wars in Italy were often represented in the field by cardinal legates as military commanders. Cardinal Robert of Geneva (afterwards Clement VII) when he captured Cesena gave the inhabitants up to three days' carnage. Even the leader of his mercenary troops was shocked, but the cardinal's cry was: "I will have more blood—kill all." Five thousand perished.[3] "The whole history of the human race affords no example of a struggle of such long duration, or one so unchanged in motive as the struggle of the Romans and Italians against the *Dominium temporale* of the Popes, whose kingdom ought not to have been of this world."[4] Lope de Soria, Charles V's minister at Genoa, wrote (25th May 1527) that the Pope's temporal power emboldened him to promote rebellion and invite the Christian princes to make war on each other. "I have now resided twenty-eight years in Italy and I have observed that of all the wars and misfortunes I have witnessed during that time the Popes have been the sole cause."[5]

Some of the Popes, not content with their own Church sovereignties, convulsed Italy with wars to make their relations secular princes. Sixtus IV set up a nephew as lord of Imola. This nephew seized Forli and put to death a son of the owner. The Pope launched a war against Ferrara, into which war all Italy was drawn, to gain

[1] *Storia d'Italia*, bk. xi, chap. viii.
[2] Sismondi gives the figures as twentythousand (*History of the Italian Republics*, chap. xiv).
[3] Sismondi, *History of the Italian Republics*, chap. viii. Creighton, *History of the Papacy* (new edition), vol. i, p. 73.
[4] Gregorovius, *History of the City of Rome*, vol. ii, p. 478.
[5] *Spanish Calendar*, vol. iii, part 2, p. 210.

further dominions for his nephew. The nephew plotted the assassination of the Medici of Florence. The two Medici brothers were attacked at the most solemn moment of mass in the cathedral. A grand-nephew of the Pope was present whom he had made cardinal at the age of seventeen. Guiliano Medici was stabbed to death, but Lorenzo, wounded, was saved by a friend at the cost of his own life. The Pope "allowed himself to become an accomplice in a scheme of assassination which shocked even the blunted conscience of Italy".[1] Infuriated at the failure of his schemes to increase his nephew's possessions, he launched war against Florence, excommunicated Lorenzo and laid Florence under an interdict. The Florentines told the Pope: "If Lorenzo had allowed himself to be slaughtered by your emissaries . . . if we had given ourselves up to you for slaughter we would have had none of this controversy with you."

Sixtus IV established another nephew by diverting to him the papal territories of Senigaglia and Mondovi.

Such establishments of princedoms led to future wars. Alexander VI's son, Caesar Borgia, attacked Imola and Forli. That was the end of the nephew's dynasty, for whom "the Pope plunged into one war after another and lavished all the resources of his temporal and spiritual authority".[2]

Alexander VI determined also that the family of the other nephew of his predecessor should be driven from Sinigaglia in order to enrich his own son. Accordingly Caesar's army seized and sacked the town. Sistus's grand-nephew escaped and afterwards became Duke of Urbino. But a later Pope, Leo X, wanted Urbino for a nephew and sent a papal army numbering twenty-thousand against it. The duke fled, and Leo X made his nephew Duke of Urbino and Lord of Pesaro.

Innocent VIII, the successor of Sixtus IV, made his son lord of two towns, from which he drove out the possessors. The story of Alexander VI's efforts to enrich his family is well known. He brought Italy into appalling ruin and suffering for this. His series of crimes is almost incredible. The King of Naples justly estimates him: "He practises all abominations in his life without respect to the seat which he holds. He cares for nothing else save to aggrandise his children by fair means or foul."[3] One of his many sons, Juan,

[1] Creighton, *Edinburgh Review*, January 1905, p. 121.
[2] Creighton, *History of the Papacy*, vol. iii, p. 102.
[3] Gregorovius, *History of the City of Rome*, vol. vii, p. 342.

was made Duke of Gandia. The papal armies fought for his advancement. Alexander bestowed on him several Italian towns. Another
son, Giofre, was married to a daughter of the King of Naples and
made a prince.

The career of Caesar Borgia was a time of nightmare horror for
Italy. Provided by his father with armies, he marched up and down
Italy spreading terror, massacre and destruction. The admiring Pope
was always planning fresh abominations for Caesar's advancement.
The treachery of these men is nearly as horrible as their cruelty.
Their allies were likely to be betrayed and destroyed if it suited the
papal advantage.

After one of Caesar's marauding expeditions, destroying and
taking possessions where he could, he was accorded a triumphant
entrance to Rome (1500). Troops came first and then rode the
Pope's son-in-law and one of the Pope's sons. Caesar followed
between cardinals,[1] attended by two hundred squires. Archbishops,
bishops and representatives of foreign kingdoms (including England)
rode in the procession. The Pope, attended by other cardinals,
waited to receive him in the Vatican. He welcomed Caesar
with rapture and presented him with the Golden Rose. Caesar
was ennobled with the titles Duke of Valence (in France), Duke
of the Romagna and of Urbino, Prince of Andria, Lord of
Piombino, made Golfaniere and Captain-general of the Holy
Roman Church.

One of the typical Borgia spoliations was the seizing of Sermonetta
and the murdering of the possessors. The Pope bestowed Sermonetta
on a son of Lucrezia Borgia. On a young son of his own, born when
he was about sixty-eight years, he bestowed Nepi and other towns.
His successor, Julius II, restored the owners. In the bull of restitution
he does not hesitate to brand his predecessor's action as unjust and
inhuman, dictated by inordinate cupidity and desire to enrich his
family by fraud and deceit.

Gregorovius writes that Alexander VI "surrendered Italy to the
Spaniards and French with the sole object of aggrandising his
bastards. He was one of the essential causes of the ruin of his
country".[2]

With this agrees the testimony of a Pope. Paul IV stated: "Our
predecessors have spent rivers of gold to exalt their bastards and

---

[1] Burchard, *Diarium*, vol. iii, p. 20 f.
[2] *History of the City of Rome*, vol. vii, p. 527 (E. T.).

nephews and on other things which displeased both God and man, and then brough ruin on their families."[1]

Leo X made his brother Duke of Nemours, tried to give him principalities belonging to the Church and make him King of Naples. He instigated devastating wars for the advancement of his Medici relations.

The states of the Church included the most fertile tracts of Italy. Centuries of warfare riveted the power of the Popes over them. It would naturally be expected that under the direct rule of the vice-gerent of God they would present a spectacle of unequalled prosperity, enlightenment and happiness. Before they shook off the papal rulership in the nineteenth-century they were almost the worst-governed in Europe. The Pope only held his subjects down by Austrian and French bayonets. Gladstone quotes from Farini's *History of Rome* of the state of things at the beginning of the century. "There was no care for the cultivation of the people, no anxiety for public prosperity. Rome was a cesspool of corruption."[2] Macaulay wrote: "The states of the Pope are, I suppose, the worst governed in the civilised world; and the imbecility of the police, the venality of the public servants, the desolation of the country, and the wretchedness of the people, force themselves on the observation of the most heedless traveller. It is hardly an exaggeration to say that the population seems to consist chiefly of foreigners, priests and paupers.[3]

[1] *Venetian State Papers* (28th August 1556), vol. vi, part 1, p. 583.
[2] *Vaticanism*, appendix viii.
[3] *Life and Letters* (1889 edition), p. 362.

CHAPTER XLVI

PAPAL PERSONALITIES

Our admiration goes forth to the many illustrious and saintly men who have been Bishops of Rome. We would like to forget the unworthy ones. But the nature of the papal claims makes this impossible. So long as it is taught that the Pope represents Christ on earth, that as supreme Pastor full power was given to him by Jesus Christ to rule, feed and govern the universal Church, then we cannot ignore the personal characters of those to whom such stupendous functions are attributed. The teaching of Christ is far from allowing us to regard orthodoxy of belief as all important and goodness of life as of secondary account. Gregory VII had a proper conception of what being Vicar of Christ involved when he asserted "that the Roman Pontiff, if canonically ordained, by the merits of Peter is without doubt rendered holy."[1]

To call attention to the flagrantly evil lives of so many occupants of the Papal See is an unpleasant duty. It cannot be shirked in examining the fantastic pretensions of the Papacy.

1

It is remarkable that the first Bishop of Rome of whom we have definite personal information, Callistus I (219–223), is described as a man of disreputable life. The learned Hippolytus, bishop and saint, was a contemporary of his and a theological opponent.[2] Even when allowance is made for partisan bias, we cannot ignore the matter-of-fact details that Hippolytus narrates at length. He describes how Callistus was a heretic, embezzler, runaway slave and convict.

The discreditable vacillations of Pope Vigilius (537–55) at the fifth General Council are told *supra*. His personal history is unsavoury. He was bought over by the Empress Theodora to support

[1] *Dictatus*, Mirbt 278, p. 146 (1934 edition.)
[2] *Refutation of All Heresies*, bk. ix.

her monophysite designs.[1] When he reached Rome a disgraceful plot deprived the Pope Silverius (a son of Pope Hormisdas) of his office and liberty, and Vigilius was unlawfully intruded in his stead. Eventually Silverius was handed over to Vigilius and exiled to the Island of Palmaria, where he was put to death—according to Liberatus—by hunger. Vigilius was regarded as responsible for this.[2] Dom. Chapman calls him "the executioner of St. Silverius".[3]

In the eighth century the condition of Rome had sunk to deplorable depths. When Pope Paul I died in 767 a soldier named Constantine was speedily tonsured, ordained, consecrated and installed as Pope. He officiated for over a year. Two prominent Church officials, Christopher and his son Sergius, by the aid of Lombard forces, had Stephen III (IV) made Pope. Constantine, his brother and a bishop who supported him had their eyes taken out. This brutality was common in Rome then. Stephen is not to be held accountable for this outrage, but he cannot be acquitted for what took place next year (769) at a Council in the Lateran under his presidency. The wretched, blinded Constantine was brought before the Pope and assembled bishops. He pleaded that compulsion was put on him by the Roman people to accept the Papacy, that there were precedents for the ecclesiastical irregularity. Prostrating himself, he implored mercy. Let Duchesne tell what followed: "They struck the poor blind pleader across the face, cast him outside and ordered that his writ of election should be burned. Having performed these graceful acts, Pope Stephen, with his faithful followers, abased themselves on the ground, confessing the sin they had committed in accepting Constantine, and beseeching penance for their misdeeds. The very angels must have smiled at the hypocritical litanies which were chanted over them."[4]

It was not long until Stephen tired of Christopher and his son. By his alliance with the Lombard king their party was overthrown. They took refuge in the basilica of St. Peter's. They were dragged from it and their eyes torn out. Christopher died a few days later; Sergius survived in prison until the Pope's brother and others had him taken out and assassinated. The verdict of Duchesne is that Stephen "basely delivered over . . . those to whom he owed his

[1] *Amore episcopatus et auri*, Liberatus *Breviarium*, c. 22. P. L. 68: 1040. Cf. Victor Tunensis, *Chronicon*. P. L. 68: 906.
[2] Liberatus *Breviarium*. Cf. Anastasius, *De Vitis Rom. Pont.*, St. Silverius. P. L. 128: 566.
[3] *The First Eight General Councils*, p. 50.
[4] *The Beginnings of the Temporal Sovereignty of the Popes*, p. 80 (E. T.).

election ".[1] Gregorovius sums up: "Such were the arts employed by the Pope to work the fall of his adversaries ".[2]

In December 799 a strange scene took place in St. Peter's when in the presence of Charlemagne charges against Pope Leo III were investigated at length and the Pope was acquitted on his publicly taking an oath of purgation. About twenty years later Pascal I underwent a similar humiliation. Two important officials, unfriendly to the Pope, were seized by members of his household (*familia S. Petri*), blinded, and put to death in the Lateran. Platina primly observes: "There were some who laid the blame of this disorder upon Pascal himself."[3] Complaints of the Pope's complicity were brought to the emperor, who sent delegates to Rome. The Pope took an oath of purgation in the presence of the imperial delegates, twenty-four bishops and the Roman people. When Pascal died the Roman citizens refused to allow his body to be buried in St. Peter's.

At the end of this century another scene took place in Rome which reveals the barbarity that existed in the surroundings of the Papacy. Pope Formosus died in 896 after being a Pope for five years. Eight months later Stephen VI, with his cardinals and bishops, held a trial on him. The corpse of Formosus was taken from the grave. Dressed in his pontifical garments, it was propped up on the throne. Pope Stephen's advocate hurled accusations at the corpse. The living Pope denounced him. Formosus was formally condemned, the papal vestments torn from him, the three fingers of his right hand with which he pronounced benediction cut off, and the body thrown into unconsecrated ground. He was afterwards thrown into the Tiber. All his ordinations were declared invalid. Before the year was finished Stephen himself was stripped of his vestment, thrown into prison and strangled. His successor Romanus, reigned for three months and the next Pope, Theodore II, for twenty days. He restored those ordained by Formosus.

2

In the tenth and eleventh centuries we find the Papacy sink to appalling depths. Infamous women made and unmade the Vicars

[1] *The Beginnings of the Temporal Sovereignty of the Popes*, p. 83. Duchesne, the eminent Roman Catholic historian, editor of the *Liber Pontificalis*, is a first-class authority on the lives of the medieval Popes. The authorised translation of his *Les Premiers Temps de l'Etat Pontifical*, by Arnold H. Matthew, is published with official *imprimatur*.
[2] *History of the City of Rome in the Middle Ages*, vol. ii, p. 336 (E. T.).
[3] *De Vitis Pont. Rom.*, Pascal i.

of Christ. Theodora was the wife of the most influential Roman. Her daughter, Marozia, even surpassed her in evil. Another daughter was named Theodora. Ecclesiastic historians like Liutprand and Baronius freely give them the name of "harlot". "To the eyes of dismayed Catholics the Church at that time resembled a brothel . . . Out of a process of decomposition such as this these women arose."[1]

In 903 Leo V was dethroned and imprisoned after a month's reign by Christopher who a few months later shared a similar fate at the hands of Sergius III. Both of Sergius's predecessors were put to death. He again annulled the ordinations of Formosus. Platina exclaims against "these monsters, by whose ambition and bribery the most holy chair of Peter was seized rather than rightly possessed".[2] They, "as monsters, were soon snatched away by a divine power".[3]

Sergius III officiated as God's vicegerent for seven years. According to him his predecessors were "wolves". Duchesne describes him as "spiteful, brutal and a scoundrel";[4] the Roman Catholic Dr. William Barry as "malignant, ferocious, and unclean".[5] It is commonly believed that he was a paramour of Marozia, and their son became Pope as John XI. Duchesne writes: "There seems to have been no secret as to his (John XI) paternity, for not only the chroniclers, such as Luitprand, but also the semi-official catalogues, by means of which *Liber Pontificalis* was continued, do not hesitate to make mention of it."[6] Platina describes John as the son of Sergius;[7] and the defensive Professor Funk calls him the son of Marozia.[8]

John XII, son of Alberic, became Pope at the age of seventeen (955). Platina considers him as "certainly the most pernicious and infamous fellow [*perniciosissimus et sceleratissimus*] of any that preceded him" and as "one that from his youth up had been debauched with all manner of vice and wickedness".[9] Duchesne agrees: "His illicit amours were a matter of public knowledge, for they were restrained neither by ties of blood nor by respect of

---

[1] Gregorovius, *History of the City of Rome*, vol. iii, pp. 256, 258.
[2] *De Vitis Pont. Rom.* (1626 edition), Benedict iv, p. 138.
[3] Ibid., Christopher, p. 139.
[4] *The Beginnings of the Temporal Sovereignty,* etc., p. 209.
[5] *Papal Monarchy*, p. 150.
[6] *The Beginnings of the Temporal Sovereignty*, etc.
[7] *De Vitis. Pont. Rom.*, John xi, p. 141.
[8] *Manual of Church History*, i, 276. Cf. *Cambridge Medieval History*, vol. iii, pp. 151, 154, 455.
[9] *De Vitis Pont. Rom.*, John xii (xiii), pp. 144, 145.

persons. The Lateran became a resort of persons of ill-fame and no virtuous woman could remain in safety at Rome. . . . We hear of a bishop consecrated at the age of ten, of a deacon ordained in a stable, and of dignitaries blinded or mutilated."[1] Some of this Pope's mutilations are too indecent to be recorded. His victims died from the savagery.

The Emperor Otto held a Council, tried and deposed him in Rome in 963. Frightful charges were put forward. The end of John was in keeping with his life: he was killed in the committal of a crime. Arnulph, Bishop of Orleans, at the Council of Rheims (991) declaimed against the abominable lives of these and other occupants of the Papal See, specifying gruesome details. "Is it to such monsters, swollen with ignominy and empty of knowledge, divine or human, that the innumerable priests of God, dispersed about the universe, distinguished for their learning and their virtues, are to be legally subject?"[2]

In 1032 there arose a Pope Benedict IX, son of another Alberic, whom Maycock thinks "was possibly the worst Pope who has ever occupied the chair of Peter".[3] It is difficult to assess the relative infamy of these degraded creatures. Benedict IX was only twelve years old when he became the infallible Head of the Church. He "had all the vices of a youth born to uncontrolled power. . . . For twelve years Benedict IX, under the protection of his powerful kindred, ruled in Rome, in the words of one of his successors, Victor III, leading a life so shameful, so foul, and execrable that he shuddered to describe it. He ruled like a captain of banditti rather than a prelate. Adulteries, homicides perpetrated by his own hand, passed unnoticed, unrevenged".[4] At length, tiring of the Papacy, he sold it for a large sum to Gregory VI; claiming it again, he destroyed the reigning Pope, Clement II. "He was a bandit, not a priest. Stained with adulteries, homicides."[5]

Cardinal Baronius, the famous sixteenth-century Roman Catholic historian, fully admits the abominations of these times. He wrote: "It is plain that scarcely anyone can believe, nay scarcely anyone can ever believe, what unworthy foul deformed, moreover what execrable and abominable things, the holy Apostolic See, upon

---

[1] *The Beginnings of the Temporal Sovereignty*, etc., p. 224.
[2] *Cambridge Medieval History*, vol. iii, p. 101.
[3] *The Papacy*, p. 41.
[4] Milman, *History of Latin Christianity* (3rd edition), vol. iii, p. 357.
[5] Dr. Wm. Barry, *The Papal Monarchy*, p. 184.

whose hinge the universal Catholic Church turns, has been compelled to suffer. . . . Oh shame! Oh grief! How monsters horrible to be seen were intruded by them (secular princes) into that see to be reverenced by angels. How many tragedies were accomplished! With what filth did it happen to her to be bespattered herself without spot or wrinkle! With what stench to be infected, with what dirt to be polluted [*inquinari spurcitiis*], and by these to be blackened with perpetual infamy!"[1] Again: "What was then the aspect of the Holy Roman Church? How utterly foul when harlots [*meretrices*] most powerful and most vile dominated Rome; at whose will sees were changed, bishops presented—and, what is horrible to hear, and unspeakable—their lovers intruded into the see of Peter; pseudo-Pontiffs who are recorded in the catalogue of Roman Pontiffs only for the sake of marking the dates. For who could maintain that persons lawlessly intruded by such courtesans were legitimate Pontiffs . . . and what sort of cardinals, deacons, and priests were chosen by these monsters?"[2] Baronius tells that all things were settled at the will of the all-powerful harlot Theodora —"*filias prostituens Pontificis Sedis Apostolicae invasoribus*".[3]

3

The characters of the Avignon Popes in the fourteenth century are discreditable. Extortion, the merchandise of sacred things, luxury, attained through them a pitch hitherto unknown. The career of Clement V was in more than one aspect repulsive. His unscrupulous and barbarous treatment of the Templars has stained his memory. He was "the creature and the tool of King Philip".[4] Clement VI provided for his nephews and his court at the expense of Christendom and said with a laugh that his predecessors had not known how to be Popes.[5]

The history of the life of an Italian Pope, Urban VI (1378–89), reveals a character of such repulsive type that the plea of insanity has been suggested for him. The cardinals who under duress selected him (except one who died soon after) denounced him as an intruder, an apostate, an accursed antichrist. Among other brutalities he

---

[1] *Annales ecclesiastici*, ann. 900: 3.
[2] Ibid., ann. 912: 8.
[3] Ibid., ann. 908: 6.
[4] Dr. Barry, *The Papacy and Modern Times*, p. 36.
[5] Creighton, *History of the Papacy* (new edition), vol. i, p. 53.

inflicted savage punishment on six cardinals of his own appointment and had five of them executed. "They suffered the rack and imprisonment and death."[1] The cautious Creighton describes him as "reckless" and "ruffianly".[2]

4

The fifty years from 1471 to 1521 saw a succession of disreputable Popes. Of Paul II, who died in 1471, Dr. William Barry writes that his fine character was "misunderstood by the Italian courts which never dreamt that a Pope could be an honourable man".[3] The crimes of Sixtus IV in instigating wars to extend his nephew's ill-gotten dominions are referred to elsewhere.[4] His excessive nepotism also led to his making several others of his nephews and relations cardinals, one of them at the age of eighteen and two of them in their twenties. "During his pontificate the cardinal college was hopelessly debased and the whole course of life in Rome was changed for the worse."[5]

Pastor writes that the serious corruption in the College of Cardinals began under Sixtus IV and that during the reign of Innocent VIII (1484–92) it increased to such an extent that it became possible by bribery to procure the election of such a successor as Alexander VI.[6]

The election of Innocent VIII was due to shameful simony. He was the father of many illegitimate children. One son, Franceschetto, lived a debauched life in Rome. His marriage with a daughter of Lorenzo Medici was openly celebrated by the Pope in the Vatican. In the next year the Pope had a grand-daughter of his own married with much pomp in the Vatican. He took part in a banquet on the occasion when his daughter and other women were present. Another grand-daughter was similarly publicly married in the Vatican a month before his death. He made the illegitimate son of his brother a cardinal and made the son of Lorenzo Medici a cardinal at the age of thirteen. It was no wonder that "the general corruption of morals in Italy advanced unchecked during his pontificate".[7] Innocent

---

[1] Prof. Francis Xavier Funk, *Manual of Church History*, vol. ii, p. 13 (E. T.).
[2] *History of the Papacy* (1897 edition), vol. i, p. 94.
[3] *The Papacy and Modern Times*, p. 77.
[4] See p. 217.
[5] Creighton, *History of the Papacy*, vol. iii, p. 114.
[6] *History of the Popes*, vol. v, p. 170.
[7] Creighton, *History of the Papacy*, vol. iii, p. 157.

granted Caesar Borgia a dispensation to receive minor orders at the age of seven. "In Rome everything appeared to be on sale."[1]

Of the next Pope, Alexander VI, there is little occasion to write. His monstrous depravity is well known. "In Alexander VI the Papacy stood forth in all the strength of its emancipations from morality."[2] "The Borgias represented the renascence of crime such as had been witnessed in the days of Tiberius and other emperors. . . . Rome was a sink of shameless vice; iniquity had reached its zenith."[3] Pastor exposes the foolishness of the attempts to whitewash Alexander and writes that "to the end of his days he remained the slave of the demon of sensuality".[4] He secured his election by "the rankest simony".[5]

His daughter Lucrezia's marriage in the Vatican was the scene of scandalous revelry. Among the ladies present was the Pope's newest mistress, the notorious Guilia Farnese. The Pope made her brother a cardinal, who afterward, as Pope Paul III (1534–49), appointed two of his own grandsons to be cardinals at an early age.[6] The marriage was dissolved in a disgraceful way four years later. Lucrezia was next married to a Neapolitan prince who was mysteriously murdered. Her next marriage was celebrated in Rome with excessive pomp. Many cardinals and bishops took part in the masses and festivities.

Perhaps the climax was reached when the universal Pastor, leaving Rome to take possession of some newly conquered fortresses, appointed Lucrezia to be his vicegerent in the Vatican. An offensive story recorded by Burchard[7] makes Gregorovius write: "What a scene for the Vatican! A young and beautiful woman, the Pope's own daughter, presiding over the cardinals in consistory. This one scene is sufficient to show to what depths the Church of Rome had sunk; it is more convincing than a thousand satires, than a thousand official reports."[8] The theory that Alexander was the vicegerent of God was once for all demolished by the appointment of Lucrezia to be his vicegerent. The accounts of some of the indecent orgies

[1] F. X. Funk, *Church History*, vol. ii, p. 28 (E. T.).
[2] Creighton, vol. iv, p. 52.
[3] Gregorovius, *History of the City of Rome*, vol. vii, pp. 430, 432 (E. T.).
[4] *History of the Popes*, vol. v, p. 363. Cf. vol. vi, p. 138.
[5] Ibid., vcl. v, p. 385.
[6] Ranke, *History of the Popes*, vol. i, p. 183 (E. T.).
[7] *Diarium*, vol. iii, p. 154.
[8] *Lucretia Borgia*, p. 173 (E. T.).

that took place in the presence of the Pope and Lucrezia are too bestial for repetition.[1] They make any tale of horror about life in the Vatican then credible. The accounts are too well authenticated to be challenged.[2] These abnormal excesses at the headquarters of Christianity spread degeneracy through Europe.

Alexander's depravity was not confined to unrestrained licentiousness. His treachery, greed and cruelty were appalling. He imprisoned the blind Cardinal Orsino, after seizing his palace and goods. The cardinal's mother had to pay the Pope 2,000 ducats and a costly pearl he had fancied for the privilege of sending the cardinal a daily supply of food. The cardinal died soon afterwards and it was commonly believed the Pope had him poisoned. Pastor cautiously writes: "The truth of this is doubtful."[3] There is less doubt about the poisoning of the rich Cardinal Michiel, whose death brought the Pope 150,000 ducats. Pastor puts the blame for this crime on the Pope's son, Caesar.[4] He admits that Alexander's conduct "was such as to shock the public opinion of a profoundly corrupt age to a degree hitherto unexampled. There seemed no end to the accumulation of scandals in the Borgia family. . . . Can we wonder that where the Borgia were concerned nothing was thought too horrible to be believed".[5]

Creighton's characteristically moderate verdict is: "However unwilling we may be to accuse a Pope of poisoning, there can be no doubt of the prevalence of the belief amongst Alexander VI's contemporaries; and the deaths of Cardinals Orsini and Michiel were accompanied by such suspicious circumstances that we cannot dismiss the belief as entirely groundless in their cases."[6]

Julius II secured the headship of the Church by bribery. "Contracts were made in public, no expense was spared, the pontificate was put up to auction for the highest bidder."[7] Gregorovius describes him as "one of the most profane and unclerical figures on the chair of Peter". He quotes the verdict of Vettori, a dispassionate contemporary. "The Popes, although calling themselves Vicars of

---

[1] Cf. Burchard, *Diarium*, vol. iii, p. 167.
[2] See Thuasne's note, Burchard, ibid. Pastor, *History of the Popes*, vol. vi, p. 108. Creighton, *History of the Papacy*, vol. iv, p. 50.
[3] *History of the Popes*, vol. vi, p. 126.
[4] Ibid., vol. vi, p. 128.
[5] Ibid., vol. v, p. 522.
[6] *History of the Papacy*, vol. iv, p. 40.
[7] Ibid., vol. iv, p. 60.

P

Christ, have introduced a new religion which has nothing of Christ in it but the name."[1]

Julius in his military campaigns was careful to have the Body of Christ carried in front of his army. He did not think it unseemly to make a triumphant entry to Rome after one of his military expeditions, on Palm Sunday, 1507. "The Romans thought that they did honour to the day by welcoming Christ's Vicar with the cry, 'Blessed is he that cometh in the name of the Lord'."[2] He was wont to live in the camp with his troops. Pastor is constrained to admit that he was carried away "to violate the *decorum clericale* in a scandalous manner".[3] When his long siege of Mirandola at last succeeded he entered the defeated city by a ladder through a breach in the walls. One of his three daughters lived in Rome and the Pope arranged her marriage with a member of the Orsini family.

Leo X (1513–21), while not so grossly revolting as some of his predecessors, was an utterly unspiritual luxury-loving prelate. His relations with the princes of his day is a long story of duplicity. For over a century all Europe was crying for the reformation of the Church in its head and members. Leo lived when the corruptions had become intolerable, but, instead of rectifying abuses, intensified them. Pastor bewails that at such a crisis a man should be chosen as Pope "who was not equal to the serious duties of his high office, who in fact scarcely knew anything about them";[4] and quotes the words of an ecclesiastic devoted to the Holy See: "Many were of opinion that it was bad for the Church that her head should be absorbed in amusements, music, the chase and buffoonery, instead of being occupied with the thought of the needs of his flock and in bewailing its misfortunes. The salt of the earth has lost its savour and nothing remains for it but to be cast out and trodden by man."

One of Leo's disgraceful actions was his bargain with the young prince, Albert of Brandenburg, aged twenty-five, to hold the vast archbishoprics of Magdeburg, Mayence and the bishopric of Halbersteat. Albert paid Leo 24,000 ducats. The arrangement for the sale of indulgences in these areas brought on the final revolt of Luther. Half of the proceeds were to go to Leo and the other half to Albert. To Pastor the impending catastrophe seems "like a

[1] *History of the City of Rome*, vol. viii, pp. 116, 117.
[2] Creighton, *History of the Papacy*, vol. iv, pp. 92, 93.
[3] *History of the Popes*, vol. vi, p. 439.
[4] Ibid., vol. vii, p. 4.

judgment from heaven".[1] The shocking imposition of the financial traffic in indulgences to supply the papal coffers was only the culminating point of countless enormities. The boundless expenditure of Leo was recouped by his agents selling release for the dead from purgatory.

The lives of many Popes can only be reconciled with Roman Catholic dogma if it be granted that morality is not vital to religion. How far gone from essential Christianity is the dogmatic position of Romanism becomes evident by the apologies, for instance, of the scholarly Pastor whose defensive *History of the Popes* is of high value. The fact that the unworthiness of priests does not invalidate the truth of religion will not avail as an excuse for the moral turpitude of the Vicars of Christ. The theory is that these Pontiffs are given to the world to take Christ's place on earth and that they have a special divine assistance to rule, feed and govern the Church. Pastor's unavailing plea is: "The supreme high priest can in no way diminish the value of that heavenly treasure which he controls and dispenses but only as a steward. The gold remains gold in impure as in pure hands. The papal office belongs to a higher sphere than the personality of its occupant for the time being, and can neither gain nor lose in its essential dignity by his saintliness on the one side or his unworthiness on the other."[2] Pastor seems to imagine that he is rebutting the arguments drawn from the lives of Alexander VI or Julius II when he tells us that Alexander "took pains on many occasions to promote devotion to St. Anne and the Blessed Virgin";[3] and that Julius "had a special devotion to the Blessed Sacrament".[4]

[1] *History of the Popes*, vol. vii, p. 333.   [3] Ibid., vol. vi, p. 145.
[2] Ibid., vol. vi, p. 141.   [4] Ibid., vol. vi, p. 599.

ADDENDUM.—Platina (d. 1481), was superintendent of the Vatican Library. Burchard was Alexander VI's Master of Ceremonies.

CHAPTER XLVII

PERSECUTION

The Popes' claims to be the true Vicars of Christ with full power to govern the Church must be tested in the light of the actual exercise of their power. One such crucial test is their record concerning religious persecution.

The enlightened Christian conscience regards punishing men with confiscation of their goods, perpetual imprisonment, torture and burning at the stake, for erroneous or independent beliefs, as peculiarly horrible and an outrage on the spirit of Christ. Yet for centuries it was the practice of the Church of Rome, and the infliction of the death penalty has been promulgated as its official teaching even in this present century. The Popes were ardent inculcators of such a practice and were directly responsible for its monstrous cruelties.

When the power of the Popes reached its zenith in the Middle Ages the frightful system for the extermination of "heretics" was elaborated.

Through the twelfth and thirteenth centuries the machinery of terrorism was constructed piece by piece. Secular authorities were compelled to co-operate under drastic penalties. Kings, if they refused, were to be excommunicated and their subjects released from fealty to them. A city which refused was to be laid under an interdict and cut off from intercourse with other cities. Innocent III in the decree *Excommunicamus* ordered: "Let Catholics who have taken the cross and girded themselves for extermination of heretics enjoy the same indulgence, and let them be fortified by the same holy privilege as is given to those who go to the succour of the Holy Land."

Innocent IV gave comprehensive instructions in his bull *Ad Extirpanda* (1252).[1] This was revised and reissued by subsequent Popes. Torture is prescribed, but it was to stop short of pulling off limbs or causing death—*citra membri diminutionem et mortis periculum*. Ruinous punishments are enacted on all who harbour

[1] Mansi, xxiii, 569–75.

or give advice or favour to a heretic. How completely the abominable system was the direct achievement of the Papacy is shown by
the clause that no change could be made without the special authority
of the Apostolic See.

Leo X in his famous bull *Exsurge Domine* (1520) denounced as
one of the errors of Luther the following: "That heretics should be
burned is contrary to the will of the Spirit." "Rome taught," writes
Lord Acton, "for four centuries and more that no Catholic could
be saved who denied that heretics ought to be put to death."[1]

In the nineteenth century Pope Gregory XVI, in his *Mirari vos*
(1832), stormed against liberty of conscience. "Out of this most
foul fountain of indifferentism flows that absurd and erroneous
opinion or rather madness [*deliramentum*] that liberty of conscience
ought to be asserted and secured by everybody."[2] Among the errors
condemned by Pius IX in his famous Syllabus (1864) are the following: "In the present day it is no longer necessary that the Catholic
religion shall be held as the only religion of the state to the exclusion of all modes of worship" (77); and: "It has been wisely
provided by the law in some countries called Catholic that persons
coming to reside therein shall enjoy the free exercise of their own
worship" (78).

Pope Leo XIII, in his encyclical *Libertas* (1888), denounces
liberty of conscience and explains how "although on account of
the extraordinary political conditions [of today] it usually happens
that the Church acquiesces in certain modern liberties, not because
she prefers them in themselves but because she judges it expedient
that they should be permitted, she would in happier times resume
her own liberty".[3] The same Pope, in his *Immortale Dei* (reprinted
in C. C. Marshall's *The Roman Catholic Church in the Modern State*),
refers approvingly to the *Mirari vos* of Gregory XVI, and agrees
with him in denying "that it is right for individuals to form their
own personal judgments about religion". He condemns the erroneous theories that the modern state should not prefer one religion
to all the rest, and "that it is bound to grant equal rights to every
creed; so that public order may not be disturbed by any particular
form of religious belief"; and that "everyone is to be free to follow
whatever religion he prefers".[4]

[1] *Correspondence*, vol. i, p. 108.
[2] Mirbt 583.
[3] Quoted in C. J. Cadoux's *Roman Catholicism and Freedom*, p. 31.
[4] Marshall, *The Roman Catholic Church in the Modern State*, pp. 386, 382.

Pius XI, in his letter to Cardinal Gasparri, announced that "liberty of conscience and liberty of discussion are to be understood and practised in accordance with Catholic doctrines and Catholic laws."[1]

In the twentieth century Professor Marianus de Luca, S.J., in his book *Institutiones Juris Ecclesiastici Publici* defends the death penalty. Professor Lepicier in his *De Stabilitate et Progressu Dogmatis* justifies the practice of the Church in handing "the heretic over to be exterminated from the world by death" (*a mundo per mortem exterminandum*). He maintains that the words in the Syllabus about employing force pertain to bodily punishments not excluding death. He supports his case by the example of the Roman Inquisition, which, if not expressly, at least equivalently, punished heretics by demanding this penalty from the secular arm and excommunicating it if it should fail in its duty. "Who dares to say that the Church has erred in a matter so grave as this?"

Honours were showered on Lepicier. Pope Pius X wrote heartily congratulating, and bestowing on him the apostolic benediction and informing him: "You have given vehement pleasure to the supreme Pontiff." He became a cardinal and was appointed papal delegate to foreign countries more than once.

Cardinal Billot was Professor in the Gregorian College at Rome. His *Tractatus de Ecclesia Christi* was published by the official press of the university. From the 1921–2 edition Dr. Coulton quotes as follows: "Therefore we must say that material force is rightly employed to protect religion, to coerce those who disturb it, and, generally speaking, to remove those things which impede our spiritual aim; nay, that force can have no more noble use than this."[2]

Rev. R. A. Knox, writing in 1939, repudiates the idea that in "our enlightened age" the Catholic Church would "waive all right of invoking the secular arm in defence of her own principles". He envisages conditions in which a Catholic Government would be entitled "to deport or imprison those who unsettled the minds of its subjects with new doctrines". "When we demand liberty in the modern state we are appealing to its own principles, not to ours."[3]

---

[1] Marshall, *The Roman Catholic Church in the Modern State*, p. 401. The letter is reprinted in full from *Current History*, August 1929.
[2] *Romanism and Truth*, vol. i, p. 82.
[3] *The Belief of Catholics*, pp. 241, 242.

CHAPTER XLVIII

THE INQUISITION

That most learned of English Roman Catholics, Lord Acton, wrote: "The Inquisition is peculiarly the weapon and peculiarly the work of the Popes. It stands out from all those things in which they co-operated, followed or assented as the distinctive feature of papal Rome. It was set up, renewed and perfected by a long series of acts emanating from the supreme authority in the Church. No other institution, no doctrine, no ceremony is so distinctly the individual creation of the Papacy, except the dispensing power. It is the principal thing with which the Papacy is identified, and by which it must be judged. The principle of the Inquisition is the Pope's sovereign power over life and death. Whosoever disobeys him should be tried and tortured and burnt. If that cannot be done, formalities may be dispensed with, and the culprit may be killed like an outlaw. That is to say, the principle of the Inquisition is murderous, and a man's opinion of the Papacy is regulated and determined by his opinion of religious assassination."[1]

About the history of the Inquisition there is not now much dispute among scholars. Lea's great works, the *History of the Inquisition in the Middle Ages* and the *History of the Inquisition of Spain*, embody immense and careful research. Little difference about facts is to be found between the writings of Vancandard and Maycock on the one side and between Coulton and Turberville on the other. It may be maintained that no human organisation was ever responsible for such appalling cruelty and misery, and for such injury to the development of the free inquiring spirit of man.

1

The methods of the Inquisition were, from the start, an outrage on elementary principles of justice. Any one could be arrested on suspicion. The trial was secret. The prisoner was not allowed to

[1] *Letters to Mary Gladstone*, pp. 185, 186.

know the accusers or witnesses. The judges were ecclesiastics with the most absolute power. The evidence of infamous persons, criminals or perjurers or heretics, was admitted so long as it was hostile. Children from the age of twelve were required to bear testimony. The prisoner had not the help of an advocate, for defence of a heretic was held guilty of the crime of fautorship of heresy. Lea considers "it may well be doubted whether, in the ordinary course of the Inquisition, counsel for the defence ever appeared before it".[1]

A person tried by the Inquisition was scarcely ever acquitted. "In the register of Carcassonne from 1249 to 1258, comprising about two hundred cases, there does not occur a single instance of a prisoner discharged as innocent."[2] Tanon, a French investigator, writes: "There is scarcely ever an acquittal, pure and simple, in the sentence of the Inquisition."[3]

2

The numbers of those burned at the stake cannot be known. Outside Spain the numbers may not have been as many as were once supposed. The frequency of accounts of burnings in many parts of Europe would point to a large number. Bernard Gui, inquisitor at Toulouse from 1307 to 1323, sentenced forty-two to death out of nine hundred and thirty tried. Gui was a careful, reputable inquisitor. On the other hand, there must have been many whose methods varied between his and those of the ferocious Robert le Bugre. This man, who is said to have conceived his mission to be "not to convert but to burn", ravaged much of France. At Peronne he burned five, at Hondancourt four, at Cambrai twenty, at Douai ten, and so on. "In one term of two or three months he is said to have thus dispatched about fifty unfortunates of either sex, and the whole number of his victims during his unchecked career of several years must have been large."[4] The excesses of the notorious Conrad of Marburg caused a general panic in Germany where he was appointed inquisitor by Gregory IX. "How great was the number of victims cannot now be ascertained."[5]

[1] *History of the Inquisition in the Middle Ages*, vol. i, p. 445.
[2] Ibid., vol. i, p. 453.
[3] See Coulton, *The Inquisition and Liberty*, p. 125.
[4] Lea, *History of the Inquisition in the Middle Ages*, vol. ii, p. 116.
[5] *Catholic Encyclopedia*, vol. iv, p. 260.

3

The minor penalties were sufficiently terrible. Gui sentenced nearly a quarter of those brought before him to wear the cross of infamy. This branded a person so severely that petitions show he could scarcely earn a livelihood.

The prisons of the Inquisition were one of the most common and atrocious penalties. Gui sentenced three hundred and seven to them. But the inquisitors could leave people in their prisons indefinitely without trial. Imprisonment would be ordered "until he shall make fuller confession of the truth". The inquisitor Eymeric in his famous *Directorium* instructs that a person believed guilty "shall be shut up in prison, strictly confined and in chains. . . . If he shows no willingness to be converted there is no need for haste . . . for the pains and privations of imprisonment often bring about a change of mind".[1] "The dungeons of the Inquisition at best were abodes of fearful misery, but where there were reasons for increasing their terrors there was no difficulty in increasing the hardships. The *durus carcer et arcta vita*—chains and starvation in a stifling hole —was a favourite device for extracting confession from unwilling lips."[2]

It happens that there is definite information about some of these prisons. Clergy and laity complained about the prison conditions in some towns in the south of France. It was stated that the cells were fitted up with divers kinds of torments. "Many through the severity of these torments lose the use of their limbs and are rendered utterly impotent. Some also, by reason of impatience and excessive pain, end their days by the cruellest death."

The, consuls of Carcassonne thus described the inquisitors' dungeons there. "Some are so dark and airless that the inmates cannot tell night from day; and thus they are in perpetual lack of air and complete darkness. In others are poor wretches in manacles of iron or wood, unable to move, sitting in their own filth, and unable to lie except on their backs upon the cold earth, and they are kept for a long time in these torments day and night."[3] The king protested that the inquisitors punished innocent folk and by newly

---

[1] Maycock, *The Inquisition*, p. 157.
[2] Lea, *History of the Inquisition in the Middle Ages*, vol. i, p. 420.
[3] Prof. Vidal, *Le Tribunal d'Inquisition de Pamiers*; see Coulton, *The Inquisition*, p. 54.

invented tortures extracted from them falsehoods about many law-abiding people, living and dead. Petitions against inhuman cruelties of the inquisitors went on for years. A Franciscan monk, Bernard Delicieux, bravely championed the sufferers. At last, in 1306, Clement V appointed two cardinals to investigate. The people who could have borne witness were terrified to do so lest the vengeance of the Inquisition would fall on them. It was pleaded that witnesses be not tortured while the case was being tried.

The cardinals found forty prisoners at Albi, including people of learning and position. The cardinals, among other reforms, ordered that certain old and sick and feeble persons "should have a change of dungeon and should be raised up from the deeper cells unto those which are higher as soon as these have been repaired". In another prison the victims were "in strict and very dark dungeons". "The said prisoners have not yet been condemned, and they have been kept in these dungeons for five years or more as they themselves have said."

Four years later we find the Pope ordering that prisoners in Albi be tried who had been eight years in prison without trial. Later again, in 1319, a man of Cordes who had been eighteen years in prison was at last tried and handed over to be burned. Another who was nine-teen years in prison without trial was allowed to escape with wearing crosses. The Inquisition prison at Carcassonne still survives. The lower dungeon is approached by a trap door. The stone pillar is worn by the prisoners' backs, and the chains are still riveted to it. There "through long years the miserable inmates endured a living death far worse than the short agony of the stake".[1]

It is significant that the Inquisition took vengeance on the man who had the almost unique courage to expose its abominations. Bernard Delicieux was arrested and was delivered over to the Inquisition. A papal commission tried him in 1319. In the inquisitorial deposi-tions against him it is alleged that "once, at Toulouse, he constantly and publicly asserted that Saints Peter and Paul would not be able to defend themselves from heresy if they were now alive and if they were examined in the fashion followed by the inquisitors". Twice he was tortured. In the record of the trial the notaries have recorded his shrieks. He was handed over to the Inquisition to be imprisoned for life, in chains, and on bread and water in the hideous Carcassonne dungeons. The judges, in view of his old age and debility, ordered that the penance of chains and bread and water be omitted. The

[1] Lea, *History of the Inquisition in the Middle Ages*, vol. i, p. 492.

Pope, John XXII, countermanded such mercy. In a short time death gave him release.

A. L. Maycock admits: "In the *Murus strictus* the horrors of solitude and the deadening weight of the chains were added to the privations and discomforts of the less severe confinement. Death under these conditions became an end devoutly to be wished. Indeed in the *Murus strictus* it was really little more than a question as to which would give out first, the mind or the body. We hear in 1273 of a prisoner who had struck himself and wounded himself in the head desiring death and seeking to kill himself."[1]

4

The most ghastly abomination of all was the system of torture. The accounts of its cold-blooded operations make one shudder at the capacity of human beings for cruelty. And it was decreed and regulated by the Popes who claim to represent Christ on earth. In 1252 Pope Innocent IV solemnly authorised it. Confirmatory or regulatory decrees about it were issued by Alexander IV, Clement IV, Urban IV and Clement V. Coulton quotes the frank statement of Mr. Christopher Hollis that the Pope's sanctioning the employment of torture is an "appalling truth".[1] There was the rack with its pulleys and windlasses, the *strappado*, which lifted the person to the roof by a rope affixed to his hands tied behind his back. Weights of varying size were tied to him. After being suspended he was allowed to crash to the floor. There was the water torture. A variety of it was to place the person horizontally, his head in a hollowed-out trough, kept in position by an iron band round his forehead. Cords that cut into his flesh bound his limbs. "A damp cloth was placed upon the tongue and a small trickle of running water allowed to fall upon it. Then by the natural actions of breathing and swallowing the cloth was drawn down into the throat, producing an agonising sensation of suffocation."[2]

Another method, quoted by Coulton from Masini's *Holy Arsenal*, is: "A fierce fire is lit; the patient is laid with his feet shackled and turned towards the fire; they are rubbed with lard or grease or any other penetrating and combustible matter. He is thus burned horribly. From time to time a screen is set between his feet and the

[1] *The Inquisition*, p. 187.
[2] Coulton, *The Inquisition and Liberty*, p. 152.
[3] Maycock, *The Inquisition*, p. 162.

brazier: this is a moment of respite which enables the inquisitor to resume his examination."[1]

"Careful notes were taken not only of all that was confessed by the victim, but of his shrieks, cries, lamentations, broken interjections and appeals for mercy. The most moving things in the literature of the Inquisition are not the accounts of their sufferings left by the victims but the sober memoranda kept by the officers of the tribunals. We are distressed and horrified just because there is no intention to shock us."[2] The inquisitors were fertile in planning agonising varieties of torture.

Confessions were supposed not to be valid if made under torture. This was circumvented by torturing the victim until he confessed. Then he was removed to another chamber where the confession was required to be repeated, and stress was laid in the record on the confession being freely given. It was the rule that torture must not be repeated. The inquisitors repeated it if the victim withdrew his confession, but called it "continuation". "The inquisitors got round every restriction placed upon their use of torture by a series of the most blatant equivocations that could possibly be imagined."[3]

Pope Clement V, who joined with Philip the Fair of France in suppressing the Knight Templars and confiscating their vast possessions, employed against them torture on a terrific scale. In 1310 he induced Edward II to allow torture to be used in England—where it was till then illegal. He warned him of the penalties of impeding the Inquisition and promised him a plenary indulgence for all his sins if he would allow the Templars to be tortured. In 1311 the Pope everywhere ordered fresh tortures. His bulls for this are styled by Lea "perhaps the most disgraceful that ever proceeded from a vicegerent of God".[4] The horrors of the tortures used may be seen from the case of a priest who had fire applied to his feet to such an extent that the bones of his heels dropped out a few days afterwards.[5] A Templar before an episcopal commission in 1309 told of his hands being tied so tightly behind his back that the blood gushed from beneath his nails. "If you put me to such tortures again I will deny everything that I now say. I will say anything you like." In one[6]

[1] *The Inquisition and Liberty*, p. 155.
[2] A. S. Turberville, *The Spanish Inquisition*, p. 93.
[3] Maycock, *The Inquisition*, p. 159.
[4] *History of the Inquisition in the Middle Ages*, vol. iii, p. 317.
[5] Ibid., vol. iii, p. 287.
[6] Maycock, *The Inquisition*, p. 225.

place thirty-six died from the effects of torture; in another, twenty-five.

5

The punishments of the Inquisition did not cease when the victim was burned to ashes, or immured for life in the Inquisition dungeons. His relatives were reduced to beggary by the law that all his possessions were forfeited.

The system offered unlimited opportunities for loot. The inquisitor Eymeric about 1375 is found lamenting that at that date in Aragon there has been such extirpation that the heretics are mostly poor folks as the Fratecelli or Waldensians, and rich heretics very rare.

This source of gain largely accounts for the revolting practice of what has been called "corpse-trials". Bernard Gui during his sixteen years in Toulouse sentenced sixty-nine persons to have their bones exhumed and burned. Twenty further trials of dead people took place. The property of these increased the spoils. Maycock admits: "That the practice of confiscating the property of condemned heretics was productive of many acts of extortion, rapacity and corruption will be doubted by no one who has any knowledge either of human nature or of the historical documents."[1] Good Catholics "felt that no man was safe whose wealth might arouse cupidity, or whose independence might provoke revenge".[2]

Under the Inquisition the technique of torture became a sort of theological science. The *Times Literary Supplement*, 8th January 1938, reported the sale for £100 of the *Repertorium haereticae pravitatis* (1494). It was an Inquisition manual including "Instructions on methods of torture and how to deal with Jews and other heretics".

[1] *The Inquisition*, p. 215.
[2] Lea, *History of the Inquisition in the Middle Ages*, vol. ii, p. 59.

CHAPTER XLIX

THE SPANISH INQUISITION

The Inquisition in Spain perpetrated horrors on a more terrific scale than in other countries; its activities were more atrocious and its hecatombs of victims more numerous than elsewhere. As the Spanish Inquisition was more under local control it is often designated by the name "royal" as distinct from the "papal" Inquisition in the rest of Europe.

It is a favourite plea that the excesses of the Spanish Inquisition were due to the State and that the Popes are not accountable for them. But the Popes had the supreme power. The authority of the Inquisition was delegated from them. They commissioned the Inquisitors General. The inquisitors were always ecclesiastics under their control. They guarded their right to hear appeals. The Inquisition was always first and last a papal institution. The Church taught the punishing of heresy with burning "to be an act so eminently pious that it accorded an indulgence to any one who would contribute wood to the pile, thus assuming the responsibility and expending the Treasure of the merits of Christ in stimulating popular ferocity".[1]

The atrocities of the Spanish Inquisition cannot be disputed. The evidence for the responsibility of the Popes is clear. The papal authorisation given for it could at any time have been withdrawn. Sixtus IV, in 1482, issued a bull decreeing that there should be free appeal from it to the Holy See with suspension of proceedings under pain of excommunication. Succeeding Popes maintained this prerogative. There is no doubt it was a profitable source of income. Alexander VI, when in need of funds for the magnificent embassy of his son to bring to King Louis XIII of France the bull of divorce from Queen Jeanne, heard appeals from two hundred and thirty Spanish heretics.[2]

Each new Inquisitor General was commissioned by the Pope, generally by a *motu-proprio*—the spontaneous act of the Holy See.

[1] Lea, *History of the Inquisition in Spain*, vol. iii, p. 184.
[2] Ibid., vol. ii, p. 114.

This in itself fixed the complicity in the Inquisition proceedings. The Popes could interpose to discipline the inquisitors.

Torquemada, the most infamous of the inquisitors for ferocity, had full papal authorisation. He was commissioned by Sixtus IV in 1483 to fuller powers. He was recommissioned by Innocent VIII in 1485. So far were the Popes from seeking to retard Torquemada's inhuman cruelties that we find them praising him and spurring him on. Sixtus IV wrote to him eulogising his zeal: "We commend you in the Lord and exhort you, cherished son, to persevere with tireless zeal in aiding and promoting the cause of faith, by doing which, as we are assured you will, you will win our special favour." Alexander VI, in 1496, two years before Torquemada's death, wrote that he "cherishes him in the very bowels of affection for his immense labours in the exaltation of the faith."[1]

The Pope could always interpose to overrule inquisitors and sovereigns. In spite of the opposition of Philip II and the Inquisition officials, Pius V insisted on Archbishop Carranza being handed over to his tribunal. He threatened to lay Spain under an interdict and he made the Inquisitor General resign. Similarly Innocent X took the Marquis of Vilalba out of the hands of local inquisitors and forced the Inquisitor General to resign his bishopric under threat of abolishing the Spanish Inquisition. In the case of a convicted Jesuit Sixtus V gave notice that if he were not handed over he would deprive the then Inquisitor General, Cardinal Quiroga, of office and cardinalate.

"In what sense," wrote Lord Acton, referring to Sixtus IV and the Spanish Inquisition, "is the Pope not responsible for the Constitution by which he established the new tribunal?"[2]

These, and similar cases, show the supremacy of the Popes over the operations of the Spanish Inquisition. The Spanish Cortes obtained an oath from Ferdinand that a *concordia*, embodying popular requirements about the Inquisition, be observed. Leo X in 1513 issued a *motu proprio* dispensing him and the Inquisitor General from their oaths.[3]

The burnings of heretics, handed over to the secular arm at Autos-da-fé, had peculiar pomp and festivity in Spain. Enormous numbers of the faithful gathered to see the Gospel of the loving

[1] Lea, *History of the Inquisition in Spain*, vol. i, p. 174.
[2] *Historical Essays and Studies*, p. 503.
[3] Lea, *History of the Inquisition of Spain*, vol. ii, p. 272.

Christ assert itself by these holocausts. Royal marriages or state visits were celebrated with these religious spectacles. Forty days' indulgences rewarded the spectators. So late as 1680 there was a gorgeous auto at Madrid at which one hundred heretics were burned. "Familiar is Voltaire's gibe that an Asiatic arriving in Madrid on such an occasion would be doubtful whether he was witnessing a festival, a religious ceremony, a sacrifice, or a massacre; it was in fact all of these."[1] Sometimes captured English seamen were burned at these orgies.

The terrible powers for destruction of inquisitors is shown by the case of the inquisitor Lucero at Cordova. Lucero was convicted of destroying people and seizing their property on a wholesale scale through fabricated evidence obtained by torture. For instance, a certain preacher was convicted. One hundred and seven of those who were said to attend his sermons were burned in a single auto-da-fé. A letter to the royal secretary in 1507 protests that Lucero and his fellow inquisitors "were able to defame the whole kingdom, to destroy, without God or justice, a great part of it, slaying and robbing and violating maids and wives to the great dishonour of the Christian religion".[2] Some of the accusations reveal diabolical atrocities. A young girl of fifteen is said to have been locked in a room stripped naked and scourged until she consented to bear testimony against her mother. A prisoner was carried in a chair to the auto-da-fé with his feet burned to the bone; he and his wife were burnt alive.[3]

It is impossible to tell the numbers of those condemned to perpetual imprisonment, the galleys, confiscation of goods or other penalties. Neither are there materials for knowing how many were burnt at the stake. A secretary to Queen Isabella gave the number burnt to 1490 as two thousand. Zurita, the historian of Aragon, estimates that prior to 1520 as many as four thousand perished in Seville alone.[4] An inscription at Seville records that from 1492 (i.e. after the first nine years of Torquemada's early ferocity) to 1524 nearly one thousand were burnt.

The history of Spain, secular and religious, is sufficient evidence of the results of the Inquisition. In that unfortunate land is to be seen the fruits of frantic devotion to the papal faith and the ruthless

[1] Turberville, *The Spanish Inquisition*, p. 113.
[2] Lea, *History of the Inquisition of Spain*, vol. i, p. 195.
[3] Ibid., vol. i, p. 211.
[4] Turberville, *The Spanish Inquisition*, p. 113.

suppression of all independent thought. The reign of terror against any criticism of Romanism or freedom of mind paralysed intellectual development. The hideous cruelties, sanctified as acts of devotion to the Deity, must have had a powerful influence in demoralising and brutalising the people. The outrages inflicted there in recent years on the clergy and religious symbols demonstrate the hatred of the Spanish populace to Christianity as they knew it. The *Analecta Ecclesiastica*, a clerical journal published in Rome, had an article (January 1895) stating: "We may certainly ascribe to the auspicious vigilance of the holy inquisitors that religious peace and that steadfastness in the faith which renders the Spanish race illustrious."[1]

[1] Coulton, *Medieval Studies*, xviii, p. 71.

CHAPTER L

GALILEO

Galileo in 1613 was a scientist whose fame resounded through Europe. Modern science reveres him as one of its most illustrious pioneers. By his study of the heavens through a telescope he was able to corroborate the theory of Copernicus that the earth revolved round the sun. Obscurantist theologians held that such views contradicted Holy Scripture and denounced him to the Inquisition.

The decision of the Inquisition theological experts ("Qualifiers") was pronounced in 1616 on two propositions extracted from Galileo's writings.

(1) The proposition that the sun is centre of the world and immovable from its place is absurd, philosophically false, and formally heretical; because it is expressly contrary to the Holy Scripture.

(2) The proposition that the earth is not the centre of the world nor immovable, but that it moves and also with a diurnal motion, is also absurd, philosophically false, and theologically considered at least erroneous in faith.

Accordingly, the Holy Office of the Inquisition ordered Cardinal Bellarmine to summon Galileo before him and admonish him to abandon such opinions and command him to abstain from teaching them under threat of imprisonment.

The cardinal gave the admonition to Galileo on 26th February 1616 in the presence of the Commissary General of the Holy Office. "The said Galileo was by the said Commissary commanded and enjoined in the name of his Holiness the Pope, and the whole congregation of the Holy Office, to relinquish altogether the said opinion, that the sun is the centre of the world and immovable, and that the earth moves; nor henceforth to hold, teach, or defend it in any way whatsoever, verbally or in writing; otherwise proceedings would be taken against him in the Holy Office: which injunction the said Galileo acquiesced in and promised to obey."

These proceedings were followed up a week later by a decree of the Congregation of the Index prohibiting and suspending until corrected the writings of Nicholas Copernicus on "The Revolutions of the Celestial Orbs", and other writers of the same views. The Pythagorean doctrine of the motion of the earth and the quiesence of the sun is declared "false and altogether opposed to Holy Scripture". The book of a Carmelite friar showing that the "aforesaid doctrine is consonant with truth and is not opposed to Holy Scripture" is altogether prohibited and condemned. Galileo had a long interview with the Pope, Paul V, soon afterwards.

In the following years the papal veto on knowledge lay heavy on the world. The genius of Galileo dare not exert itself. His resentment at the shackles which bound him can be seen in a letter he wrote to the Archduke Leopold of Austria sending him a treatise on the tides. Referring to the prohibited book of Copernicus, he writes that he held it "to be true until it pleased those gentlemen to prohibit the work and to declare that opinion to be false and contrary to Scripture. Now knowing as I do that it behoves us to obey the decisions of the authorities and to believe them, since they are guided by a higher insight than any to which my humble mind can of itself attain, I consider this treatise which I send you merely to be a poetical conceit or a dream and desire that your Highness may take it as such, inasmuch as it is based on the double motion of the earth". He complains that his treatise was written before the condemnation. He had intended to have added new proofs, "but a voice from heaven has aroused me and dissolved all my confused and tangled fantasies in mists". When an attack was made on the Copernican theories Galileo wrote a reply. He said that they were not rejected from a disbelief of their probability but "from reverence for Holy Scripture as well as zeal for religion and our holy faith". His friends persuaded him not to venture to publish his work. (Kepler, who published a reply, had his book put on the Index.)

In 1631 Galileo published the Dialogues, which were to cause the greatest tragedy of his life. He had complied with all the vexatious rules of the censorship and obtained an official *Imprimatur*. In this book he is careful not to teach the proscribed doctrine of the movement of the earth. He supposes it to be discussed *pro* and *con* by the personages in the book. The device did not save him. Pope Urban VIII was infuriated and personally directed the prosecution. He thought that some of the arguments refuted in the book were ones that he had himself put forward against the motion of the earth! The Inquisition prohibited the sale of the Dialogues. The Pope appointed a commission to examine it. The commission reported adversely. In September 1632 an order was issued: "His Holiness charges the inquisitor at Florence to inform Galileo, in the name of the Holy Office, that he is to appear in the course of the month of October in Rome before the Commissary General."

Galileo, an old, infirm man of nearly seventy years, was dismayed at the prospect of appearing before the dreaded Inquisition. That all his achievements should have caused him to be branded as a criminal made him curse the time he had given to them. So ill was he that he pleaded it was not likely he could journey then to Rome alive. "The desire to live" made him implore the intercession of a friendly cardinal with the Holy Father. He besought that he might be tried before the Inquisition in Florence. It was in vain. The Inquisition considered the letter on 11th November in the presence of the Pope who ordered that the writer must be compelled to come to Rome. The Grand Duke's ambassador solemnly assured the Pope that Galileo was in such a state that he might die on the way. In December the Florentine inquisitor reported that Galileo was in bed ill and not in a condition to travel. He forwarded a certificate in which three doctors testified to the weak state of Galileo, that he had frequent attacks of giddiness, melancholy, sleeplessness, pains. "We also observed a serious hernia with rupture of the peritoneum. All these symptoms are worthy of notice, as under the least aggravation they might become dangerous to life." The merciless reply from the Pope and Holy Office was that, unless Galileo set out, a commissioner and physician would be sent from Rome and if he were found in a condition to travel he would be brought as a prisoner in chains. If the journey had to be postponed then as soon as the danger was over he would be brought as a prisoner in chains. He would have to pay the expenses of the commissioner and physician. The Grand Duke had done his utmost to protect his friend the famous scientist, who brought honour on Florence. Italian rulers were then powerless before the tyranny of the Papacy.

Galileo arrived in the Grand Ducal litter at Rome in February 1633, and was allowed to stay at the Florentine embassy with injunctions to stay indoors and see no one.

It was not until 12th April that Galileo was summoned before the Inquisition as a prisoner. The Florentine ambassador had seen

Pope Urban VIII and, finding him implacable against Galileo, had persuaded the scientist not to defend himself but "to submit to what shall be prescribed to him to believe respecting the motion of the earth".[1] Galileo was in such profound dejection that his friends were anxious for his life. He yielded and took the line of submissiveness before the tribunal that could imprison him for life or send him to the stake. He pleaded that in his book he had not maintained the movement of the earth and had given the arguments against it. He was confined in apartments in the quarters of an Inquisition official. One of his judges visited him and persuaded him to give up his plea of not having taught the objected-to doctrine. On 30th April the wretched, terrified man condemned the argumentation of his book and declared that he sincerely held the reasons he had advanced to be false, inconclusive, and admitting of refutation. On 10th May he appeared again before the Inquisition and pleaded piteously for mercy, urging his age and ill-health and anxiety.

Galileo's fate was decided at a private meeting of the Inquisition, the Pope presiding. All through the proceedings it is the Pope who plays the chief part and it is he who directs every step. Galileo was summoned to appear on 21st June. He denied he held the doctrine of the movement of the earth since the command was given him to abandon it. Threatened with torture, he abjectly protested his obedience. He was ordered to be "sent back to his place". On 22nd June 1633, in the presence of his judges, the ten cardinals, who were Inquisitors General, "special deputies of the holy apostolical chair against heretical depravity" and of a large assembly of cardinals and prelates, the sentence arrived at before the Pope was read to him.

The sentence specifies how Galileo was denounced to the Holy Office in 1615 for holding as true the false doctrine of the movability of the earth; for instructing pupils so; for maintaining a correspondence on it with German mathematicians; for answering the objections produced from Holy Scripture according to his own meaning; for publishing a letter containing propositions "contrary to the true sense and authority of the Holy Scripture". The sentence goes on to recall how it "was decreed in the Holy Congregation held before his Holiness on the 25th day of February 1616, that his eminence the Lord Cardinal Bellarmine should enjoin you to give up altogether the said false doctrine"; and how he was dismissed on promising obedience.

[1] J. J. Fahie, *Galileo*, p. 293.

"And in order that so pernicious a doctrine might be altogether rooted out, nor insinuate itself further, to the heavy detriment of Catholic truth, a decree emanated from the Holy Congregation of the Index, prohibiting the books which treat of this doctrine; and it was declared false and altogether contrary to the Holy and divine Scripture." Then Galileo's offence in publishing his Dialogues is set forth. As it appeared he had not disclosed the whole truth with regard to his intention, "we thought it necessary to proceed to the rigorous examination of you . . . in which you answered like a good Catholic".

"Invoking therefore the most holy name of our Lord Jesus Christ and of His most Glorious Virgin Mother Mary by this our final sentence", Galileo, as "an examined and confessed criminal", is pronounced vehemently suspected of the heresy "contrary to the Holy and divine Scripture, namely that the sun is the centre of the world and that it does not move from east to west and that the earth does move"; also that an opinion can be held as probable, after it has been declared and finally decreed to be contrary to the Holy Scripture. Galileo has incurred all the penalties enjoined against delinquents; "from which it is our pleasure that you be absolved, provided that, first, with a sincere heart and unfeigned faith, in our presence, you abjure, curse, and detest the said errors and heresies, and every other error and heresy contrary to the Catholic and apostolic Church of Rome, in the form now shown to you". That his grievous and pernicious error may not go unpunished and that he may be a warning to others, his book is prohibited, "and we condemn you to the formal prison of this Holy Office for a period determinable at our pleasure; and by way of salutary penance we order you during the next three years to recite once a week the seven penitential psalms".

The form of the abjuration which the unhappy man had to sign was drastic and horrible. Kneeling, he had to admit that after it had been signified to him that the false doctrine of the mobility of the earth was repugnant to Holy Scripture he had adduced reasons with great force in support of it without giving any solution. "With a sincere heart and unfeigned faith I abjure, curse and detest the said error and heresies . . . and I swear that I will never more in future say or assert anything verbally, or in writing, which may give rise to a similar suspicion of me." He had also to swear that if he knew any "heretic" he would denounce him to the Inquisition. "So may

God help me and His holy Gospels which I touch with my own hands."

It is a shocking story. Only utter terrorism could have made Galileo perjure himself. He abjured under threat of torture and fear of life-long imprisonment and perhaps of being burned at the stake. The phrase occurs in the sentence of the inquisitors that they thought it necessary to proceed to "the rigorous examination" of him to discover his intention. This is the regular phrase for examination by torture. In Galileo's case probably the inquisitors did not proceed beyond the initial stage of threat, but that was sufficient to break the nerve of the old feeble man. He knew how a man of genius, Giordano Bruno, who also held the Copernican doctrine, was burned at Rome in 1600; and how the body of Antonio de Dominis, who died in the Inquisition prison in Rome in 1624, was burned. In his lifetime Pietro Carnesecchi, protonotary and secretary to Clement VII, was burned there and countless others.

Galileo spent the rest of his life miserably under the control of the Inquisition. He never regained entire liberty. He was unable to publish his researches. He was at first detained in the house of the friendly Archbishop of Siena and then allowed to move to his country house at Arcetri. There he was subjected to the harsh control of the Inquisition. His disease needed medical treatment at Florence. On applying for leave to go there the Inquisition Vicar informed him "of a mandate from the Holy Office that I must in future abstain from asking permission to return to Florence or they would take me back to Rome and put me in the actual prison of the Holy Office. From this answer it seems to me that in all probability my present prison will only be exchanged for that narrow and long-enduring one which awaits us all". This savage mandate was dictated by the Pope at a meeting of the Holy Office on 23rd March 1634.[1]

In 1638 the local inquisitor reported that to execute his Holiness's commands he went, accompanied by a physician, to see Galileo. He wanted to see whether if he was allowed to return to Florence he was in a condition "to propagate the condemned doctrine of the double motion of the earth". He found him entirely blind from cataract. "He has, besides, a severe rupture and suffers from continual weariness of life and sleeplessness which, as he asserts (and it is confirmed by the inmates of his house), does not permit him one hour's sound sleep in the twenty-four. He is, besides, so reduced

[1] J. J. Fahie, *Galileo*, p. 341.

that he looks more like a corpse than a living man." His house was a long way from the city and so inconvenient of access that he could seldom, and then with expense, have medical aid. The inquisitor advised that "if his Holiness in his boundless mercy" would allow him to live in Florence he was so prostrated that it would be easy to keep him in check.

The Pope at a meeting of the Congregation allowed him to go to Florence to his son's house but under orders not to go out in the city under pain of imprisonment for life and excommunication; not to speak with any one of the condemned doctrines; not to receive suspicious visitors. His confinement was so severe that at Easter a special permission from Rome had to be obtained before he could attend a church one hundred yards from his house. His life-long friend, Professor Castelli, was—after an interview with the Pope—only allowed to see him in the company of an Inquisition official and forbidden under severest penalties to converse with him on the forbidden subject.

In 1639 Galileo went back to Arcetri, and stayed there until his death in 1642. He used to address his letters from "my prison at Arcetri", "my continued exile prison". There Milton visited "the famous Galileo, grown old, a prisoner to the Inquisition for thinking in astronomy otherwise than the Franciscan and Dominican licensers thought".[1] His power, as one vehemently suspected of heresy, to make a will was questioned, as was the right to bury him in consecrated ground. Preparations were being made for a public funeral and a monument, but these had to be cancelled when the Pope sent for the Florentine ambassador and forbade them.

Papal apologists try to exonerate the Pope from complicity in these proceedings against Galileo and the doctrine of the earth's mobility. What has been written shows the leading part the Pope took in them. Further evidence, if needed, could be given. In the many efforts for relaxation of Galileo's sufferings it is always to the Pope personally that appeal is made. Repeated intercessions were made to the Pope and nearly always in vain. The fact is that it was not the cardinals—several of whom were Galileo's friends—but "the Father and Teacher of all Christians" who was directly responsible for the enormity.

The supreme Judge of the faithful exerted his fullest authority against the "heresy". "If he did not speak infallibly then, it will

[1] *Areopagitica.*

be impossible to know that he ever speaks infallibly."[1] In 1633 Pope Urban directed that in order that these things might be known to all, copies of the sentence on Galileo were to be sent to all apostolic nuncios, and all inquisitors. They were to summon professors of mathematics and read the sentence to them. The sentence had the words: "That so pernicious a doctrine might be altogether rooted out, nor insinuate itself farther to the heavy detriment of Catholic truth, a decree emanated from the Holy Congregation of the Index prohibiting the books which treat of this doctrine; and it was declared false, and altogether contrary to the Holy and divine Scripture." In Florence, for instance, the inquisitor read the sentence in the church of Sancta Croce, notices having been served to attend on the professors and on others who were known to be friends and adherents of Galileo. The 1616 decree of the Index is expressly stated in the sentence to have been passed at a meeting held before the Pope himself.

The infallible Popes long continued their fulminations against the heresy of the earth's mobility. The Index of 1704 prohibits "all books that teach the mobility of the earth or the immobility of the sun". When what is known as the Jesuits' edition of Newton's *Principia* was published a proviso had to be inserted by the editors disclaiming credence in Newton's teaching of the earth's movement. "We profess to pay the obsequious reverence which is due to the decrees pronounced by the sovereign Pontiffs against the motion of the earth." This is an instance of how Roman dogma produces concealed scepticism. The names of Galileo, Copernicus, Foscarini, appeared on the Index of 1828. It was not until the accession of Gregory XVI (1831) that the prohibition was withdrawn and the earth received papal permission to move.

The excuse that the decree of 1616 had not the confirmatory signature of the Pope is futile in the face of the known facts. The confirmation laid stress on was not customary at the time and seems not to have been used before 1729. The Catholic Dictionary writes: "This view is untenable in view of the fact that in any decree of one of the Sacred Congregations confirmed and ordered to be published by the Pope it is the Pope himself who speaks—not the cardinals merely—if not always in his capacity of universal Doctor, yet always in that of supreme Pastor or Ruler. That this decree was not confirmed by Paul V there is not, so far as we know, the smallest

---

[1] Salmon, *Infallibility of the Church* (3rd edition), p. 248.

shred of evidence for maintaining."[1] Nor will the plea of a distinction between the Pope as Governor and as infallible Teacher hold good. The doctrine was expressly treated as "formally heretical", detrimental to Catholic truth and contrary to Scripture. It is only another proof that the Pope is not a reliable expositor of Scripture. Pope Urban declared: "It was not merely a question of mathematics but of Holy Writ, religion and the faith."[2] In any case, the desired papal confirmation was formally given by Pope Alexander VII. We are told that the gift of truth was conferred by heaven upon the successors of Peter that by them the flock of Christ might be "kept away from the poisonous food of error".[3] So Alexander VII in 1664 exercised the gift by republishing the decree: "With apostolic authority we confirm and approve of all and each in this contained, according to the tenor of these presents."

The claim to infallibility is shattered by the case of Galileo and its consequences. For over two centuries the Popes in the most authoritative way condemned belief in the mobility of the earth. They acted not as private individuals but with the whole force of their positions as Heads of the Church and supreme and universal Pastors. When Pope Boniface VIII decrees that "it is absolutely necessary to salvation that every human creature should be subject to the Roman Pontiff", or when Pius IX decrees that the Virgin Mary in the first instant of her conception has been "preserved and exempted from every stain of original sin", that she is "the safest refuge for all who are in peril", that "she stands exalted above all the choirs of angels" at the right hand of Christ, we have no scientifically exact proof to bring of their errors. But when they deny the mobility of the earth their teaching can be brought to a decisive test. Salmon is justified in suggesting to Roman apologists that their only hope of vindicating papal infallibility is to consider again whether it may not be possible to maintain that the sun actually does go round the earth.

"The history of Galileo makes short work of the question. Is it possible for the Church of Rome to err in her interpretation of Scripture, or to mistake in what she teaches to be an essential part of the Christian faith? She *can* err, for she *has* erred. She has made many errors more dangerous to the souls of men, but never

---

[1] Article on Galileo (2nd edition), p. 362.
[2] Pastor, *History of the Popes*, vol. xxix, p. 60.
[3] Vatican Decrees, chap. 4.

committed any blunder more calculated to throw contempt on her pretensions in the minds of all thinking men, than when she persisted for about two hundred years in teaching that it was the doctrine of the Bible, and therefore an essential part of the Catholic faith, that the earth stands still, and that the sun and planets revolve daily round it."[1]

[1] Salmon, *Infallibility of the Church*, p. 252.

CHAPTER LI

THE GREAT SCHISM

The argument that it is inconceivable that God would have left His Church without a living infallible Guide breaks down again and again when confronted with the actual facts of history. One of the most shattering disproofs of it is the Great schism from 1378 to 1417. In that period there were two and sometimes three rival Popes, fiercely denouncing each other. If the Church was to be secured against error by the simple rule of cleaving to the Bishop of Rome then the Church could not be left in ignorance of who was the Bishop of Rome. Yet the Christian world was divided between the claims of the contestants for the office, and each of these rival Popes was emphatic in proclaiming that adherence to his opponent brought eternal damnation.

At the death of Gregory XI (1378) the Roman populace rose in revolt against the succession of French Popes who lived in Avignon. They surrounded the conclave of cardinals riotously clamouring for a Roman or at least an Italian Pope. An Italian was elected by the terrorised conclave, who took the title of Urban VI. After the election nearly all the cardinals fled for safety to strongholds or away from the city, and all (except one who died) present at the election of Urban joined in receiving Clement VII as Pope.

Then ensued two conflicting lines of Popes. To Urban succeeded Boniface IX, Innocent VII and Gregory XII. Clement, the opposing Pope at Avignon, was succeeded by Benedict XIII. The confusion was so complete that the ordinary people could not be expected to decide who was the real Pope. Most of Italy, England, Germany, Hungary, Flanders and the northern kingdoms held to Urban. France, Scotland, Savoy, Naples, Spain, were for Clement. St. Catherine of Siena and St. Catherine of Sweden were for Urban. St. Vincent Ferrar and St. Colette championed Clement. The Blessed Peter of Aragon and the Blessed Ursuline of Parma maintained the side of Urban, and the Blessed Peter of Luxemburg that of Clement. Which of these forfeited salvation by giving an impostor the place of the Vicar of Christ?

The denunciations of the one Pope against another were terrifying. As the Roman Catholic historian, Professor Francis Xavier Funk of Tubingen, writes: "The whole of Christendom was under excommunication since each Pope anathematised the other and his followers."[1] Pope Urban VI declared Pope Clement VII and his part of the Church to be schismatics, apostates, blasphemers, heretics. Even any who would give them Christian burial was to be excommunicated and could only be absolved by disinterring them with his own hands. Anyone who supplied them with food or fuel or money was also excommunicated. The subjects of princes who favoured Clement were released from their obedience. All who would undertake a crusade for the extermination of Clement's party were to have the privileges and indulgences granted to those who fought against the heathen in the Holy Land. The military Bishop of Norwich obtained from Urban a bull appointing him leader of such a holy crusade, and the bishop carried out a fruitless campaign in Flanders. Eight years later Boniface IX bestowed a similar commission as crusade leader on the Earl of Huntingdon.

The enmity of the rival Pontiffs was not confined to apostolic fulminations. The unfortunate land of Italy was desolated by barbarous warfare. Each Pope strove to overcome the other by force of arms. Sanguinary contests were waged even at the walls of Rome. "It was one horrible feature of the schism that it called for the spirit of persecution and intolerance as much as if some great principle had been at stake."[2]

At length it was apparent that the successors of St. Peter were bound to destroy the Church if they were not coerced into decency. Both Benedict XIII and Gregory XII had solemnly pledged themselves by oath to end the schism, but resisted all practical methods. In 1408 the cardinals summoned a Council to meet next year at Pisa. Both Popes quite naturally protested against such an infringement of their divinely given prerogatives. Benedict excommunicated the cardinals and their adherents. The Council was largely attended. The best thought of the age supported its work. Peter d'Ailly, the illustrious Bishop of Cambrai, cardinal, taught the sound Protestant doctrine that, in unity with Christ, not with the Pope, does the unity

[1] *A Manual of Church History* (Eng. trans.), vol. ii, p. 12.
[2] Creighton, *History of the Papacy* (new edition), vol. i, p. 92.

of the Church consist, and that the primitive Church used the power of assembling Councils, and in the Council of Jerusalem it was not Peter but James who presided. The Council on 5th June 1409 deposed the two Popes, "called by some Benedict the Thirteenth and Gregory the Twelfth". It decreed that "the aforesaid Angelus Corrarie and Petrus de Luna, pretenders to the Papacy, have been and are notorious schismatics; nourishers, defenders, approvers and pertinacious maintainers of the ancient schism; that they are also notorious heretics and have departed from the faith and are guilty of the notorious and enormous crimes of breaking their oaths and vows in most evident and manifest manner, by their incorrigible conduct and contumacy notoriously scandalising God's holy and universal Church." The Council went on definitely to deprive both Popes and to declare null and void their sentences of excommunication.

A few weeks later the cardinals (numbering twenty-four) elected the Archbishop of Milan, who took the title of Alexander V. The result was that henceforth there were three Popes instead of two. The new Pope lived less than a year and was succeeded by one of the strangest and most disreputable men ever raised to the Papacy, Balthasar Cossa. He "began his career as a piratical adventurer".[1] He was an unscrupulous military leader. He possessed "all the qualities of a successful condottiere general. . . . He was more at home in a camp than in a church; his private life exceeded even the bounds of military licence; it was a grotesque and blasphemous incongruity to look upon such a man as the Vicar of Christ".[2]

Soon the third rival Pope, John XXIII, was launching his excommunication against the other two and their adherents, and publishing a new crusade against his enemies. The scandal became so intolerable that the famous Council of Constance had to be assembled to end it. The eminent Roman Catholic historian, Pastor, admits the practical impossibility for the people then to be sure who was the Vicar of Christ. "It is extremely difficult for those who study the question in the present day with countless documents before them, and the power of contemplating the further development of the schism, to estimate the difficulties of contemporaries who sought to know which of the two Popes had a right to their obedience. The

---

[1] Creighton, *History of the Papacy*, (new edition) vol. i, p. 230.
[2] Ibid., vol. i, p. 268.

extreme confusion is evidenced by the fact that canonised saints are found amongst the adherents of each of the rivals. . . . All the writings of the period give more or less evidence of the conflicting opinions which prevailed, and upright men afterwards confessed that they had been unable to find out which was the true Pope."[1]

[1] *History of the Popes*, vol. i, pp. 138 ,139.

CHAPTER LII

THE COUNCIL OF CONSTANCE

The Council of Constance assembled in November 1414. It was one of the greatest Church Councils ever held and drew together in an impressive way the Western Church.[1] It was attended by twenty-nine cardinals, three patriarchs, thirty-three archbishops, about one hundred and fifty bishops, one hundred abbots, three hundred doctors of theology, one thousand eight hundred priests, more that one hundred dukes and earls, and two thousand four hundred knights. Pope John XXIII authorised its assembling. Popes Gregory XII and Benedict XIII sent legates to it.

At one of its sessions Gerson, Chancellor of Paris University, preached a sermon teaching that a General Council is the authority which all, even the Pope, are bound to obey. When John XXIII fled from Constance the Council passed momentous decrees. It declared at its fifth session that it, as "a General Council legitimately assembled in the Holy Spirit, representing the Catholic Church militant, has power immediately from Christ, which anyone of whatever rank or dignity, even the papal, is bound to obey in these things which pertain to the faith and the extirpation of the aforesaid schism, and general reformation of the Church of God in its head and members".

The Council further declared that every one of whatsoever condition, rank or dignity, even the papal, who contumaciously refuses to obey the commands of this Holy Synod or any other General Synod legitimately assembled, shall be subject to condign punishment. Also it ruled that all acts done by Pope John to the hurt of the Council are made null and void by the authority of the Synod.

The Council summoned the fugitive Pope to appear and on his refusal suspended him from the Papacy. Commissioners were appointed to examine witnesses and draw up charges against him. A frightful list of seventy crimes were catalogued. "Never probably

[1] "It was in a certain sense a congress of the whole West"—Funk, *Manual of Church History*, vol. ii, p. 16.

were seventy more awful accusations brought against man than against the Vicar of Christ."[1] Sixteen, of appalling depravity, were dropped "out of respect not to the Pope but to public decency", and on the remaining fifty-four he was declared deposed. The Pope made no attempt to answer the charges. He formally submitted to the Council. The sentences of deposition pronounced against him in May 1415 was milder than the accusations warranted. "Our Lord Pope John was, moreover, a notorious simoniac; a waster of the goods and rights not only of the Roman Church but others, an evil administrator both of the spiritualities and temporalities of the Church, causing notorious scandal to the Church of God and Christian people by his detestable and unseemly life and manners both before and since his accession to the Papacy." He was therefore deposed as "unworthy, useless and harmful".[2]

The Council proceeded to appoint a new Pope. Gregory XII made little or no resistance and died during the Council. Benedict XIII defied the Council and disregarded its sentence of deposition. He made two new cardinals and kept up the assertion of his rightful Papacy in the only Catholic Church until his death in 1424. He had a successor in Clement VIII. The new Pope of the Council, Cardinal Colonna, was elected in November 1417 and took the name Martin V.

The proceedings at Constance are a full and comprehensive rebuttal of the Vatican Decrees that the Pope is placed over the universal Church, that there is no superior authority to his, and that it is unlawful to appeal from his judgments to an Oecumenical Council as to a higher authority. It deposed two Popes and compelled the third to resign. Some one of them must have been the true successor of St. Peter. The legitimacy of Martin V and all his successors to the present day depends on the lawful authority of the Council over the Popes. Further, as we have seen, it declared in the most explicit way that its authority was "immediately from Christ" over every person in the Church, including the Popes. It also ascribed a like authority to other General Councils. There is no avoiding the finality of such a judgment. By it the constitution of the Roman Church was decided. As Funk admits, these decrees "to a certain extent were a historical necessity. After the late experiences the Council alone seemed to be in a position to bring about unity in

---

[1] Milman, *History of Latin Christianity*, vol. viii, p. 277.
[2] Creighton, *History of the Papacy*, vol. i, p. 343.

R

the Church, and as its right was questioned by the Popes it could only act by having power above that of the Papacy ".[1]

Martin V declared that he would inviolably keep and never in any way contravene each and every thing regularly determined, concluded and decreed in matters of faith by the Council: he gave definite witness to his acceptance of Constance as an Oecumenical Council. In his bull, *Inter Cunctas*, he wrote: "The General Council of Constance had banished from the Church John Wiclif, John Huss, and Jerome of Prague as heretics." He also in this bull laid down tests for orthodoxy such as: "Do you believe, hold and maintain that every General Council, and especially that of Constance, represents the universal Church? Do you believe that all the faithful are obliged to approve and believe what the holy Council of Constance representing the universal Church has approved and approves touching the faith and the salvation of souls, and what it condemned and condemns as contrary to the faith and good morals?"[2] As Bishop Maret has written: "Can there be anything more formal, more decisive than these words in favour of the indivisible authority of the Council of Constance?"[3]

---

[1] *Manual of Church History*, vol. ii, p. 17.
[2] Gieseler, *Compendium of Ecclesiastical History*, vol. iv, p. 307 (E. T.).
[3] *Du Concile Général et de Paix Religieuse*, vol. i, p. 399.

CHAPTER LIII

THE VATICAN COUNCIL

1

The Vatican Council of 1869–70 has no valid claim either in its constitution or procedure to rank as oecumenical. It represented only a section of the Church. The great Reformed Churches took no part in it. The Eastern Churches were invited but refused to attend. The Patriarch of Constantinople wrote in reply that if the Pope of Rome had respect to apostolic equality and brotherhood as an equal among equals, though first by canonical right and rank of his see, he should have consulted the patriarchs and Synods of the East, as to how, where, and in what conditions they would agree to the assembling of a Council. But this should have been done as a brother to brethren and not in a dictatorial form.

2

The decisions arrived at did not obtain the virtual unanimity that is requisite to authenticate articles of the faith. It is an accepted principle of Councils that they are not for the inventing of new dogmas but for the promulgation of what has always been believed by the faithful. The bishops do not attend as legislators to enact fresh laws but as witnesses to testify to traditional faith. It is plain that if the Vatican Council was not practically unanimous in admitting that the dogma was part of the "revelation or deposit of faith delivered through the apostles", then its decision by a majority vote is destitute of force. Many of the most learned and celebrated leaders of the Church strenuously opposed its adoption. So great was the opposition to it at the Council that the closure had to be applied. Three cardinals and several leading archbishops and bishops, to the number of eighty, signed a written protest. When the critical vote was taken on 13th July 1870, four hundred and seventy-one voted *placet* (affirmative), eighty-eight *non placet* and sixty-two *placet juxta modum* (i.e. accepting the principle but not agreeing to details). Seventy-six at least of the bishops in Rome abstained from voting.[1] Before the final vote came on fifty-five bishops wrote to the Pope stating that, while renewing and confirming their previous opposition votes, they decided to remain away from the session on 18th July. Here was no virtually unanimous agreement on what was the belief of the Church.

Vigorous protests were made at the Council against deciding such a question by a majority. It was urged that the practice followed in Oecumenical Councils should be adhered to, and dogmas of faith be defined not by a numerical majority but by a moral unanimity, a principle so fully accepted by Pius IV that at Trent, when an important question of dogma was being dealt with, he said "he wished to define nothing but what should be decreed by the unanimous consent of the Fathers". And so vital was the point thought to be, these bishops declared, that if it were not conceded "their conscience would be weighed down with an intolerable burden, and they would fear that the character of the Council might be called in question and its authority undermined as lacking liberty".[2]

Dr. Darboy, Archbishop of Paris, protested to Cardinal Antonelli, Papal Secretary of State. "I say from the depth of inner conviction that if decrees are passed by such methods as these occasion will be given for the gravest suspicions as to the validity and freedom of the Vatican Council. . . . That decrees can be passed this way is indisputable. You can do anything by force of numbers against reason and against right."[3]

To Newman the absence of moral unanimity made the validity of the Council exceedingly doubtful. Dealing with the numbers who voted against it he wrote: "If the fact be so, that the Fathers were not unanimous, is the definition valid? This depends on the question whether unanimity, at least moral, is or is not necessary for its validity? As at present advised, I think it is. . . . I do not, cannot, see that a majority in the present Council can of itself *rule* its own sufficiency without such external testimony"[4] (i.e. history and precedent).

---

[1] Quirinus gives the number of absentees as ninety-one. Newman says "more than eighty".
[2] Butler, *The Vatican Council*, vol. i, pp. 250, 251.
[3] Quoted from *Quirinus* by Sparrow Simpson, *Papal Infallibility*, p. 259.
[4] *Letter to the Duke of Norfolk*, pp. 97, 98.

Strossmayer told the Council that the exacting of dogmas by a numerical majority would present a handle for saying that liberty and truth were wanting in the Council. He declared his inmost conviction that such a method would deprive the Council of authority to bind the conscience of the Catholic world.[1]

3

Another fatal flaw to the freedom of the Council was the predominant influence of Pope Pius IX. Through long ages the power of the Pope had been growing until it reached an extent that made a free Council on the model of the ancient ones entirely impossible.

In the primitive Church Councils were not assembled on the summons of the Bishops of Rome; they did not preside at them; they were regarded in them as on an equality, though holding a premier place, with other bishops; they could be overruled and even condemned as heretics.

At the time of the Vatican Council the Bishop of Rome had secured a supremacy that revolutionised the ancient constitution of the Church. It was plainly impossible for discussions to be conducted on the primitive basis. The rights of the episcopate had become unconstitutionally impaired. All the bishops present had to take at their consecration the oath by which they were bound to maintain, defend, increase and advance the rights, honours, privileges and authority of their lord the Pope, and to obey his rules and mandates with all their power. The modern relation of the bishops to the Pope annihilates the freedom of deliberating and deciding that gives authority to a Council. As Lord Acton wrote: "It was certain that any real attempt that might be made to prevent the definition could be overwhelmed by the preponderance of those bishops whom the modern constitution of the Church places in dependence on Rome."[2]

Bishop Moriarty admitted to Newman this bar to a valid Council: "The presence and presidence of the Romanus Pontifex necessarily takes from the Council the *pouvoir constitutif* [constitutive power] —we cannot be *une assemblée constituante*; we have only the power of discussion and opposition and declamation."[3]

The upsetting of the ancient order of the Church by the papal

---

[1] Acton, *History of Freedom*, p. 542.   [2] Ibid., p. 524.
[3] Butler, *The Vatican Council*, vol. ii, p. 40.

seizure of arbitrary power was of long standing. It had been gradually built up through unscrupulous aggression and forged documents which in times of ignorance could not be exposed. Even the strongest minds in the Middle Ages were imposed on.

Thus it became possible for Gregory VII to decree that the Pope or his legates can depose bishops and that he can translate bishops from one see to another.[1]

Thus Innocent III could declare that the authority of giving validity in spiritual as well as temporal appointments resided in the Roman Church.[2] He could claim for himself the plenitude of power over the whole Church, but that because he is not able personally to exercise his solicitude everywhere he has called the bishops and other ministers "into a share of the charge so that the weight of such an office may be the more easily borne by the acts of subsidiaries [subsidiarias actiones]".[3]

Thus Bellarmine could maintain that all bishops must receive jurisdiction from the Pope and that the Pope can cancel or alter their jurisdiction. He explains why the constitution of the Church is monarchical.[4]

The Vatican Council was only a simulacrum of a Council. The Pope had made himself the absolute master of a subject episcopate. The independent rights of bishops no longer existed as when Cyprian wrote of the bishops who preside over the Church and prove the episcopate one and indivisible; or that the episcopate is held by each in joint tenure;[5] or when Augustine could write to Pope Boniface: "The pastoral watchtower is common to all of us who have the office of the episcopate, although that on which you stand is of a loftier height."[6]

The pitiful subserviency of the bishops to the Pope, and their acknowledgment of their helplessness, were distressing features, revealing how far gone the Roman Church was from primitive freedom.

Before the final vote some of the leaders of the minority had an interview with Pius and besought him to make certain concessions. Ketteler, Bishop of Mainz, threw himself on his knees before him

[1] *Dictatus*, Mirbt 278.
[2] *Per Venerabilem*, Mirbt 324.
[3] P. L. 214, 459.
[4] *De Potestate Summi Pontificis*, iv, 24 and i, 5.
[5] *De Unitate*, 5.
[6] *Ad Bonifium contra duas Epp.* P. L. 44: 551.

and with tears said: "Good Father, save us, and save the Church of God." It was a pitiable scene demonstrating how the main elements of a free Council were lacking. Pius was obdurate.[1]

The letter written to the Pope by fifty-five bishops before the final session, explaining the reasons for their absence and their departure from Rome, witnesses eloquently to the impossibility of a valid Council being held in the modern Roman Church. They state: "The filial piety and reverence which very recently brought our representatives to the feet of your Holiness do not allow us in a cause so closely concerning your Holiness to say *non placet* openly and in the face of the Father."[2]

4

The manner in which Pius IX used his predominant authority to overawe the members opposed to admitting his infallibility was highly indecorous, even childish. He strove ceaselessly to obtain a verdict for one party. Those who published writings favouring his being infallible received laudatory rescripts. In some of these he even used unseemly and abusive language about writers who did not so interpret history. One who controverted Bishops Maret and Dupanloup he praised for "showing up their hatred, violence and artifices (*simultatem, violentiam et artes*)". To one who wrote in flamboyant terms of the Pope's infallibility ("In a council the Pope is the chief party which defines as a sovereign in the name of all the others. He is the whole.") Pius wrote: "Nothing is more useful than to present a just conception of things"; and he denounces the efforts of the "powers of hell" at the Council. These are typical utterances. In a brief to Dom Gueranger the Pope attacks the opponents of his infallibility as men "who show themselves completely imbued with corrupt principles and who no longer know how to submit their intelligence to the judgment of the Holy See. . . . Their folly mounts to this excess that they attempt to remake the divine constitution of the Church in order to bring down more easily the authority of the supreme Head whom Christ has set over it and whose prerogatives they dread".[3] The megalomania of the credulous old man brought him to indefensible tactics. Distributing

[1] Butler, *The Vatican Council*, vol. ii, p. 157.
[2] Ibid., vol. ii, p. 159.
[3] Friedrich, *Documenta*, vol. i, p. 184.

decorations to his dependent vicars, apostolic and oriental bishops, he told them: "It is necessary for you to defend the truth with the Vicar of Jesus Christ. My children do not abandon me."[1]

Butler is plainly unhappy about such excesses of propaganda. He asks—without giving an answer—about the part played by the Pope: "Did it amount to undue influence? That at the final stages he exerted his personal influence to the utmost cannot be questioned, for it was quite open."[2] "It might with show of reason be held that many of the bishops were swayed by what is known as reverential fear towards a beloved superior, an old man, the object in a very unusual measure of the devotion and affection of all."[3] A bishop wrote: "See what more than aught else destroys our liberty; it is crushed under the respect we have for our Head."[4] It is admitted that even bishops who took a neutral or moderate line were scolded by the Pope in personal interviews and told "they are not on his side; they are among his enemies; they are damaging the good cause; their loyalty is not sound".[5]

Cardinal Guidi, Archbishop of Bologna, made a speech accepting infallibility but urging that the Pope in deciding should take counsel with the bishops as to the tradition of the Churches. The cardinal was sent for by the Pope and upbraided. He pleaded that he only maintained bishops were witnesses of tradition. "Witnesses of tradition," said the Pope, "there's only one; that's me."[6]

The independence of a Council under these conditions is more than doubtful. An even worse case of tyranny was that of the Roman Catholic Patriarch of Babylon, Mgr. Audu. He had made an inoffensive speech in defence of the old method of appointing Oriental bishops. The Pope sent for him at once, denounced him, and under threat of deposition compelled him to sign a paper promising to consecrate two bishops nominated by the Pope. The patriarch did not feel himself bound by a signature extorted under such conditions, and a schism resulted.[7] Bishop Hefele included "how violently the Pope himself thirsts for the dogma of infallibility and publicly stigmatises those who oppose it" as among the influences that "work like devastating gunpowder upon the courage of many

[1] Friedrich, *Documenta*, vol. i, p. 185.
[2] Butler, *The Vatican Council*, vol. ii, p. 198.
[3] Ibid., vol. ii, p. 199.
[4] Ibid., vol. ii, p. 199.
[5] Ibid., vol. ii, p. 202.
[6] Ibid., vol. ii, p. 98.
[7] Ibid., vol. i, pp. 225, 226.

bishops".[1] "The Pope is resolute and obstinate,"[2] wrote Moriarty, Bishop of Kerry. "The Pope," wrote Ullathorne, Bishop of Birmingham, "takes every opportunity of expressing his views on the infallibility both in audiences and letters that at once get into the papers."[3] When Antonelli, Cardinal Secretary of State, and the other cardinals begged Pio Nono to withdraw the infallibility proposal, the answer was in effect: Full steam ahead. "I have the holy Virgin with me; I will go on."[4]

5

The membership of the Council was another scandalous defect. According to the pamphlet *The Liberty of the Council and the Infallibility*, believed to have been written by Mgr. Darboy, Archbishop of Paris, Italy had two hundred and seventy-six bishops while the rest of Europe had only two hundred and sixty-five. Butler admits that Italy had "over two hundred and fifty bishoprics" and that the ecclesiastical map of Central Italy is a network of bishops' sees.[5] The twelve million German Roman Catholics were represented by nineteen bishops. Salmon states (and Butler does not correct him here) that the seven hundred thousand inhabitants of the papal states were represented by sixty-two, and that three bishops of the minority represented five millions.[6]

Another anomalous feature was the large numbers who were not diocesan bishops at all, and many of whom were dependent on the Pope. The writer of the pamphlet gives the number of non-episcopal Cardinals as twenty-three, the bishops *in partibus infidelium*, i.e. bishops not in possession of constituted dioceses, including Vicars Apostolic, one hundred and twenty ("*révocables ad nutum*"), superiors of religious orders forty-five, and some others, comprising one hundred and ninety-five in all. Butler is in substantial agreement though he points out that several of the non-diocesan bishops had, in reality, authority over extensive communities. He analyses the actual voting at the largest session, sixty were Vicars Apostolic, ten were coadjutors, thirty-six were mere titulars, sixty-four were not bishops—comprising one hundred and seventy.

[1] Quoted by Coulton, *Papal Infallibility*, p. 124.
[2] Butler, *The Vatican Council*, vol. ii, p. 30.
[3] Ibid., vol. ii, p. 199.
[4] Ibid., vol. ii, p. 22.
[5] Ibid., vol. i, p. 264: "The enormous preponderance of Italian bishops."
[6] *Infallibility of the Church* (3rd edition), p. 323.

Much complaint was made about "the Pope's boarders". He maintained a great number in Rome of the bishops attending. It seems impossible now to find the number precisely. Quirinus says that three hundred enjoyed the Pope's hospitality and that they cost him £1,000 a day. Butler does not attempt an estimate, though he prefers Ullathorne's figure of the cost at £200 a day. The author of the pamphlet above quoted considers a great number were so "lodged, fed, supported by the Pope", and he asks: "Was there not a difficult conflict between delicacy of feeling and gratitude on the one side, and conscience on the other?"[1]

Comparisons have inevitably been drawn between the mentality and knowledge of the individual bishops of the majority and of the minority. Undoubtedly the minority included prelates of in general far higher qualifications. Döllinger tells his archbishop that the bishops from the Latin countries, Spain, Italy, South America and France, who formed the majority in the Council, had been led astray by the books taught them in college—that the quotations they relied on from the books are for the most part false, fabricated or garbled—that the immense majority of these Latin bishops lacked either the will or the proper discernment for separating truth from falsehood. Hundreds of these bishops could, without blushing, he writes, appeal to the inviolable authority of Liguori.[2]

Bishop Moriarty reflects also on the fitness of many of the bishops. "The majority represents the Curia Romana, Italy, Spain, Belgium, Ireland, South America. It is composed of men who have not come into contact with the unbelieving mind or with the intellectual mind of the time. When I read the school of theology in which they were trained I am not surprised that they treat every doubter as a heretic."[3] With this we may compare Newman's outcry about "the capacity possessed by bishops drawn from all corners of the earth to judge what is fitting for European society".[4]

One has only to glance at the speeches of many of the majority bishops at the Council to see the puerile nature of their arguments. Similarly, the elaborate reply of the deputation *de Fide* and its recommendation of certain books as answering the embarrassing cases of Vigilius and Honorius are evidences of their want of scholarship or candour. Some of the books they appealed to as

[1] Friedrich, *Documenta*, vol. i, p. 169.
[2] *Declarations and Letters*, pp. 84, 97.
[3] Butler, *The Vatican Council*, vol. ii, p. 29.
[4] *Ward's Life of Newman*, vol. ii, p. 288.

explaining away the condemnation of Honorius[1] give contradictory accounts. The vaunted expedient of the latest (at the time of the Council), Pennacchi, is contemptuously dismissed by a favourite modern Romanist apologist, Dom Chapman, as "absurd".[2]

In the momentous Vatican Decrees at least five times the testimonies adduced from ancient authorities are vitiated by insolent tampering with the documents or gross misrepresentations of the sources appealed to.

Chapter 2 has, as subject, the perpetuity of St. Peter's prerogatives in the Roman Pontiff—a manifestly unprovable claim. Four authorities are directly quoted.

(1) A grandiloquent statement by one of the Pope's legates, the priest Philip, is cited as if it were the decision of the Council of Ephesus. "It would not be more false if a modern writer so quoted a counsel's speech as to make us believe he was quoting from a judge's decision."[3]

(2) Eight words are omitted from the sentence and twelve interpolated. Some of these smuggled-in words are especially reprehensible. Philip had audaciously claimed that Peter lived and exercised judgment in his successors (*vivit et judicium exercet*). The Pope has inserted the words "and presides" (*et praesidet*) and has expanded "successors" to "the bishops of the Holy See of Rome which was founded by Him and consecrated with His blood".

(3) Irenaeus is quoted in a mutilated form and in a sense incompatible with his meaning.[4]

(4) The words of Irenaeus are strangely incorporated with a sentence from the Council of Aquileia which contains more interpolated words than genuine ones. Coulton quotes the comment of Professor Schulte on these brazenly misleading references. "We cannot believe the actual forger of these documents, promulgated by Pius IX, in the most solemn Council of modern times, to have been the Holy Ghost."[5] The argument from the Council's words is misleading. The only other authority quoted from is Pope Leo!

(5) Pope Gregory the Great is cited in the third chapter in a sense flagrantly contrary to his meaning.[6]

[1] Friedrich, *Documenta*, vol. ii, p. 311.
[2] *Condemnation of Pope Honorius* (Catholic Truth Society), p. 16.
[3] Coulton, *Romanism and Truth*, vol. ii, p. 230.
[4] See p. 90 ff.
[5] *Romanism and Truth*, vol. ii, p. 231.
[6] See p. 203 ff.

The methods by which the proceedings of the Council were ordered aroused intense indignation. The Pope reserved to himself the complete mastery over the business to be brought forward. The appointment of officials and regulation of procedure were taken out of the hands of the members.

From the beginning the tactics adopted by the infallibilists were discreditable. The deputation *de Fide* was the most important of the Council. It had far-reaching powers. No one known to be unfavourable to the decree was allowed on it. Bishop Ullathorne calls this an "intrigue". The chief intriguer was the convert Manning. The English bishops put forward Grant of Southwark as their representative. He was not elected but Manning was. Butler charges Manning with falsehood. "It was not that the Italian bishops put him on their list, but that he was on the list circulated by himself."[1] This successful intrigue appears to Butler the "one serious blot"[2] on the Council's doings. The election was "engineered" to exclude all but one party. Ullathorne writes of Manning being "manœuvred upon it". This incident is illuminative. Yet Dupanloup was told by the Pope: "We know that the Council is under the guidance of the Holy Ghost."

[1] *The Vatican Council*, vol. i, p. 175.   [2] Ibid., vol. i, p. 172.

CHAPTER LIV

ROMAN CATHOLIC OPPONENTS OF THE DECREE

1

It was not in numbers only that the minority at the Vatican Council was impressive. Among them were many bishops pre-eminent in learning and celebrated as foremost champions of the Church. Their exposures of its errors were unanswerable. Among them was Hefele, Bishop of Rottenburg, who is described by Dom Butler as "perhaps the most learned bishop of the Council in the domain of Church history and patrology. His *History of the Councils* is the classical work on the subject".[1] During the Council he published a tract on Pope Honorius, devastating in its demonstration of papal fallibility.

Hefele's observations on the first appearance of the *schema* of the decree at the Council are outspoken and decisive. He denied that the Biblical testimonies which were brought forward witnessed to the infallibility of the Pope; Luke xxii. 32 was not relevant. The patristic references were only by an unworthy artifice applied to the infallibility of the single person of the Roman Pontiff. "In short, the doctrine of the infallibility of the Roman Pontiff does not seem to me to be based on Holy Scripture or on ecclesiastical tradition. Altogether to the contrary; unless I am mistaken, Christian antiquity obstructs the doctrine, and not a few doubts against the declaration of the new dogma arise from Church history and the words of the holy Fathers."

He goes on to show how in the primitive Church when controversies arose appeal was made, as Vincentius Lerinsis witnessed, to universality, antiquity, consent. "No one ever imagined that there was the short cut of obtaining an infallible decision on a controversy from any one single individual." He gave instances from history—the investigation that Leo's letter to Flavian received at Chalcedon

[1] *The Vatican Council*, vol. i, p. 133: "With whom no Roman divine will bear comparison for a moment." Acton, *Correspondence*, vol. i, p. 95.

—the contradictory dogmatic judgments of Vigilius, and of other Popes, the whole history of the condemnation of Honorius, the statements of the Greek and Latin Fathers irreconcilable with the dogma.[1]

The speech that Hefele delivered at the Council in the main debate was short but crushing.[2] The dogma would involve, he declared, the greatest dangers and most certain injuries to the Church. If ever there was a papal epistle that could be considered *ex cathedra* it was the Tome of Leo. Yet the Fathers at Chalcedon subjected it to their examination as to whether it was orthodox or not. "If the doctrine of pontifical infallibility was known to them they could not have dared to do this. They would not have passed judgment but would have suppliantly and humbly accepted it. They treated it as on an equality with the epistle of Cyril." All the bishops were required on oath to testify if they found Leo's statement conformable and harmonious with the Nicene and Constantinopolitan symbols. Thus they were solemnly called on to adjudicate about Leo's epistle and orthodoxy. If they believed him to be the infallible Pope it is evident they were bound to act differently from this. It was not said to them, "Here is a dogmatic letter of the Pope: hear it and submit", but "Hear it and judge". The Bishops of Illyricum and Palestine thought that three passages were of questionable orthodoxy. "No one said, 'Why do you act so indiscreetly; it is not lawful to have such doubts'." No one questioned their right to be doubtful.

Pope Agatho's letter to the sixth General Council was subjected to a similar investigation as to whether his doctrines were upheld by the authority of the primitive Fathers, and after the scrutiny was carried out the epistle was approved and praised. The seventh and eighth General Councils acted similarly regarding the formularies of Hadrian I and Hadrian II. Is it said that a Council has the right to approve of a papal decision but not to dissent from it? "He who has the right to approve has also the right to dissent, otherwise the right to approve is plainly fictitious."

He urged that the historical obstacles to the dogma must be faced. He represented the attitude of the majority as "the infallibility of the Roman Pontiff is a truth divinely revealed. Therefore all historical facts which seem to block it are either false or should be so explained or arranged that they do not block it."

---

[1] Friedrich, *Documenta*, vol. ii, p. 220.   [2] Mansi, lii, 80 ff.

He held up to ridicule the books recommended formally by the committee that drew up the *Schema* as meeting the difficulties about Vigilius and Honorius. As an example of the authors so relied on he took the book of Pennacchi. This apologist's expedient was that Honorius was not judged by the Council but only by the Oriental members of the Council. Even if this were true, it showed the Oriental half of the Council was not aware of the infallibility of Honorius. He exposed the dishonesty of the plea by pointing out that Pope Agatho's three legates subscribed to the condemnation and so did the deputies present from the Roman Council. "Therefore they also did not hold the doctrine." He protested his obedience and reverence to the Pope: "But I do not believe it lawful to proceed to a declaration of his infallibility." "We are not arbiters of, but witnesses to, Church doctrine." He appealed for loyalty to "the constant practice and faith of the Church".

2

This is one of many protests which prove how contradictory of history it was to claim the dogma was divinely revealed. Cardinal Schwarzenberg, in his written Observations, stated that the Scriptural texts alleged were insufficient to prove the personal infallibility, and that by several approved interpreters they were not applied to the infallibility of the Pope at all. The testimonies of the Fathers did not teach the infallibility apart from the Council of the bishops.[1]

Many of the bishops in their Observations instanced the case of Honorius as fatal to the claim. One wrote that there was no escape from it except by holding that the records of the sixth General Council and the letters of Leo II were forged and therefore the other Councils and Popes were deceived.[2] Another vouched that in his diocese to the present day there was not a trace of tradition about papal infallibility.[3] Another declared that the doctrine was new and unheard of, swarming with the greatest historical difficulties.[4] Another boldly declared that the doctrine could be proved by no certain arguments from Scripture or tradition and that "this definition would change the constitution which Christ gave to His Church".[5] Four of the bishops joined in showing that the doctrine

---

[1] Friedrich, *Documenta*, vol. ii, p. 221.   [3] Ibid., vol. ii, p. 223.
[2] Ibid., vol. ii, p. 240.   [4] Ibid., vol. ii, p. 228.
             [5] Ibid., vol. ii, p. 245.

was not even part of the Roman tradition of revealed truth, "by what means, then, can what is not revealed be declared to be a dogma of the faith?"[1] Bishop Clifford said it would be a stone of stumbling to not a few Catholics. He stressed that before emancipation in England was granted the bishops (among whom were two predecessors of Cardinal Cullen of Dublin) and the theologians publicly declared that the Pope could not define dogmas without the consent of the Church.[2] Archbishop Purcell pictured Protestants in the United States being able to say to them: "Up to the present this doctrine has been preached by you as if it were a free opinion in the Church; now you assert it is a doctrine of the faith: therefore either formerly you spake falsely, or the doctrine of the Church has changed." Then he added: "How our variations will be laid to our charge." Many of the authorities on which the dogma rested were false and spurious; others not interpreted in the true sense.[3] Another bishop said that "nothing more disastrous than this unfortunate proposal is able to be imagined; nothing more fatal to the authority of the Church and the Apostolic See."[4]

3

The leaders of the opposition are stated by Butler to have been the two Austrian cardinals, Schwarzenburg, Archbishop of Prague, and Rauscher, Archbishop of Vienna. They had "proved themselves pillars of the Church".[5] Rauscher was a man of wide erudition and regarded as "one of the glories of the Council".

With them were the Archbishops of Salzburg (Primate of Germany), Munich, Olmutz, Bamberg—the archbishops of all the great sees of Germany and the Austrian Empire,[6] and Ketteler, Bishop of Mayence.

All the Hungarian bishops supported the minority, headed by Simor, Archbishop of Esztergom (Primate of Hungary), and Haynald, Archbishop of Kaloesa, "both of them learned theologians and apostolic bishops".[7]

---

[1] Friedrich, *Documenta*, vol. ii, p. 253.
[2] Ibid., vol. ii, p. 258.
[3] Ibid., vol. ii, p. 260.
[4] Ibid., vol. ii, p. 257. Archbishop Downey states emphatically that at the Vatican Council "the question as to whether the doctrine of papal infallibility be true or not was never discussed" (*The Papacy*, p. 192).
[5] Butler, *The Vatican Council*, vol. i, p. 132.
[6] Ibid., vol. i, p. 205.
[7] Ibid., vol. i, p. 134.

Archbishop Melchers of Cologne was the leading German bishop present, "a great bishop and Catholic leader in Germany". He was one of the strongest opponents of the definition.

Strossmayer, Bishop of Bosnia and Sirmium, was an outspoken and unsparing opponent. In one of the first debates he protested against the title of the constitution. "Pius, Bishop, Servant of the Servants of God, with the approval of the Sacred Council." He urged that, as at Trent, all decrees should be promulgated not as the Pope's but as the Council's. When he objected to carrying the definition by a majority instead of by moral unanimity a disgraceful scene occurred. His words were inaudible in the clamorous uproar. In vain he protested. The bishops left their seats, shouting: "He is Lucifer, anathema, anathema." "He is another Luther; let him be cast out." Such an atmosphere was not conducive to the calm witnessing on the essentials of the faith.[1]

The most influential of the French minority bishops was the brilliant Archbishop Darboy of Paris, who afterwards was shot by the Communards and died blessing his executioners. Before going to the Council he issued a pastoral in which the significant words occur: "It is incredible that five or six hundred bishops will affirm in the face of the world that they have found in the convictions of their respective Churches that which is not there."

Dupanloup, Bishop of Orleans, was a foremost figure of the opposition. He had a notable career as Rector of the Episcopal College of Paris, Vicar General and Canon of Notre Dame. His books and pamphlets made him famous and influential in France. Butler describes him as "the chief Catholic champion in all public controversies, the recognised spokesman of the bishops, the most prominent bishop in France, and one of the most prominent bishops in the whole Catholic world".[2] He was a powerful champion of the Pope's temporal sovereignty. The Pope often turned to him for help, and a printed volume of near three hundred pages is made up of rescripts and letters of Pius IX to him in recognition of his manifold services to religion. This is the man who was the chief driving force in resisting the definition of infallibility. He insisted that the Church has lived for eighteen centuries without defining a principle now declared essential to her existence. "How explain the fact that she has formulated all her doctrines, produced her

[1] A speech, much circulated, ascribed to Strossmayer, is not authentic.
[2] Ibid., vol. i, p. 66.

S

teachers, condemned all heresies without this definition."[1] His zeal in opposition roused the resentment of the Pope, who wrote him an extraordinary letter.

Other French opposing bishops were Cardinal Matthieu, Archbishop of Besancon, Meignan of Chalons (afterwards Archbishop of Tours), and Cardinal Ginoulhiac of Grenoble, said to have been the first theologian of the French bishops.

On the eve of the Council Maret, Bishop of Sura, wrote a very learned and powerful book against papal infallibility—*Du Concile générale et de la paix religieuse.* Maret was dean of the Catholic theological faculty of the Sorbonne. A copy of his book was sent to every bishop of the Roman Catholic communion. It is a valuable résumé of the historical evidence against papal infallibility. "The Pope does not possess a sovereignty pure, indivisible and absolute. And if infallibility is identical with sovereignty the Pope does not possess infallibility absolute and separate."[2] His investigation of the facts of history is lucid and competent. For instance, in dealing with Pope Honorius his summing up is: "A Pope whose doctrine and whose person are condemned by three General Councils, as by his successors, evidently possesses neither absolute sovereignty nor infallibility."[3]

Of the English bishops, Clifford of Clifton and Archbishop Errington were with the minority; as were from Ireland Archbishop McHale of Tuam, Bishops Moriarty of Kerry, Furlong of Ferns and Leahy of Dromore.

From America there were opponents of the definition in Archbishops McCloskey of New York, Purcell of Cincinnati, Kenrick of St. Louis, Connolly of Halifax, and nineteen U.S. bishops, including Bishop Verot of Savannah. Verot in his speech[4] showed from Acts xi that Christians educated by the apostles were not taught that Peter was infallible. Otherwise they would not have contended with him. Neither would St. Paul have withstood him (Gal. ii) and held that he was reprehensible and walked not uprightly. "Why are we then so precipitate as to define after eighteen centuries that the successor of Peter is infallible?" After other cogent Scriptural and historical evidences, he said : "I conclude that the pontifical

---

[1] Quoted in Sparrow-Simpson's *Roman Catholic Opposition to Papal Infallibility*, p. 170.
[2] vol. ii, p. 64.
[3] vol. i, p. 292.
[4] Mansi, lii, 289 ff.

infallibility is not an apostolic tradition but an opinion introduced by a piety and zeal not according to knowledge. Therefore for me to give my vote for it would be a sacrilege." The Council which often interrupted him refused to hear him further.

Archbishop Kenrick has been called "perhaps the stiffest opponent of the definition". He was a distinguished prelate. When the speech he had prepared could not be delivered owing to the closure he printed it as a *concio habenda et non habita*.[1] This is a powerful and comprehensive refutation of the unscriptural, unhistorical nature of the infallibility. When prelates such as these witnessed against the definition its validity is open to grave question from any point of view. Their individual reputations were superior to those of their opponents.

4

From many of the speeches delivered at the Vatican Council overwhelming arguments against the infallibility definition can be drawn. Cardinal Schwarzenberg of Prague asked if all their catechisms were to be corrected as incomplete and feeble, for that would follow from the definition.[2] Cardinal Rauscher of Vienna said that if it had pleased God to make the successors of Peter infallible witnesses of revealed truth then the occasion for innumerable controversies and dangers would have been removed. By such provision of divine benevolence the faithful would have been so instructed that they would not have been exposed to doubt. The holy men of old could not have been ignorant of it nor even neglected to inculcate it. All that would have been necessary was to approach the Roman Pontiff and learn the truth from him. If the definitions of the Roman Pontiffs about faith and morals are infallible then Cardinal Orsi was right when he said there was no need for Oecumenical Councils and all that labour was uselessly called forth in the Church. Everyone believed that in controversies about the faith Councils should be held. No one either in East or West rose up to say: why so much journeying, trouble and danger? Let us go to the Roman Pontiff; his decrees concerning the faith will avail as much as the definitions of the most numerous Synod gathered from all the world. He denied that any single writer of the first

[1] Friedrich, *Documenta*, vol. i, pp. 189–246. See Coulton's *Papal Infallibility*, chap. xiii.
[2] Mansi, lii, 100.

eight centuries had proved that the Church was bound to receive as divinely revealed truth the decisions of the Pope made apart from the consent of the Church.[1]

Archbishop Simor, Primate of Hungary, pointed out that not even the word "infallibility" was mentioned at the Council of Trent nor in the Acts of any ancient Council.[2]

Bishop Ketteler of Mayence stated that if the Pope was declared to be independently infallible then all the other bishops had no function as witnesses to the truth but to repeat what he said because he said it. Then the decision of the whole college of bishops would be worth neither more nor less than an example of perfect subjection.[3]

But arguments and history were of no avail against the ignorance and delusions and fears and submissiveness to authority of so many. Acton, writing to Gladstone (1st January 1870),[4] can only think of possibly two bishops prepared to defy excommunication. He overestimated the number by two. One of those he mentioned, Hefele, is a painful example of how helpless a bishop of the Roman Church is if in opposition to the Pope. After returning from the Council he declared he would "never recognise the new dogma without the limitations which we demand; and I shall deny the validity and the freedom of the Council. The Romans may then suspend and excommunicate me, and put an administrator in my place". A month later he is writing: "As to recognising for divine revelation a thing which is essentially untrue, let those do that who can; as for me, *non possum*." In November 1870 he is still firm: "I cannot conceal from myself . . . that the new dogma has no really veracious foundation in Scripture or tradition and that it is incalculably harmful to the Church, so that she never suffered any more cruel and fatal blow than on 18th July." Of a bishop who thought with him he writes that he "will do as I am doing so long as he can, but when once the knife is put to his throat he will submit". "I thought that I was serving the Catholic Church; and I was serving the caricature that Romanism and Jesuitism have made of her. It was only when I got to Rome that I saw quite clearly how all that is commonly done there bears only the name and outward semblance of Christianity."

Soon the knife was approaching his own throat and he had not

---

[1] Mansi, lii, 108, 109.
[2] Ibid., lii, 141.
[3] Ibid., lii, 210.
[4] Lord Acton, *Correspondence*, vol. i, p. 96.

the fortitude to stand by the truth he had proclaimed. In March 1871 there is the pathetic cry: "The position of a suspended and excommunicated bishop seems to me horrible and I could scarcely bear it. I would far sooner make up my mind to cede or resign and gladly would I lay down that pastoral staff which has made a broken and miserable man of me." Only a month later and the broken man gave in, "casting my own subjectivity at the feet of the supreme ecclesiastical authority"[1]—in other words, sacrificing his intellect and honour.

5

The protests of two notable Roman Catholic ecclesiastics outside the council attracted much attention.

(1) The Rev. J. H. Newman's grief and indignation—indeed consternation—are poignantly expressed in his letter to Bishop Ullathorne. It was written on 28th January 1870. He deplores that the great Council is infusing into the Church "little else than fear and distrust". "I look with anxiety at the prospect of having to defend decisions which may not be difficult to my private judgment but may be most difficult to maintain logically in the face of historical facts. What have we done to be treated as the faithful never were treated before? When has definition of doctrine *de fide* been a luxury of devotion and not a stern, painful necessity? Why should an aggressive, insolent faction be allowed to make the heart of the just to mourn whom the Lord hath not made sorrowful?" He pictures the distress of some of the truest minds, one day ready recklessly to believe the Pope is impeccable; another day tempted to believe the worst that *Janus* says; others doubting about the capacity of bishops drawn from all corners of the earth to judge what is fitting for European society, "and then again angry with the Holy See for listening to the flattery of a clique of Jesuits, redemptionists and converts. Then again think of the store of pontifical scandals in the history of eighteen centuries which have partly been poured out and partly are still to come. . . . All I do is to pray those great early Doctors of the Church, whose intercession would decide the matter —Augustine and the rest—to avert so great a calamity. If it is God's will that the Pope's infallibility should be defined, then it is His blessed will to throw back 'the times and the moments' of that

[1] See Coulton, *Papal Infallibility*, pp. 200–2.

triumph which He has destined for His kingdom; and I shall feel I have but to bow my head to His adorable, inscrutable Providence."[1]

To other correspondents he wrote similarly: "I cannot bear to think of the tyrannousness and cruelty of its advocates."[2] "I don't give up hope till the very end, the bitter end."[3] "Anxious as I am, I will not believe that the Pope's infallibility can be defined at the Council till I see it actually done."[4]

(2) Père Gratry was a priest of the Oratory in Paris, member of the Academy, Professor of Moral Theology at the Sorbonne. He published four letters addressed to Mgr. Deschamps, before the Council, which are memorable for their incisive rebuttal of ultramontanism. They made a great sensation at the time and are often still quoted. He demolishes the erroneous arguments drawn from the Fathers in trenchant style. For instance, dealing with the "elaborations on St. Augustine's 'Rome has spoken; the matter is finished'" he remarks: "But the objection to this is that St. Augustine never said that at all." He emphasised the condemnation of Pope Honorius. It is his scathing denunciations of Roman forgeries and concealments of truth that are most often cited. He shows how the ultramontane case has been "gangrened with fraud". "Had then the Catholic religion—had the word of God—need of this monstrous imposture in a solemn judgment? O ye men of little faith, of low minds, of miserable hearts, have not your cunning devices become the scandal of souls?"

Such are the audacious falsifications made use of that he can understand people "should be seized with giddiness and cry out, 'What then can we believe now?'". "Are we preachers of falsehood or apostles of the truth?"

---

[1] Ward, *Life*, vol. ii, pp. 288, 289.
[2] Ibid., vol. ii, p. 289.
[3] Ibid., vol. ii, p. 290.
[4] Ibid., vol. ii, p. 293.

CHAPTER LV

DÖLLINGER AND ACTON

I

Johann J. Ignaz von Döllinger was the greatest Roman Catholic historian in Germany. His books commanded universal respect. He became Professor of Canon Law and Ecclesiastical History in Munich University in 1827. Under him Munich became the centre of Roman Catholic ecclesiastical learning in Europe. He was "the great champion of the Catholic cause in Germany".[1]

When the infallibility dogma was mooted he became the chief protagonist in Germany against it. He is largely responsible for the book *Janus*—an overwhelming impeachment of papal absolutism. It is the fashion to decry it by Romanist writers, but the comparatively few errors that have been proved against it do not by any means cancel the devastating force of the book as a whole. When the fullest allowance is made for all the mistakes that can be found in *Janus* it remains a storehouse of impregnable proofs against the infallibility delusion. In October 1869 Döllinger published *Considerations for the Bishops of the Council Respecting the Question of Papal Infallibility*. He shows that the dogma was altogether unknown in the Church for many centuries and has never been admitted in the Eastern Church; that no heretic of old was accused of discarding the authority of the Popes in matters of faith; that the ancient Fathers who treat of the rule of faith make no reference to the supreme judgment of the Roman See; that the doctrine only appeared in the West at a late period and then in consequence of a series of forgeries. He gives grounds for his statement that "to the adherents of the theory of infallibility the history of the ancient Church in the first millennium must appear as an incomprehensible problem". He was a true prophet when he wrote that if the doctrine be decreed "it will present an incalculably weak point to the separated Churches—the

[1] Butler, *The Vatican Council*, vol. ii, p. 185.

Graeco-Russian and the Protestant. So far as can be foreseen, the whole controversy, as it has hitherto been carried on against the Catholic doctrine and Church, would concentrate itself more and more on this one doctrine".[1]

Döllinger was one of the few Romanists who, after demonstrating that infallibility was a myth, had the courage to stand by his principles. When called upon by his bishop to submit to the decree, he pleaded (28th March 1871) to be allowed to appear before a Board of the bishops and undertook to demonstrate that the new dogma was without Biblical or historic foundations; that it rests, "as I am ready to prove, on a complete misunderstanding of ecclesiastical tradition in the first thousand years of the Church, and on a distortion of her history; it contradicts the clearest facts and evidences".[2]

The whole lengthy letter to the Archbishop of Munich is a thorough-going attack on the truth of the Vatican Decrees, and on the means by which they were passed. If the bishops cannot receive him, he pleads that a commission of members of the Cathedral Chapter discuss the points at issue with him. Referring to the archbishop's pastoral, he writes: "I will enter into an engagement to prove it contains a long series of misunderstood, garbled, mutilated or invented evidences which, together with the suppression of important facts and opposing evidences, forms a picture that is altogether unlike actual tradition."[3] He reminds the archbishop that "in an address delivered to the Pope on 12th January, and signed by you, the bishops of the minority declared that 'the sayings and actions of the Church Fathers, the genuine documents of history, and even the Catholic conception of doctrine presented some serious difficulties which were opposed to the proclamation of the doctrine of infallibility". His conclusion is: "As Christian, as theologian, as historian, as citizen, I cannot accept this doctrine."[4]

The request to be heard in his own defence at a conference was ignored, and Döllinger was excommunicated on 23rd April 1871 when he was seventy-two years old. He lived to be ninety, dying on 10th January 1890. In 1873 he was made president of the Munich Academy.

---

[1] *Declarations and Letters on the Vatican Decrees*, pp. 30, 31 (E. T.).
[2] Ibid., p. 84.
[3] Ibid., p. 92.
[4] Ibid., p. 103.

In the years between his excommunication and his death repeated and urgent efforts were made to induce him to be reconciled to the Church. His submission was many times wrongly announced. In one of the contradictions of this that he had to publish he wrote (4th May 1879): "Having devoted during the last nine years my time principally to the renewed study of all the questions connected with the history of the Popes and the Councils, and, I may say, gone again over the whole ground of ecclesiastical history, the result is that the proofs of the falsehood of the Vatican Decrees amount to demonstration. When I am told that I must swear to the truth of those doctrines my answer is just as if I were asked to swear that two and two make five and not four."[1]

To a lady who wrote imploring him to save his soul from eternal punishment he replied: "I am now in my eighty-first year and was a public teacher of theology for forty-seven years, during which long period no censure, nor even a challenge that I should defend myself or make a better explanation, has ever reached me from ecclesiastical dignitaries either at home or abroad." Then came 1870. "It was in vain that I begged they would let me remain by the faith and confession to which I had hitherto been faithful without blame and without contradiction. Yesterday still orthodox, I was today a heretic worthy of excommunication, not because I had changed my teaching but because they had considered it advisable to undertake the alteration and to make opinions into Articles of Faith. I ought, as the favourite expression of the Jesuits runs, 'to make a sacrifice of my intellect' [Sacrificio dell' intellecto]. This is what your ladyship also demands of me. But if I did so, in a question which is for the historical eye perfectly clear and unambiguous, there would then no longer be for me any such thing as historical truth and certainty; I should then have to suppose that my whole life long I had been in a world of dizzy illusion and that in historical matters I am altogether incapable of distinguishing truth from fable and falsehood." He explains to her that "with the same inward certainty with which you are convinced of the existence of Napoleon and of the principal facts of his life, a certainty that no authority in the world can shake, I know that the Vatican Decrees are untrue". The oath required would be to him a double perjury. He would have to break the oath

---

[1] *Declarations and Letters on the Vatican Decrees*, p. 125.

laid on him at the entrance upon his official duties—to expound the
Scriptures in agreement with the interpretation of the Fathers; "and
second, in the required oath I should have to carry out a moral self-
destruction on myself".[1]

The importance attached by Rome to the adhesion of a scholar so
venerated through the world as Döllinger is shown by the touching
appeals made to him by the new Archbishop of Munich and by the
papal nuncio, Archbishop of Petra. They write to him in terms of the
highest admiration. The Archbishop of Munich addressed him as
"the teacher of my youth towards whom I have always preserved
my earlier admiration and sense of gratefulness". "There are
but few days which pass without my thinking of you with
the old love and sympathy." On Döllinger's eightieth birthday
he assures him that the Pope would gladly stretch out the
hand of peace to him and that thousands are yearning for his
return to the Church.

Döllinger's unshakable loyalty to the truth appears again and
again in his replies. He explains to the Archbishop why he cannot
receive "the new Articles of Faith which have been fabricated
eighteen centuries after the time of the apostles". On these Articles
the whole Catholic doctrinal edifice is to rest. The ancient principle
of adhering to tradition is now turned into the opposite. "In order to
be consistent all the older text-books of theology ought now to be
rewritten or prohibited." His prolonged study of the question makes
it clear that the building stones in which the Vatican system has
been raised "were taken from a series of forgeries and fictions".
"Here I now stand, and your Grace may yourself imagine with
what feeling I must accept such suggestions as yours and those the
present Pope has sent to me three times already. I say to myself
daily that I am a frail man, constantly prone to err in many ways. . . .
I am conscious that I have never obstinately closed my eyes to a
better judgment; at all events I cannot call such a case to mind.
Though at first with a heavy heart, I have renounced even cherished
ideas as soon as it was clear to me that they were untenable. Now it
is of course possible that a derangement of my mind has set in which
makes me incapable of understanding historical facts." So he begs
the archbishop to choose but one or several of the learned clergy
of his diocese and let him meet them in discussion. If he is refuted he
solemnly promises to submit and to recant and to spend the remainder

---

[1] *Declarations and Letters on the Vatican Decrees*, pp. 131-4.

of his life in refuting his own writings. He gives instances of men in the past like Pelagius, Abelard, Huss and Jerome who were allowed to plead their cause fully and in detail. The matters at issue are not mysteries of the faith but questions of history and fact. "These are things which can be cleared up and expounded in such a way that every well-educated and well-instructed man can form his own judgment of the justice or injustice of the one side or the other even without having gone through any course of theology."[1]

He declares that "the exposition given at Rome in 1870 to the passages which were quoted as Biblical proof differs entirely from that of the Fathers and has not been advanced by a single one of the commentators that belong to the early patristic age". To take the oath demanded of him would be to "call upon God to witness that I was willing to believe and teach a dogma and its contrary at the same time. Can you seriously exact anything of this sort from me? Am I to appear before the eternal Judge with a double perjury on my conscience?"

Similarly, in his reply to the papal nuncio's solicitation later on in the same year, he says that he was excommunicated because "I refused to change my faith; I refused to believe and to teach a new dogma, the contrary of which I had been taught in my youth and the falsity of which I had learned by the study and research of fifty-six years." "Sixteen years have passed since the anathema was launched against me. I have employed the time in giving myself to study and repeated researches to examine the sources, to follow the tradition from one century to another. An exhaustive examination of the alleged witnesses which have been compiled in the works written in support of the Council have made me see there a mass of alterations, fictions, falsifications, the greater part of which had been already recognised as such in the seventeenth century."

2

The most learned English Roman Catholic of his day was Lord Acton, Regius Professor of History, Cambridge. He took

---

[1] *Declarations and Letters on the Vatican Decrees*, pp. 145-51.

a strenuous part against the definition and condemned it in severe terms. To him it was "this great calamity", "this insane enterprise".[1]

The official documents issued during the Council showed the papal absolutism "in its hostility to the rights of the Church, of the state and of the intellect. We have to meet an organised conspiracy to establish a power which would be the most formidable enemy of liberty as well as of science throughout the world".[2] The opposition included, he said, "the most enlightened bishops of France, Germany and America".

Acton was in Rome during the Council and in close touch with what was taking place among the bishops. He writes as a man seeing an abhorrent tragedy being accomplished. He describes the mental position of the ultramontane majority—"after Scripture was subjugated, tradition itself was deposed; and the constant belief of the past yielded to the general conviction of the present. . . . Divines of this school, after preferring the Church to the Bible, preferred the modern Church to the ancient and ended by sacrificing both to the Pope".[3] "Authority must conquer history" was their standpoint.

He condemns scathingly the inclination to get rid of evidence, which inclination, he says, was specially associated with the doctrine of papal infallibility,—as the suppression of the *Liber Diurnus*.[4]

He describes how the minority at the Council were baffled "by the serene vitality of a view which was impervious to proof". No appeal to revelation or tradition, to reason or conscience, appeared to have any bearing on the issue.

Acton writes with evident regret about the conduct of the bishops of the minority. In the Observations they sent in against the decree some of them "testified that it was unknown in many parts of the Church, and was denied by the Fathers, so that neither perpetuity nor universality could be pleaded in its favour; and they declared it an absurd contradiction, founded on ignoble deceit and incapable of being made an article of faith by Pope or Council".[5] "But it was certain that there were men amongst them who would renounce

---

[1] *Correspondence*, vol. i, p. 109.
[2] *Correspondence*, vol. i, p. 91.
[3] *History of Freedom*, p. 514.
[4] *supra*, p. 202.
[5] *History of Freedom*, p. 546.

their belief rather than incur the penalty of excommunication, who preferred authority to proof, and accepted the Pope's declaration *La tradizione son' io.*"[1]

The protest of two such men as Döllinger and Acton, of profound historic knowledge and sincere attachment to their Church, is destructive of the claim that papal infallibility is a doctrine of the Catholic faith.

[1] Ibid., p. 549.

CHAPTER LVI

EX CATHEDRA

1

The Roman claim to have infallible guidance in matters of faith has an attractiveness for some. Advocates of Romanism exalt this prerogative of their Church. They represent the necessity and security of certitude through the infallible organ divinely provided. One "Catholic Truth" writer states: "No reasonable being can rightly be asked to yield assent to assertions which reason cannot verify unless they come from a trustworthy source. No source of supra-rational truth can be thought trustworthy unless its infallibility is satisfactorily guaranteed."[1]

Another argues that without infallibility everything is reduced to a mere opinion. "Your doctrines are no longer certain. I can't believe in a thing which may be false."[2]

Another parades the varying beliefs of Protestant teachers and contrasts the ensuing want of certainty with the blessing of having an inerrant guide. In the Roman Catholic Church there is a teacher who is "protected from falling into error when he teaches the Church by the Holy Spirit of God which watches over him". "The teacher assigned is not the Pope as a mere man but the Pope under the special guidance of the Holy Spirit, so that the real teacher is God."[3] "God has given the Pope the gift of infallibility so that we may all be sure and certain of the truth which the Church teaches."[4]

How wonderfully simple and easy it all is! The world-old searchings of the human mind for the discovery of religious truth are needless and impertinent since God has provided the Bishop of Rome with supernatural gifts to declare it.

But when we ask how we are to know when this infallible teaching is given we find ourselves at once in difficulties. The most authoritative Romanist theologians are not in agreement. All inform us that it is

[1] Rev. Joseph Keating, S.J., *The True Church*, p. 7.
[2] Rev. Edmund Lester, S.J., *Dialogues of Defence*, p. 2.
[3] Rev. Sydney F. Smith, S.J., *Papal Supremacy and Infallibility*, pp. 22, 24.
[4] *The Catholic Faith*, a compendium authorised by H. H. Pope Pius X, p. 25.

when the Pope speaks *ex cathedra*. But how can we tell when he is speaking *ex cathedra*? Then hesitations, contradictions, confusion appear.

The Vatican Decrees should be conclusive. It formulates that the Pope speaks *ex cathedra* "when in discharge of the office of Pastor and Doctor of all Christians, by virtue of his supreme apostolic authority he defines a doctrine regarding faith or morals to be held by the universal Church".

We see that the infallibility is hedged round with conditions. The Pope to give infallible teaching (1) must be using the apostolic authority of his office as supreme Pastor and Doctor; (2) he must be defining a doctrine; (3) the doctrine must concern faith or morals; (4) it is a doctrine to be held by the universal Church.

The privilege of enjoying the absolute certitude of belief is not, after all, so easily secured. There must first be certitude that all these conditions are scrupulously fulfilled. How can the ordinary member of the Roman Catholic Church be sure of that?

Take the second condition of defining a doctrine. On that there are hopelessly conflicting views among the best-informed Roman Catholics. Cardinal Manning, who had such a leading part in having the dogma decreed by the Vatican Council, tells us that the word "definition here signifies the precise judgment or sentence in which a traditional truth of faith or morals may be authoritatively formulated". He declares that we are to take the word not in its forensic and narrow sense but in its wide and common sense. "The wide and common sense is that of an authoritative termination of questions which have been in doubt and debate, and therefore of the judgment or sentence thence resulting. . . . *Definire* is *finem imponere* or *finaliter judicare*. It is therefore equivalent to *determinare* or *finaliter determinare*. It signifies the final decision by which any matter of faith and morals is put into a doctrinal form."[1]

The Rev. Vincent McNabb, O.P., appears to agree generally with this view. "This intention to settle, close, or define the doctrinal discussion must be made sufficiently clear before the faithful are bound to give interior assent. Yet there is no necessity upon the Council or Popes to use the formal phrase 'we define'. It is enough if their words make clear that the period of discussion is over and has given place to the period of explicit consent."[2]

---

[1] *The Vatican Council and Its Definitions* (1870), pp. 87, 88. (*Petri Privilegium.*)
[2] *Infallibility*, pp. 69, 70.

Again, the very high authority of Bishop Gasser, "the official spokesman of the deputation *de fide*" at the Vatican Council, agrees. It was he who was entrusted with the proposing of the final formula to the Council. His speech took four hours to deliver. He explained that the word *definit* was not to be taken in a forensic sense but as meaning that the Pope "directly and terminatively issues his sentence about a doctrine of faith or morals, so that every one of the faithful can be certain of the mind of the Apostolic See, of the mind of the Roman Pontiff; in such a way that he knows for certain that this or that doctrine is held by the Roman Pontiff to be heretical, or almost heretical, certain or erroneous. This is the meaning of the verb *definit*".[1]

Cardinal Hergenrother agrees with this view. He was one of the most learned scholars in the Roman Church of his day. He was one of the "consultors" invited to Rome by Pius IX for the preliminary work of the Vatican Council. He tells that infallibility is to be seen wherever the Pope unmistakably announces that he, as supreme Shepherd, Teacher and Judge, "wishes to decide a question and to bind the conscience of all believers. Hence definitions may be recognised by the customary expressions without this or that formula being absolutely needful".[2]

One might naturally think that in following the teaching of such eminent authorities as these he is on safe ground in being able to detect what are the infallible *ex cathedra* utterances. Their interpretations seem commonsense ones, natural and obvious. But he will soon find that just as eminent theologians, some of whom took part in framing the Vatican Council formula, reject such explanations. They insist that "define" must be taken in its narrow technical sense.

Bishop Ullathorne voted for the decree at the Vatican Council. In a pastoral issued on his return explaining the doctrine of it he stresses and italicises the word "defines", evidently attaching vital importance to it. Butler considers his a studiously moderate interpretation of the doctrine and contrasts it with Manning's.[3]

Bishop Fessler was General Secretary of the Vatican Council. Butler considers him the most authoritative interpreter of the infallibility decree. His treatise *The True and False Infallibility of the Popes* ran into several editions and was much translated. Pius IX

---

[1] Butler, *The Vatican Council*, vol. ii, p. 144.
[2] *Anti-Janus*, p. 57.
[3] *The Vatican Council*, vol. ii, pp. 210, 212.

wrote him a personal letter of thanks and approval as "having brought out the true meaning of the dogma of papal infallibility". His central position is that the definition must be interpreted and applied on strict theological and legal principles. Fessler lays it down that only what Popes have "defined" (*definit* is the well considered word of the Vatican Council") are infallible *ex cathedra* utterances. Butler emphasises how this teaching is "counter" to that of Manning. "The burden of his tract is the necessity of definition."[1]

Dom. Cuthbert Butler, formerly Abbot of Downside, is a historian of considerable repute. His *History of the Vatican Council* is "the best English book on this subject from the Roman point of view".[2] He strongly advocates the "minimising" technical interpretation of Ullathorne and Fessler.[3]

He cites Pére Lucien Choupin, S.J., "a recognised authority on the subject" who stands for a strict legal interpretation of the definition.[4]

Butler also cites with approbation Pére E. Dublanchy, author of an article on infallibility in the *Dictionaire de Théologie Catholique*, in refusing to regard as infallible the decree of Pope Leo XIII against "Americanism" because it "seems to contain nothing of the nature of a formal doctrinal definition".[5] The decree on Anglican Orders concludes with a decision that seems definite enough: "*Motu proprio, certa scientia*, we pronounce and declare that the ordinations carried out by the Anglican rite were wholly invalid and altogether null." This fully satisfies Manning's requirements for an infallible pronouncement, but Dublanchy will not admit it, and Butler agrees with him.

The decree *Lamentabile* was confirmed by the Pope and excommunication was pronounced on the errors condemned in it. Here is how Abbot Butler writes of this: "Some theologians held that this condemnation raised the *Lamentabile* to the position of an *ex cathedra* condemnation. Other eminent theologians held that it did not confer on the decree that which was wanting to it in order to be a strictly and formally papal decision."[6] Similarly the important

---

[1] *The Vatican Council*, vol. ii, pp. 214–16.
[2] Coulton, *Papal Infallibility*, p. vii.
[3] *The Vatican Council*, vol. ii, pp. 213 circa.
[4] Ibid., vol. ii, p. 221.
[5] Ibid., vol. ii, p. 223.
[6] Ibid., vol. ii, p. 225.

papal pronouncement *Pascendi* against Modernism is denied by
Butler, and the learned theologians he cites to rank as infallible—
even though it contains the vital term "we define"! They only
admit it to be regarded as "the highest act of pontifical magisterium
next to *ex cathedra* definition".[1] And this in spite of the fact that
in the encyclical *Pascendi* the Pope at the end of a long denunciation
of Modernist errors declares: "Looking at the entire system in a
single view no one will wonder if we define it thus, affirming it to be
a collection of all the heresies." It is hard on a Roman Catholic,
assured of the security of infallible guidance against heresy, to be
told by leading authorities of his Church that he must not assume
this papal condemnation of all the heresies is really *ex cathedra*.

What has become of the promised assurance of infallible guidance?
An answer given by the theological expert who conducts the enquiry
bureau of the Roman Catholic journal *The Universe* (2nd February
1945) illustrates the confusion. Pope Eugenius IV in his famous
instruction to the Armenians gave questionable teaching on important subjects, embarrassing to later Romanism. Pope John XXII
advocated views on the Beatific Vision that aroused fierce condemnation. His successor was Benedict XII. Here is the answer given
to a querist about both controversies.

(1) Opinions differ as to the infallible character of the decree of
Pope Eugenius IV to the Armenians. The older scholastics for the
most part regarded it as infallible document, but many modern
theologians, such as Gasparri and Van Rossum, regard it as merely
a practical instruction and not as an infallible definition.

(2) As to the bull *Benedictus Deus*, issued by Pope Benedict XII
in 1336, it seems clear that it was this Pope's intention to settle
finally the question whether the souls of the blessed enjoy the
Beatific Vision immediately after death, and hence this is regarded
by most, if not all, as an infallible pronouncement. Moreover, it
was "addressed to the universal Church, whereas the former 'decree
for the Armenians' was addressed only to a particular section".

It really seems impossible for the ordinary Roman Catholic to
be "sure and certain" even when he is given what seems authoritative
papal pronouncements. Leo XIII issued a sweeping condemnation
of Anglican Orders (*Apostolicae Curae*). He announced that his

[1] *The Vatican Council*, vol. ii, p. 226.

"intention had been to pass a final judgment and settle [the question] forever"—*absolute judicari*—that his decision was valid and irrevocable in perpetuity. Yet the eminent Jesuit writer, Sydney F. Smith, cannot describe its infallibility as beyond question. His halting conclusion is that "it belongs to a class of *ex cathedra* utterances for which infallibility is claimed on the ground not indeed of the terms of the Vatican definition but of the constant practice of the Holy See, the consentient teaching of the theologians as well as of the clearest deductions from the principles of faith".[1]

2

All this reveals that the ordinary Roman Catholic is very far from possessing the boasted blissful certainty in accepting what is presented for his belief. Not only the *modus operandi* of infallibility is obscure. The scope of the Pope's infallibility is also beset with impenetrable fog.

Cardinal Manning instructs the faithful that under the term "definitions" are included all dogmatic judgments, i.e. "all judgments in matters of dogma; as, for instance, the inspiration and authenticity of sacred books, the orthodoxy or heretodoxy of human and uninspired books. . . . All censures whether for heresy or with a note less than heresy . . . all legislative or judicial acts so far as they are inseparably connected with his doctrinal authority; as for instance all judgments, sentences and decisions which contain the motives of such acts as derived from faith and morals. Under this will come laws of discipline, canonisation of saints, approbation of religious Orders, of devotions and the like".[2]

This is the view of infallibility that agrees with the arguments about the advantage of belonging to a Church that has an infallible Teacher. But a host of high Romanist authorities emphatically discard it. The official spokesman for the decree at the Vatican Council, Bishop Gasser, expressly disagrees with it. He discussed the question: were "dogmatic facts"—truths required for guarding intact the deposit of revelation—to be included within the scope of infallibility? He declined to assert they were. Are papal decisions infallible in defining truths that pertain to the safeguarding of the deposit? He answers: "It seems right to the Fathers of the deputation

---

[1] *Catholic Encyclopedia*, vol. i, p. 498.
[2] *The Vatican Council and Its Definitions*, pp. 88, 89. (*Petri Privilegium*.)

with unanimous agreement that the question be not defined now but be left in the state in which it is."[1]

Bishop Fessler directly contradicts Cardinal Manning. "A dogmatic definition *ex cathedra* will not be made as accessory matter to the condemnation of a book." "The Pope has the gift of infallibility only as *supreme teacher of truths necessary for salvation as revealed by God*; not as supreme legislator in matters of discipline, not as supreme judge in ecclesiastical questions, not in respect of any other question over which his highest governing power in the Church may still in other respects extend."[2]

When foremost prelates, so prominently concerned in drawing up the momentous decree, thus disagree as to what it involves how can the ordinary public be "sure and certain"?

3

Naturally in the face of all this dissension it follows that there is hopeless confusion as to what documents can be received as genuinely infallible. Where or how can the inerrant, living Voice be heard? What use, after all, is an inerrant Teacher if we do not know when, if ever, he is teaching inerrantly? Manning and Ward and others held a great number of papal decrees to be infallible. Cardinal Newman wrote, on the other hand: "Definitions obligatory on our faith are of rare occurrence and this is confessed by all sober theologians. Father O'Reilly, for instance, of Dublin, one of the first theologians of the day, says: 'The papal infallibility is comparatively seldom brought into action'."[3]

Bishop Ullathorne says: "The occasions for such an exercise of authority are comparatively few and occur but now and then." Bishop Fessler writes: "Dr. Schulte finds a great number of papal *ex cathedra* utterances. I, in accordance with the theological faculty, find only a few."[4]

The specifying what even these few infallible utterances are has proved too difficult an enterprise for the Roman Church. Yet it should be very easy for the supreme Doctor of all Christians to remove the doubts on so tremendously important a matter.

[1] Mansi, lii, 1226.
[2] Butler, *The Vatican Council*, vol. ii, p. 217.
[3] *Letter to the Duke of Norfolk*, p. 124.
[4] Butler, *The Vatican Council*, vol. ii, pp. 214, 215.

Great stress was laid at the time of the Vatican Council on the need for defining papal infallibility. The Pope declared the motive of the Council to be "to find an extraordinary remedy for the extraordinary evils of the Christian world". Since 1870 Christianity has been confronted with problems and dangers of extreme magnitude. Has there been a single act of infallible guidance in that period? We have only to read the cautious pages of Abbot Butler to see the hesitations and hair-splittings of theologians in their discussions about this. He seems to endorse Dublanchy's opinion that "it is doubtful whether since the Council there has been any infallible *ex cathedra* utterance of a Pope".[1]

4

In addition to all this perplexity, the faithful Roman Catholic, striving to find mental security, is confronted with another and a baffling puzzle. Even supposing that somewhere infallible utterances do exist, he must not presume to imagine he can identify them!

Fessler makes it plain that it is a matter of almost insuperable difficulty to ascertain when the Pope is speaking infallibly. "We shall look in vain if we wish to find from history or theology that papal *ex cathedra* utterances are to be recognised, sometimes from the words used, sometimes from the circumstances and sometimes from the definition itself as though each of these marks was of itself sufficient to establish the fact." Only a body of experts can ascertain where the mysterious *ex cathedra* element comes in. It does not seem as if even bishops and priests had sufficient analytical science for the investigation. "If there is no authentic explanation [whatever that means] of a papal *ex cathedra* utterance, the theological faculty, which has been for centuries engaged on this question, has to be heard upon the marks of a real *ex cathedra* utterance."[2] It is no wonder Fessler found in history "only a few" *ex cathedra* utterances.

It is in accordance with Fessler's warnings that we should be taught by other Romanist theologians that ordinary people cannot presume to understand papal utterances. Cardinal Newman warns the faithful of their utter unfitness to know when the much gloried-in certainty is being vouchsafed. In his *Letter to the Duke of Norfolk*

[1] Butler, *The Vatican Council*, vol. ii, p. 226.
[2] Ibid., vol. ii, p. 217.

he writes: "None but the *Schola Theologorum* is competent to
determine the force of papal and Synodical utterances, and the exact
interpretation of them is a work of time."[1]

Who are the competent theologians? The cardinal, who can be so
lucid at times, leaves us in doubt. He explains that theology is a
science of a special kind with methods and a language of its own.
"A really first-class theologian is rarely to be found." Only some of
its rules are known to priests, but "even this general knowledge is
not possessed by laymen". He stresses "the necessity of a scientific
education to understand the value of propositions".[2] We can only
interpret sagely "in the light of certain rules which arise out of
what is called the *stylus curiae*".[3]

Again, what has become of the assurance of certainty in the faith?
We cannot be sure any teaching of the Pope is *ex cathedra* unless
some unidentified body of theologians have certified it. We have
seen how the highest theologians contradict each other on the most
vital concerns of infallibility. Even if they should be in agreement,
how are we to know they are right, since the infallibility decree does
not guarantee their infallibility? The old question remains un-
answered—what is the value of an inerrant guide if we cannot know
when he is speaking inerrantly? It looks as if we have to resort, after
all, to reliance on private judgment.

Devoted Roman Catholics have shown alacrity in seizing such
excuses as Newman puts forward for by-passing papal pronouncements they felt were wrong. Wilfrid Ward delighted in this kind of
refuge from the plain words of the *Pascendi*. He held that the ordinary intelligent Catholic cannot understand its guidance by taking the
obvious sense of it. Theologians must collate it with other authoritative utterances that may at first sight seem to contradict it. When
this collation is carried out then the *Pascendi* "may prove so different
from what it seems to us that it need not closely concern us at
present".[4]

Again, we see the amazing—and amusing—confusion in the
Roman Church as to how the infallible teaching is to be discovered.
"Can one conceive," cried Fr. Fawkes, "a divine authority teaching
the world in terms which require specialist interpretations?"[5] The

---

[1] *Letter to the Duke of Norfolk*, p. 4.
[2] Ibid., p. 92.
[3] Ibid., p. 93.
[4] *Insurrection versus Resurrection*, p. 276.
[5] Ibid., p. 277,

difficulty of understanding the Delphic oracle was not more puzzling than what is here required.

Dr. Salmon gives the apt comparison of the daughters of the Vicar of Wakefield being given by their mother a guinea apiece because the honour of the family required that they should always have money in their pocket, but that each was under strict conditions never to change her guinea. "The Pope seems to possess the gift of infallibility on the same terms. The 'honour of the family' requires he should have it, but obvious considerations of prudence constantly deter him from using it."[1] The supposed indispensable infallibility keeps eluding our view as we seek to find it. Alice remonstrated with the Cheshire Cat: "I wish you wouldn't keep appearing and vanishing so suddenly: you make me quite giddy." It will be remembered that Alice had applied to the Cat for guidance on "which way I ought to walk from here".

If anyone thinks the illustrations too flippant he may be reassured by knowing how intelligent Roman Catholics themselves jest about their infallible oracle. For instance, Wilfrid Ward, editor of the *Dublin Review*, who was offered a professorship at Ushaw, writes that in some quarters the joke about the hell of liberal Protestants was applied to the infallibility. "It was said they were too orthodox to deny hell but too liberal to admit that any one went there. 'Hell was a place of eternal torment, eternally untenanted.' So, too, infallibility was a gift ensuring freedom from error in utterances which the Pope never made."[2]

Abbot Butler practically abandons the claims to infallibility, so confidently proclaimed by many of his co-religionists, when he writes: "We are not so sensitive or so exacting in this matter of infallibility as our forefathers were. . . . Nowadays Catholics have for the most part settled down into a middle position and are prepared to accept as right and true a great body of teachings and judgments of the Popes, without requiring to know that it is guaranteed infallible, trusting to the Providence of God over the teaching authority of the Church and the promised guidance of the Holy Spirit, satisfied that such pronouncements will not be made rashly or without proper care and prayer."[3]

What is the difference between this and the Anglican position?

[1] *Infallibility of the Church*, p. 187.
[2] *The Wilfrid Wards and the Transition*, p. 180.
[3] *The Vatican Council*, vol. ii, p. 227.

"Trusting to the Providence of God . . . and the promised guidance of the Holy Spirit." The best historian of the Vatican Council, within his Church, at the end of his book reverts to the old common Catholic reliance on the Holy Spirit's normal guidance of the Church. He falls back on something very like private judgment.

It does not seem to occur to Romanists that all such doubts and disagreements could be dissipated by the Pope announcing which of his decisions are to be regarded as *ex cathedra*.

The conflicting theories about *ex cathedra* reduce the supposed prerogative to futility. They are only artificial refinements to avoid the difficulties that arise if many of the most responsible acts of the Papacy cannot somehow or other be side-stepped.

The Rev. Vincent McNabb, O.P., wrote a clever little book to smooth away the objections to the infallibility. At the end, after setting forth the distinctions between what is and what is not an infallible dictum, he has to deal with the objection (which is, he admits, "not without a show of reasonableness") that such distinctions and logical refinements as he has been making "have an air of artifice, or that simple minds cannot grasp them, or that they merely irritate the common sense of modern thought, or that it is wrong to tone down such unpalatable truths as papal infallibility in our thirst for unity among Christians". How does he face the issue? He has nothing to answer except a feeble and obviously irrelevant *tu quoque*: "To allay these teasing difficulties it should be remembered that all legislation whether political or theological is proverbially technical. To the simple citizen an Act of Parliament seems plain and obvious, yet it will give occasion to bulky commentaries and wearisome discussions and prolonged lawsuits when handed over to the care of the men of the law. Moreover, explanations, or, if you will, refinements, greater than these, must now be resorted to by all religious bodies claiming continuity through a historic past."[1]

When that is the best that so plausible an apologist as Father McNabb in his much recommended book can offer, then it is plain that the Vatican Council decree is an embarrassing heritage for the Roman Catholic Church.

[1] *Infallibility*, p. 70.

THE ENCYCLICAL "LUX VERITATIS"

Pope Pius XI issued an encyclical in 1931, *Lux Veritatis*, in which he appeals to "history, the guide of life", and maintains that the Fathers of the Council in the whole celebration of the Ephesian Synod make "luminously manifest to the eyes of all" the dogma that "in matters of faith and morals the Roman Pontiff has a God-given authority, supreme, perfect, and subject to none, over the faithful of Christ, all and several". He stresses the history of this Council as a medium by which those who dissent from the Apostolic See may be moved "to return to the one fold and the one Shepherd". The unfounded assumptions and perversion of the evidence are amazing in this encyclical.

It is disconcerting to find so deliberate an utterance of the Head of that Church to be abounding with the grossest errors. Since in it the appeal to history is put in the forefront, and views different from it are denounced as a "fabric of falsehood clothed with a specious appearance of truth", and since this alleged falsity can, it is said, be readily seen by anyone who "looks at the faithful record of fact and diligently examines the documentary evidence", then the wrong statements made are the more inexcusable.

1

The Council of Ephesus by the very fact of its Assembly is, as we have seen, a conclusive refutation of papal claims. Its existence meant the treatment as null and void of the Pope's decision. How solemnly that decision was promulgated is set forth in the encyclical: "Celestine . . . having summoned a Roman Synod and weighed the matter maturely in virtue of his supreme and absolute authority over the whole of the Lord's flock, made and solemnly sanctioned" his decrees against Nestorius. If Celestine held the sovereign position claimed why then hold the Council of Ephesus at all? Why did no bishop in the whole of Christendom protest? Why did Celestine himself acquiesce and send representatives to it if "none may reopen the judgment of the Apostolic See, than whose authority there is none greater, nor can any lawfully review its judgment".[1]

By Celestine's decision the see of Constantinople had been vacant since the preceding December. All that the Fathers at Ephesus had to decide was—had Nestorius submitted to Celestine's orders? "Five minutes would have sufficed for proving that he had done the very contrary."[2]

2

We have seen how abundantly clear it is that the Council regarded Nestorius as Bishop of Constantinople until his trial and condemnation, on evidence tendered, took place before itself.

The trial of Nestorius began and proceeded for some time without any mention whatever of his having been already condemned by the Bishop of Rome. Cyril's appeal for a pronouncement on the orthodoxy of his second letter was heard and voted on and Nestorius anathematised without anyone referring to the decision of Celestine. Battifol admits the significance of this. " Up to that point no mention was made of the opinion of Rome. Cyril had caused approval for his faith from the Council and reprobation of that of Nestorius without invoking any other authority than the faith of Nicaea. It is then only that Juvenal of Jerusalem asked that there be read the letter to Nestorius of the very holy and very religious Archbishop of the Romans, Celestine."[3]

The encyclical represents the legates as demanding, when they appeared at the Council, "that all things decreed previously should be submitted to them that they might be confirmed and ratified in the name of the Apostolic See". Then, after quoting the grandiloquent speech of Philip, it is stated: "What more need be said? Did the Fathers of the Oecumenical Council make any objection to this manner of acting adopted by Celestine and his legates or oppose it in any way? By no manner of means. On the contrary, written documents remain which plainly show their own dutiful observance and reverence."

On reading this, the Pope's own stricture rises to one's mind— "a fabric of falsehood clothed with a specious appearance of truth".

---

[1] Vatican Decrees, chap. 3.
[2] Dr. Bright, *Roman See in the Early Church*, p. 156.
[3] Batiffol, *Le Siège Apostolique*, p. 373.

The manner of the papal legates confirming what was decreed (without waiting for their presence) was the ordinary way of proceeding, and involved not the slightest proof of dutiful "observance and reverence" for papal authority. It simply meant that the representatives of Rome joined with the bishops in condemning Nestorius —that the assent of Rome, just like that of any other see, was formally given. Of course the bishops, who by the third session on 11th July were in a very troubled state, with the Court treating their proceedings as invalid, rejoiced naturally at receiving the influential co-operation of the bishops of the West.

The "written documents" show how the opposite of what the papal encyclical states is the fact. For when the legates announced their agreement the acute Cyril demanded that "the representatives of the Apostolic See *and of the whole holy Synod of the venerable bishops of the West*"[1] sign "in token of canonical agreement with us all". Exactly. The Council had now received a tremendous accession of strength from the bishops of the Western Empire. One of them, in signing, is recorded to have assented "to the just judgment" of the Council.

A study of the records makes it so clear that no idea of papal supremacy was in the minds of any of those taking part that it passes comprehension how Pope Pius XI could write that the documents "prove so expressly and significantly that already throughout the universal Church there was a strong and common faith in the authority of the Roman Pontiff over the whole flock of Christ, an authority subject to no one and incapable of error".

At the risk of wearying readers who may well think that sufficient documents have been quoted, let me call attention to a few more.

When the emperor refused to acknowledge as valid the actions of the Council that Cyril presided over, then it is obvious the Council should have claimed the infallible authority of the Pope if that was the "strong and common faith of the universal Church". This they never do. They profess, instead, that they have "followed the ancient tradition of the holy Fathers, apostles, evangelists, and of the three hundred and ten of Nicaea".[2] They have the holy bishops of the world on their side, the "Bishop" of Rome and the "Archbishop" Cyril. "The whole West is consenting with us." They number more than two hundred, "collected out of all the earth".[3]

---

[1] Mansi, iv, 1300. [2] Ibid., iv, 1421. [3] Ibid., iv, 1425.

Darker days followed for the Council. The emperor sent a high official with a decree accepting the deposition pronounced by John's assembly against Cyril and Memnon. These two leaders were cast into prison. The bishops then sent urgent pleas to the emperor. They appealed to him with every argument they could use. They were the real "Oecumenical Synod which had all the West and your great Rome and the Apostolic See participating with them, also all Africa and Illyricum";[1] the fewness and ill-doings of the opposing bishops are told at length; they themselves have been loyal to the faith of Nicaea, and so on. Not once do we find them urging what, if the encyclical's statements were true, would obviously have been their prime and sufficient excuse, viz.: that they were bound to obey the Roman Pontiff who had "a God-given authority, supreme, perfect, and subject to none, over the faithful of Christ".

Evidence of how it was the belief of the Church that it was a General Council and not the Roman bishop that had authority in matters of faith is forthcoming from the "supplication" presented to the emperor by the archimandrite Basil and the monks of Constantinople before the Council met. They deplore the confusion caused by the errors of Nestorius and beg the emperor to call a sacred Council at once which would "correctly confirm and build up what was shaken or fallen down".[2] By it the peace of the Church may be restored. Later, when the findings of the Council were being challenged, they petitioned him "that the decision of the majority, which has also authority in accordance with the sees, should be confirmed by you".[3] They appeal to the authority of the "majority" and of the "sees"—not of one see.

There is no possible doubt as to what was the "strong and common faith of the Church" in 431.

3

(1) Cyril is represented as acknowledging the supreme authority of Celestine and addressing most dutiful letters to "the most blessed Father Celestine, beloved of God". This is misleading. Similar titles of respect were common in the Eastern Church. Cyril addresses Nestorius's successor in Constantinople as "My most holy and worshipful Lord, Archbishop Father Maximian".[4]

---

[1] Mansi, iv, 1433.
[2] Ibid., iv, 1108.
[3] Ibid., iv, 1456.
[4] Migne. P. G. 77: 253.

There is a constant tendency in Roman apologists to found arguments on the polite and rhetorical complimentary expressions that were common at one time, especially in the East. What Cyril was capable of in this way may be seen in his letter to the weak emperor, Theodosius, when he wanted to enlist him against Nestorius.[1] "Heaven and earth," he tells him, "are full of the glory of God, but the emperor is His similitude upon earth." Milman describes as servility and impiety the "Oriental tone of adulation".[2] Sixtus III, Celestine's successor, tells Cyril that the whole Church owes him so much that "all are subject to you".[3]

It would have been very strange if Cyril did not write to the Bishop of Rome. A doctrinal struggle between the Bishops of the second and third sees in Christendom should not be carried on without consulting the occupant of the first see. In the bitter conflict it was all-important for either to win the support of the metropolitan of the West. When forces were fairly evenly matched the support of the Western Church might well turn the scale. Deposition, banishment, and perhaps a miserable death (as happened to the unfortunate Nestorius), were the consequences of defeat.

As Milman writes: "Both parties, Nestorius and Cyril themselves, could not but look with earnest solicitude to Rome. She held the balance of power."[4] Controversies between Eastern bishops inevitably elevated the importance of the Bishop of Rome.

It is wrong to read into Cyril's letter to Celestine a recognition of the Pope's supreme jurisdiction. The learned Roman Catholic bishop, Hefele, describes his procedure. After mentioning Nestorius's threat to bring Cyril before a Synod, he writes: "For this reason, and also because Nestorius himself had first applied to Rome in regard to the question of Theotokos, and, on the other hand, the Pope also had made enquiries on the subject of Cyril, the latter had felt bound to inform the Pope on the subject of the new heresy."[5]

Lux Veritatis conceals the fact that it was Celestine who wrote first to Cyril and that Cyril ordered his statement of the case not to be delivered to Celestine unless his messenger found that Nestorius

---

[1] Mansi, iv, 617.
[2] *History of Latin Christianity*, vol. i, p. 192.
[3] Mansi, v, 374.
[4] *History of Latin Christianity*, vol. i, p. 194.
[5] *History of the Councils*, vol. iii, p. 24 (E. T.)

had already written to him.[1] Cyril, writing to John of Antioch, stresses how it had been "necessary" for him (Cyril) to communicate with Celestine since Nestorius had done so.[2] Similarly he explains to Juvenal of Jerusalem how Nestorius tried to mislead the Roman Church and how Celestine wrote to himself.[3] He seems anxious to show he did not approach Celestine of his own accord, but to protect him against being led astray.

(2) *Lux Veritatis* claims Cyril as one "who understood and strenuously maintained the authority of the Roman Church". The only proof cited of this is his letter to Celestine—a letter not warranting such inference. Cyril asked Celestine to let him know "what he thought" of his contemplated breaking off of communion with Nestorius. He even states that he had practically made up his mind, "but we do not publicly break off communion with him before communicating these things to your Holiness".[4]

There is a letter extant from Cyril dealing with Nestorius's alleged sanctioning of an anathema on anyone who said Mary was Theotokos. Cyril asks what is to hinder him from pronouncing a counter anathema. He implies that he is quite free to do so but that it would be more useful to rally the other bishops of the Church to the cause first—"the godly bishops of the East and West".[5] To claim Cyril as a maintainer of papal authority is very unfortunate. For several years of his episcopate he had obstinately preferred to remain out of union with Rome rather than acknowledge that St. Chrysostom was to be reckoned a Catholic bishop. Never in his many writings does he acknowledge the sovereignty of Rome or that the bishops there held prerogatives from Peter. Nay more, he interprets the Petrine texts in a manner contradictory to the basal Roman claims. He holds that the apostles were equal with one another. "Peter and John were both apostles and saints and adorned with equal honours and powers."[6]   The Rock text is taught to mean that the Church is founded on the "disciple's immovable and firm faith".[7] "He called the Rock, I consider, the unshaken faith of the disciple."[8] Attention has already been

---

[1] Mansi, iv, 1130.
[2] Ibid., iv, 1052.
[3] Ibid., iv, 1060.
[4] Ibid., iv, 1016.
[5] Ibid., iv, 1000.
[6] Migne. P. G. 76: 65. *Adv. Nest.* (ἰσομέτροις τιμαῖς).
[7] See p. 48.
[8] P. G. 70: 940. *In Isaiah*, lib. iv, oratio 2.

called to how utterly in conflict with papal exegesis is Cyril's teaching on John xxi. 15–17 that "Feed My lambs" is "a renewal of the apostolate already conferred".[1]

No better evidence is required that Cyril gave no countenance to papal claims than the series of forgeries concocted as his on which St. Thomas Aquinas relied when establishing the case for the Papacy.

(3) "Nor was Nestorius ignorant of the supreme authority of the Roman bishop over the universal Church."[2] His letters to Celestine are appealed to in proof of this. A more startling misrepresentation it would be hard to find. Nestorius as Bishop of Constantinople wrote to the Bishop of Rome on Church affairs in terms of complete equality, and indeed casually. He addresses Celestine as "brother" and remarks: "We ought to have fraternal communications with each other in turns in order that by obtaining concord we may oppose the Devil, the enemy of peace."[3] He goes on to advocate interchange of information: "Let us narrate our affairs to each other as brothers to brothers."[4] There is a letter from Nestorius in which he tells how Cyril has betaken himself to Celestine—"a man too simple to be able to understand acutely the sense of the dogmas".[5] Nestorius afterwards showed clearly enough his contempt for the authority of Celestine.

(4) It is asserted by Pius XI that when the Emperor Theodosius summoned the Council "the judgment of Celestine had not yet arrived at Constantinople and nothing was known about it there". When this judgment was formally served on Nestorius, in December 430, why did not Theodosius cancel the summons since the supreme Judge had spoken?

Celestine wrote his judgment direct to Nestorius on 11th August. According to Professor Ramsay[6] it took twenty-four days to travel from Rome to Constantinople. If we allow double this time, it would have been known in Constantinople at the beginning of October. The summonses to the Council were dated 19th November.

(5) In spite of the reckless statements above we are not prepared for the Pope's assertion that Celestine announced as "his legates who were to preside at the Council, namely the Patriarch Cyril,

---

[1] See p. 54.
[2] *Lux Veritatis*, p. 8.
[3] Mansi, iv, 1021.
[4] Ibid., iv, 1023.
[5] Ibid., v, 762.
[6] Hastings, *Dictionary of the Bible* (extra vol.), p. 387.

the Bishops Arcadius and Projectus and the priest Philip ".[1] Celestine did not nominate Cyril as his legate. He never refers to Cyril as his legate to the Council. The Council, in writing to Celestine, described Arcadius, Projectus and Philip as those who "filled the place of the Apostolic See ".[2] The legates of Celestine never presided.

4

Finally it is necessary to call attention to some mistranslations resorted to in this papal encyclical.

(1) It is not correct to state Celestine "ordered the fathers of the Council to execute the sentence passed by himself". The sentence will not bear that construction. He did order his legates to maintain (*exequantur*) what he had already decided. Of course, that is partly why they were sent to the Council. But his tone to the bishops was very different. "We do not doubt that your Holinesses will manifest your consent to this when you perceive that what has been done was decreed for the security of the universal Church."[3] Any bishop who felt strongly and had committed himself to a declaration could ask no less.

(2) The commission of Celestine to Cyril is thus rendered: "Wherefore in virtue of the authority of our see, and acting in our stead, you will strictly enforce this sentence." What Celestine wrote was "wherefore the authority of our see having been joined with yourself".[4] Celestine's authority was to be combined with Cyril's. Cyril showed conclusively how he understood it, for instead of transmitting the sentence direct he not only sent it in the name of his own as well as of the Roman Synod, but altered it out of knowledge by formulating twelve dogmas of his own to be adopted. Indeed, writing to the monks of Constantinople informing them of what he had done he represents the edict as coming first from his own Synod, "which is sent on behalf of ourselves and . . . the Bishop of Great Rome".[5]

(3) The encyclical states : "When they came to the condemnation and rejection of Nestorius the same Fathers of the Council did not think that they were free to judge the whole cause afresh." This is misleading. The encyclical proceeds to state that they "openly

---

[1] *Lux Veritatis*, p. 11.
[2] Mansi, iv, 1337.
[3] Mansi, iv, 1287.

[4] Ibid., iv, 1019 (συναφθείσης σοι).
[5] Ibid., iv, 1097.

profess that they are anticipated and 'forced' by the sentence of the Roman Pontiff: 'Understanding that he [Nestorius] thinks and preaches impiously, and compelled by the sacred canons and by the letter of our most holy Father and fellow-minister, Celestine, the Bishop of the Roman Church, we came of necessity and with tears to this lamentable sentence against him.' "

There are three mistranslations here.

(a) The Council did not say it was "forced" or "compelled". The word used[1] means "urged" or "impelled". Archbishop Chrysostom of Athens protests against the misinterpretation and prefers the sense of "persuaded".[2] In Liddel and Scott's Lexicon the meanings are given of "urge", "impel", "stimulate", "hasten".

(b) It should not be "by the sacred canons and by the letter of our most holy Father", but "impelled by the canons and in accordance with the letter, etc.". The papal translation ignores the change of prepositions; that referring to the canons is ἀπό and that referring to the letter is ἐκ.

(c) The words "of necessity" are misplaced. They are transferred to follow the reference to the letter of the Pope as if, owing to that letter, the condemnation was necessary, whereas the first word in the clause is "necessarily", and so properly refers to the authority of the canons.

(4) The letter of Cyril to Celestine is translated as asking him to "vouchsafe therefore to prescribe what you feel in this matter so that it may be clearly known to us whether we must hold communion with him or whether, etc.". A more correct translation would be: "Be so good as to signify what you think."[3] The word rendered "must" should be "ought" or "fitting" (χρή).[4] This is clear from the context, for immediately afterwards Cyril uses the same word in recommending Celestine to write his views to the other bishops. If "must" be used in the one place why not in the other? And so Cyril tells the Pope what he must do!

This chapter has not been a pleasant one to write. It is grievous to think that so respected a prelate as Pius XI was responsible for the indefensible misrepresentations in the encyclical. He was a scholar, and a very short investigation of the documents or a glance

[1] Mansi, iv, 1212 (καταπειχθέντες).
[2] The Third Oecumenical Council, p. 38.
[3] καταξίωσαν τυπῶσαι τό δοκουν Duchesne: "Let Celestine give his advice", (Early History of the Church, vol. iii, p. 234).
[4] Battifol, "si nous devons", Le Siège Apostolique, p. 350.

U

at the works of some scholars of his Church (e.g. Bossuet, Fleury, Tillemont, Maret, Duchesne, Battifol) would have shown him how misleading are not only many of his assertions but his main thesis. Pius XI, however, seems to claim that the encyclical is directly his own work. He refers to the studies of two committees of distinguished men on the Council of Ephesus and states: "We feel that it becomes the office committed to us by God that we ourselves should speak with you in these encyclical letters concerning this most important matter."

The encyclical is entitled "the light of truth", and in it the Pope, speaking of Christ, adds, "whose Vicar on earth we are". Since this encyclical represents what the Head of the Roman Church proclaims as truth, then we can only despair of a Church that solemnly sets forth error as truth and endeavours to support it by perverting history.

BIBLIOGRAPHY

Whilst it is impossible to mention the immense number of sources and authorities connected with this subject, the author wishes in particular to acknowledge his indebtedness to the following:

ACTON, Lord — Historical Essays and Studies; History of Freedom; Lectures on Modern History; Letters to Mary Gladstone; Correspondence.

ADDIS and ARNOLD — Catholic Dictionary.

ALLIES, T. W. — The See of Peter.

ALLNATT, C. F. B. — *Cathedra Petri.*

BARONIUS, Cardinal — *Annales Ecclesiastici.*

BARROW, Isaac — Treatise on the Pope's Supremacy.

BARRY, Wm. — The Papacy and Modern Times; Papal Monarchy.

BARTOLI, Georgio — The Primitive Church and the Primacy of Rome.

BATTIFOL, Mgr. Pierre — *Cathedra Petri; Le Siège Apostolique; Catholicisme et Papauté.*

BELLARMINE, Cardinal — *De Summo Pontifice.*

BENSON, Archbishop — Cyprian.

BOSSUET, Bishop — *Defensis Declarationis Cleri Gallicani; Gallia Orthodoxa.*

BRIGHT, Wm. — The Roman See in the Early Church; Waymarks in Church History.

BRINCKMAN, Arthur — Notes on the Papal Claims.

BRYCE, Lord — Holy Roman Empire.

BURCHARD, J. — *Diarium.*

BURY, J. B. — History of the Papacy in the Nineteenth Century.

BUTLER, Dom. Cuthbert — History of the Vatican Council.

CADOUX, C. J. — Catholicism and Christianity.

Cambridge Medieval History, The

Catholic Faith, The; A Compendium authorized by Pius X

CHAMBAT, Dom Lucien — *Le Royaute du Christ.*

CHAPMAN, Dom John — Bishop Gore and the Catholic Claims; The Condemnation of Pope Honorius; The First Eight General Councils and Papal Infallibility; The Papacy; Studies in the Early Papacy.

CHRYSOSTOM, Archbishop of Athens — The Third Œcumenical Council and the Primacy of the Bishop of Rome.

COULTON, G. G. — The Inquisition and Liberty; Medieval Studies; Papal Infallibility; A Premium upon Falsehood; The Roman Catholic Church and the Bible; Romanism and Truth; The Scandal of Cardinal Gasquet; Sectarian History; The Inquisition.

CREIGHTON, Mandell — History of the Papacy.
CYPRIAN, St. — De Unitate Catholicae Ecclesiae.

DARBOY, Archbishop — La Liberté du Concile et l'Infallibilité.
DE LUCA, Marianus — Institutiones Juris Ecclesiastici Publici.
DEL VAL, Merry — The Truth of the Papal Claims.
DENNY, E. — Papalism.
DI BRUNO, J. F. — Catholic Belief.
Dictionaire de Théologie Catholique
Dictionary of Christian Biography
Dictionary of Christian Antiquities
DOLLINGER, J. J. I. von — Declarations and Letters on the Vatican Decrees; Fables about the Popes.
DOWNEY, Archbishop — The Papacy.
DUCHESNE, Mgr. L. — The Beginning of the Temporal Sovereignty of the Popes; Early History of the Christian Church; Fastes Espicopaux de l'Ancienne Gaule.

EUSEBIUS — Historia Ecclesiastica.

FAHIE, J. J. — Galileo.
FIGGIS, Neville — Hopes for English Religion.
FLEURY, Claude — Histoire Ecclesiastique.
FOAKES-JACKSON, F. J. — Peter, Prince of Apostles.
FORTESQUE, Adrian — The Early Papacy.
FRIEDRICH, Johann — Documenta.
FUNK, F. X. — Manual of Church History.

GIESELER, Johann C. L. — Compendium of Ecclesiastical History.
GILLE, Albert — A Catholic Plan for Reunion.
GLADSTONE, W. E. — Rome and the Newest Fashions in Religion.
GORE, Bishop Charles — Belief in God; The Church and the Ministry; Leo the Great; Roman Catholic Claims.
GOUGAUD, Louis — Les Chrétientés Celtiques.
GREGOROVIUS, F. — History of the City of Rome; Lucretia Borgia.
GUICCIARDINI — Storia d'Italia

HEADLAM, Bishop A. C. — The Doctrine of the Church.
HEFELE, Bishop — History of the Councils.
HENDERSON, E. F. — Select Documents of the Middle Ages.
HERGENROTHER, Cardinal — Anti-Janus.
HINSCHIUS, Paulus — Decretales Pseudo-Isidorianae.
HIPPOLYTUS, St. — Refutation of all Heresies.
HOUTIN, Abbé — Une Vie de Prêtre.
HUGEL, F. von — The Petrine Claims.

INGE, W. R. — Christian Ethics and Modern Problems.

JALLAND, T. G. — The Church and the Papacy.
JANUS — The Pope and the Council.
JOHNSON, Vernon — One Lord, One Faith.

KEATING, Joseph — The True Church.
KENNEY, James F. — The Sources for the Early History of Ireland.
KERR, Wm. Shaw — Independence of the Celtic Church in Ireland.

KIDD, B. J.	History of the Church; The Roman Primacy.
KNOX, R. A.	The Belief of Catholics.
LEA, H. C.	History of the Inquisition in the Middle Ages; History of the Inquisition of Spain.
LEPICIER, Alexius M.	*De Stabilitate et Progressu Dogmatis.*
L'EPINOIS, Henry de	*Les Pièces du Procès de Galileè.*
LESLIE, Charles	The Case Stated.
LESTER, Edmund	Dialogues of Defence.
LETO, Pomponio	Eight months at Rome (Vatican Council).
LIGHTFOOT, Bishop J. B.	Apostolic Fathers; Commentary on Philippians.
LITTLEDALE, R. F.	The Petrine Claims.
LODGE, R.	The Close of the Middle Ages.
LOOMIS, L. R.	The Book of the Popes (*Liber Pontificalis*).
LOWTHER-CLARKE, W. K.	The First Epistle of Clement to the Corinthians.
LUNN, Arnold	Now I See.
MACAULAY, Lord	Life and Letters.
MALDEN, P. H.	Anglo-Catholics—Have they grasped the Point?
MANNING, Cardinal	*Petri Privilegium:* Temporal Mission of the Holy Ghost; The Vatican Council and its Definitions.
MANSI, J. D.	*Concilia.*
MARET, Bishop	*Du Concile Général et de la Paix Religieuse.*
MARSHALL, C. C.	The Roman Catholic Church in the Modern State.
MAYCOCK, A. L.	The Inquisition; The Papacy.
McNABB, Vincent	Infallibility.
MERRILL, E. T.	Essays in Early Church History.
MILMAN, H. H.	History of Latin Christianity.
MILNER-WHITE and KNOX	One God and Father of All.
MILTON, John	*Areopagitica.*
MIRBT, C.	*Quellen zur Geschichte des Papsttums.*
NEWMAN, Cardinal	The Arians of the Fourth Century; Letter to the Duke of Norfolk.
OULTON, J. E. L.	History of the Church of Ireland.
PASTOR, Ludwig	History of the Popes.
PAUL, F. J.	Romanism and Evangelical Christianity.
PETRE, M. D.	Modernism.
PLATINA, B.	*De Vitis Pontificum Romanorum.*
PULLER, F. W.	Primitive Saints and the See of Rome.
QUIRINIUS	Letters from Rome on the Council.
RANKE, Leopold von	History of the Popes.
RENOUF, Peter le Page	The Case of Pope Honorius.
REYNALDUS	*Annales Ecclesiastici.*
ROBERTS, W. W.	Pontifical Decrees against the Motion of the Earth.
SABATINI, Rafael	Torquemada and the Spanish Inquisition.
SALMON, G.	Infallibility of the Church.

SHOTWELL and LOOMIS   The See of Peter.
SIMCOX, J. V.   Is the Roman Catholic Church a Secret Society?
SISMONDI, J. C. L.   History of the Italian Republics.
SMITH, Sydney F.   Papal Supremacy and Infallibility.
SOCRATES SCHOLASTICUS   Ecclesiastical History.
SOZOMEN, Hermias   *Historia Ecclesiastica.*
SPARROW-SIMPSON, W. J.   Roman Catholic Opposition to Papal Infallibility.
STREETER, Burnett H.   The Primitive Church.

TERTULLIAN   *De Praescriptione Haereticorum.*
TILLEMONT, Sébastien   *Memoires.*
TURBERVILLE, A. S.   Medieval Heresy and the Inquisition; The Spanish Inquisition.
TURNER, C. H.   Catholic and Apostolic.
TYRRELL, George   Medievalism; Life.

ULLMANN, Walter   Medieval Papalism.

VINCENT, St. of Lerins   *Commonitorium.*

WARD, Maisie   Insurrection versus Resurrection; The Wilfred Wards and the Transition.
WARD, Wilfred   Life of Newman.
WHATELY, Archbishop   Cautions for the Times.
WILHELM and SCANNELL   Manual of Catholic Theology.
WILLIAMS, N. P.   Our Case as against Rome.
WOODLOCK, F.   Constantinople, Canterbury and Rome.
WORDSWORTH, Bishop Christopher   St. Hippolytus and the Church of Rome.
WORDSWORTH, Bishop John   Ministry of Grace.

PERIODICALS

Catholic Layman (Ed. A. E. Gayer)
Church Quarterly Review
Church Times
Daily Telegraph
Dublin Review
Journal of Theological Studies
North British Review
Spectator
Times Literary Supplement
The Tablet
The Universe

INDEX

SCRIPTURE REFERENCES